Rewired

David Hudson
in association with eLine Productions

Macmillan Technical Publishing, Indianapolis, Indiana

Rewired

By David Hudson

Published by:
Macmillan Technical Publishing
201 West 103rd Street
Indianapolis, IN 46290 USA

Printed in the United States of America 1 2 3 4 5 6 7 8 9 0

Library of Congress Cataloging-in-Publication Number: 96-78514

Warning and Disclaimer

This book is designed to provide information about the Internet. Every effort has been made to make this book as complete and as accurate as possible, but no warranty or fitness is implied.

The information is provided on an "as is" basis. The author(s) and Macmillan Technical Publishing shall have neither liability nor responsibility to any person or entity with respect to any loss or damages arising from the information contained in this book or from the use of the disks or programs that may accompany it.

Publisher	**Don Fowley**
Publisher's Assistant	**Rosemary Lewis**
Publishing Manager	**Jim LeValley**
Marketing Managers	**Kourtnaye Sturgeon** **Mary Foote**
Managing Editor	**Carla Hall**

Acquisitions Editor	**Jim LeValley**
Acquisitions Coordinator	**Amy Lewis**
Senior Editors	**Sarah Kearns**
	Suzanne Snyder
Development Editor	**Ali Karp**
Project Editor	**Noelle Gasco**
Copy Editors	**Keith Cline**
	Matt Litten
Assistant Marketing Manager	**Gretchen Schlesinger**
Cover Designer	**Michael Wilson**
Cover Production	**Aren Howell**
Cover Illustration	**Michael Wilson**
Book Designer	**Michael J. Nolan**
Manufacturing Coordinator	**Brook Farling**
Director of Production	**Larry Klein**
Production Team Supervisors	**Laurie Casey**
	Joe Millay
Production Analyst	**Erich J. Richter**
Production Team	**Tricia Flodder**
	Christopher Morris
	Daniela Raderstorf
	Megan Wade

About the Author

David Hudson regularly tackles current issues arising in online culture for the *Rewired* web site. His articles have appeared in publications ranging from *A.N.Y.P.*, a European arts review, to the Vienna daily *Der Standard*, from computer publications such as *Mac Home Journal* to such stalwarts of the alternative press as the *L.A. Weekly* and the *San Francisco Bay Guardian*. Mr. Hudson's fiction and poetry has been published widely, his music videos broadcast narrowly, and his screenwriting realized on the indie film circuit and on German television. After graduating from the University of Texas in Austin with a BS in Radio-TV-Film and an MA in English, he hooked up with Munich performance artists minimal club with whom he wrote and performed for six years. Mr. Hudson then spent a year in San Francisco, helping to create an online service for architects, and is now slated to head story development for a new television series in Berlin.

eLine Productions is a San Francisco-based development company specializing in web applications and enterprise solutions.

The company made its mark in 1993 by creating one of the world's largest virtual communities focused entirely on a particular metropolitan area— San Francisco—and went on to apply the concepts behind online conferencing to the business environment in the form of "user base management systems." While eLine has developed numerous custom and "shrink wrap" technology solutions, the company has yet to shake its interest in the cultural implications and real-world applications of the technology we now live with. eLine devotes significant time to exploring the interplay of arts, culture, and technology through an in-house lecture series, maintenance of five vibrant online communities, and continued participation in numerous experimental projects.

Although considered a "Technology Firm" by most, eLine views itself as a cross between a community center and think-tank for those concerned with the directions and implications of the emerging technology. eLine will continue to foster this environment that has attracted such talented minds as David Hudson.

Trademark Acknowledgments

All terms mentioned in this book that are known to be trademarks or service marks have been appropriately capitalized. Macmillan Technical Publishing cannot attest to the accuracy of this information. Use of a term in this book should not be regarded as affecting the validity of any trademark or service mark.

Dedication

To Dagmar, Adrienne, and Ian, who had to make do with a virtual husband and father for too many months.

David Hudson

Acknowledgments

First and foremost, my appreciation goes to Andrew Sullivan, whose input and support have been tremendous. Andrew has been right there, every step of the way, intricately involved in all the pesky, finite logistics. But more importantly, many of the essential ideas you'll find here originally sprang from Andrew's fast and clear mind.

Also, this book would never have happened if Bruce Rinehart hadn't set the wheels in motion.

I'd also like to thank Jim LeValley for recognizing the potential and the need for a sober look at online technology and the culture that has evolved from it—and for placing his faith in this team to pull it off.

Portions of this book have appeared in different forms in the *San Francisco Bay Guardian*, the *L.A. Weekly*, *nettime*, *Rhizome*, and of course, on the *Rewired* web site.

David Hudson

Table of Contents

Introduction

Let's Get Sober

We've had the eureka phase in all its euphoric glory. Then the backlash. Now that we're beginning to get over the Internet emotionally, we may be entering the phase in which our brains finally kick in and get to work.

It's about time. For a while there, the hype was getting out of hand. No need to run down all the utopian claims made for the Net at the moment; we'll touch on several of them later as we need them, even if only for the fun of comparing and contrasting them with a rapidly emerging reality. Besides, you have heard the bulk of it from just about every mass media outlet online and off. For now, suffice it to say that the Net was to be at the forefront of a digital revolution that was to radically change everything—lifestyles, politics, the economy, media, even human nature itself. Everything.

The great arc of hype peaked, conveniently enough, smack dab in the middle of the decade. 1995 was the year the Internet—specifically the web—hit the public consciousness big time. Granted, the mass media snowball had already started rolling long before, and certainly the most coveted Christmas gifts of 1994 were computers or accessories to spiff them up with. It was in 1995, however, that the Net became a steady fixture of the American landscape and began to make a serious dent on landscapes elsewhere.

When, in the election of 1992, vice presidential candidate Al Gore spoke of paving the information superhighway, few people in the audiences along the campaign trail knew what he was talking about. The issue did not stir the hearts and minds of the voters. In fact, Gore's concern for the matter only contributed to his image as a policy wonk dealing with pie-in-the-sky irrelevancies, and after a while, Gore's speeches highlighted a different set of themes.

But by the time Newt Gingrich was swept to power in the November 1994 elections, the public was ready to listen to Gingrich's abstract talk of an Information Age. In 1995, the new Speaker of the House had no qualms about going on in public about passing out laptops to the poor (even while promising to do away with the welfare state in the same breath). The Internet was the future, and America had darn well better be ready for it.

What happened? Besides the fact, of course, that the Internet had doubled in size a couple of times between the two politicians' play on the buzzword of the 90s, information. Or that the online population was no longer a fringe society of computer geeks and white coats, but instead was supposedly made up of just plain folks. These factors alone can't explain the change in the mind of the public, especially when we consider that the online population is still quite definitively a minority.

What happened to the Internet is what has happened to other abstract concepts in our culture such as "the deficit" and "Michael Jackson." It got hot. It hit the papers, and as the wave of hype was just starting to crest, made for great wacky human interest spots on TV. Following *Newsweek*'s special issue "TechnoMania" (February 27, 1995), a cover-to-cover announcement that the Information Age had arrived, *Time* released its special Spring 1995 issue, "Welcome to Cyberspace." "Cyberspace" was one of those terms like "online" or even "Internet" itself that was knowingly thrown around a lot, often out of context or misapplied entirely, to catch an eye or an ear. These words were suddenly sexy (sometimes, as with the case of "Cyberporn," *Time*'s other splashy cover, too sexy), and, as the old phrase goes, they sold papers.

The difference between the Net and Michael Jackson is that the Net is not likely to fade away from public consciousness, especially now that so many powerful entities have begun to invest in it, some of them staking their futures on its future. Online technology is here to stay and be tampered with, and will no doubt continue to evolve in surprising, unpredictable ways. Few would question the single most ubiquitous truism of our time: The advent of this technology, spearheaded by the almost accidental explosion of the Internet, will have a tremendous social, cultural, political, and economic impact.

But how much exactly? What is the true nature of this impact? Well, several answers have been put forward, and they vary widely. It all depends on who you listen to. Anyone who tells you he or she knows precisely what the future holds should probably be handled with extreme caution. Be very nice, but slip out of the room the moment you get a chance.

More likely, you will run into forecasters who are either very careful in their assessments or have a vested interest in an extremely positive or negative reading of that impact. So if you're skimming the papers and run into a quote such as, "I don't see how the Internet can be considered overhype when we are talking about something as fundamental as communications," check the source. In this case, it's Netscape chairman James Clark. Aha.

Surely one of the most rosy portraits of what it is all going to be like has got to be Nicholas Negroponte's *Being Digital*, probably not coincidentally one of the bestselling books on the Net and all its related technologies. Even though Negroponte takes a lot of flack for being a techno-utopian, that's really only half fair because he is pretty up front throughout the book about the mode of rampant speculation he has flown into trance-like page by page. There are a lot of what-ifs going on here. "Imagine an electronic newspaper delivered to your home in bits. Assume it is sent to a magical, paper-thin, flexible, waterproof, wireless, lightweight, bright display." Well, just imagine! Typically, these objects of techno-desire are made to seem a shade more plausible with a bit of "here's how we'd pull it off" talk, and one listens because, after all, this is the director of the famous MIT Media Lab talking, and he ought to know. The sentence that immediately follows: "The interface solution is likely to call upon mankind's years of experience with headlining and layout, typographic landmarks, images, and a host of techniques to assist browsing." That just about clears it up, doesn't it?

Little is actually technically nailed down in *Being Digital*, from the Dick Tracy video-conferencing gadgets you will wear on your wrist to the now famous example of the refrigerator that calls up your car to tell it to remind you that you're out of milk, would you please pick up a carton on the way home. But it is an exhilarating read nonetheless so long as you keep it all in perspective. It is only when Negroponte does venture out onto thin ice and makes a tentative prediction with real numbers and all, such as, "My guess is that 1 billion people will be connected by the year 2000," that he gets into trouble. Business-of-the-Net writer David Kline called him on this one in a column for *Wired* magazine's web site "HotWired," noting that before a billion people could log on to the Net, they need access to a phone line. "Currently, there are only about 750 million to 800 million telephone lines worldwide. Even in Asia, where phone usage is growing the fastest, experts are predicting the installation of only 15 million to 20 million new lines annually over the next six years." Details, details...

But Kline didn't stop there. The numbers kept coming. 160 million telephones in the U.S., but only around ten percent of that number on the Net. Because obviously, you need a lot more hardware than a phone (and "what about the 80 to 90 percent of the world that is not affluent?"), and perhaps most crucially, the desire to get out there and join the revolution. "[S]ignificantly, less than half of all owners of computers with modems even choose to go online."

Having spoiled Negroponte's "Over a billion served" scheme, Kline still wasn't finished with him. He'd caught "*Wired* magazine's Utopian in Residence" (Negroponte writes a back page column for the magazine and was one of *Wired*'s earliest and most critical financial backers as well) on National Public Radio by saying, "he believes that there is really no division between rich and poor in who uses the Internet. It's generational, he said; all the young people are using the Net." This "from a man, incidentally, who makes upwards of US$30,000 per one-hour speech."

Unfortunately, two columns later, David Kline's "Market Forces" column was discontinued by "HotWired." You can only go so far. There is a lot to be read between the lines of this story, little observations about who's pumping the hype machine, what they would have to gain out of it, and where the level of tolerance for pesky facts registers in their consciences and pocketbooks. But the point that stands out clearest is that Kline is no extremist. He is a good capitalist who would like to see commerce flourish on the Internet, but like so many mainstreamers, not to mention those suspicious or even terrified of all that the digital revolution is said to represent, he'd had enough. The hype had gotten out of hand; it was way off base.

So when the inevitable backlash hit, for the most part, it missed the mark just as widely. Interestingly, the backlash took to the form of books more than any other medium, and the most prominent to stand out in a wide field would have to be Clifford Stoll's *Silicon Snake Oil*, another big seller. In the summer of 1996, Stoll was on the radio in Berlin, a quick stop along his Beware the Internet world tour, and among the quotes that leapt out at me was: "I could feel my life dribbling away through the modem." And this gem: "Why would anyone spend hours downloading grainy pornographic pictures? People ought to be out in the real world having real sex with each other." I kid you not.

Neither the hype nor the backlash are any help whatsoever in the face of the challenges to the qualities of the online experience that have brought tens of millions of people to check it out. The most important of these is surely maintaining the Net's unique many-to-many model of communication. In the immediate wake of this overriding concern are issues such as the feasibility of universal access, privacy, censorship, community building, individual and cultural identity, and that's just for starters. These are still the salad days of the Net and other forms of online communication, and the decisions we make or fail to make now will have repercussions for generations to come.

So let's sober up. The party's over; we've tossed out the stale hors d'oeuvres; it is morning on the Internet. Fortunately, as we wake in the harsh light of reality, we find that we are not alone.

At about the same time Stoll was sending snappy sound bites over the Berlin airwaves, hundreds of participants in the sixth annual conference of the Internet Society gathered in Montreal for INET '96. The theme of the conference was "The Internet: Transforming Our Society Now," and although that may sound like yet another clarion call for a collective back-patting session, that is not how it turned out.

With all those voices, there are certain to be a few dissenters, but in his paper, "The 1996 Internet Counterrevolution: Power, Information, and the Mass Media," Chris Adams of Goldfarb Consultants put his finger right on the general trend discernible throughout most of the proceedings. "If the first half of the 1990s was the soil in which the Internet social revolution was planted, the second half will sprout the counterrevolution."

Adams outlines what he sees as the rapid deterioration of the Net's many-to-many model, that aspect of the communications medium that makes it truly unique. Instead of newspaper publishers, movie moguls, or television broadcasters sending out their one-way messages to you, everybody is talking to everybody on the Net. All voices are equal. At least they were for a while.

Although still intact theoretically, in practice, the model is fading fast, the old elitist power structures encroaching on the new. Adams places the blame squarely on the almost immediate acquiescence to the commercialization of the Net aided significantly by commercial online services and the essential nature of the web. He reminds us that it wasn't all that long ago when the Net was governed by Acceptable Use Policies (AUPs), which "explicitly banned Internet usage aimed at profit-making."

Although I doubt that Adams has anything against business on the Net per se, he is rightfully concerned with raising our awareness of the effects of its glowering presence. It is one thing to speak your mind in a commercial-free environment, and quite another to speak the same words in a forum "hosted" by a party with a financial interest in what is said there. Not to mention the fierce competitiveness unleashed onto the "level playing field," whereby whoever has the deepest pockets can out-spend, out-banner, out-sponsor, and so on anyone of lesser means, regardless of the actual value contributed to the discourse the Net is supposed to be all about.

Adams's is one of the many voices representing that general morning-after feeling detectable in several key papers delivered at the conference. Some of the more notables place the Net in historical perspective, specifically comparing and contrasting previous declarations of inevitable social transformation that never happened with the one not happening now. Hans Klein of the Institute of Public Policy sums it up best: "The launch of new communications technologies is usually accompanied by bold predictions of positive social change. With the successive creation of telephone, film, radio, television, cable television, and now the Internet have come optimistic predictions of empowerment, enlightenment, and broad social benefits. Yet as each of these technological revolutions has receded into the past and its historical record of social change has become available for study, that record has frequently disappointed expectations."

Klein did, however, leave out the airplane. That's right, the airplane. Although not exactly a communications technology, its invention set the public imagination on fire. Think of it. Flight! To me, a machine that gets me off the ground, above the clouds, and from one continent to the next in the time it would take to drive across a modest European country beats the heck out of any web site on the wow scale. And the people who witnessed the airplane's invention thought so, too.

"Not a man but felt that this was the beginning of such a mighty era that no tongue could tell its import, and those who gazed felt awestruck, as though they had torn aside the veil of the future and looked into the very Holy of Holies..." Nice. So nice and so durable, I'm quoting Graham Rayman, quoting historian Joseph Corn, quoting Mary Parker who originally wrote it in 1910. Rayman offers several examples of people allowing their common sense to take off with those new flying machines, evangelists who thought the airplane would bring you closer to God, and others who thought the machine was a step toward our own godliness, such as Alfred Lawson, who wrote a book in 1916 describing a race of "Alti-men" living in the skies above "Ground-men" who would dwell "at the bottom of the atmospheric sea like a crab or an oyster." How quickly these new inventions redraw class lines.

Rayman has also written on the general hysteria that greeted the telephone, noting such oddities as the 1881 *Scientific American* article portraying the telephone as the harbinger of a new "kinship of humanity" in that people would no longer be separated by geographical distance. Sound familiar? How about these predictions Rayman has dusted off: "Science fiction writer H. G. Wells said the telephone would reduce traffic jams. Futurist Herbert Casson held that the phone would enhance the bonds between citizens. Sociologist Charles Horton Cooley said it would subvert local ties in favor of nationalistic concerns."

Rayman then picks up the book, *America Calling*, by historian Claude Fischer, written in 1992. Fischer had set out to document the changes the phone had wrought in American society over the decades, but ended up writing, "The telephone did not radically alter American ways of life; rather Americans used it to more vigorously pursue their characteristic ways of life." The more things change...

Meanwhile, back at INET '96, Mark Surman draws in the paper he delivered to the conference, "Wired Words: Utopia, Revolution, and the History of Electronic Highways," similar parallels between the broken promises of cable TV and those not-yet-broken of the Net. "Here is a piece of advice—beware of self-styled, wired revolutionaries bearing gifts. You probably know who I'm talking about. If you don't, you'll know them when you see them. They'll be carrying all sorts of shiny parcels with words like democracy, plenitude, equity, and knowledge emblazoned across the wrapping in big, fluorescent orange letters." Yes, Mr. Surman, I believe we know who you're talking about. "Faith, revolution, and the wired world," he continues, "this is a combination that rules our popular mind in the mid-1990s."

Surman notes three specific signs of techno-utopianism to be on the look out for, signs that have appeared with each consecutive wave of definitively life-transforming innovations: "1) that massive and positive social change will emerge from the introduction of a new communications technology; 2) that these changes will be caused by the inherent technical properties of the hardware; and 3) that the social revolution occurring as a result of the new technology is of a scale not seen for hundreds, or even thousands, of years." Later in the paper, Surman notes that in *Wired's* debut issue, "publisher Louis Rossetto related the Digital Revolution to '...social changes so profound their only parallel is probably the discovery of fire.' (*Wired* 1.1, p.10.) In typical *Wired* style, Rossetto had to prove that his revolution was bigger, better, and cooler than anyone else's."

Surman doesn't deny that there is a communications revolution going on. But when you take all the factors of its making into account, it is a long, drawn-out revolution, begun over a century ago and far from over. Reading his version of how he sees it put together, I couldn't help but think of the industrial revolution. What are the dates on that one exactly? There aren't any exact dates, of course, which makes it difficult to classify it as a revolution in the sense that the American, French, and Russian revolutions had definite first and last shots defining their beginnings, their ends, and the clear differences between what life was like before and after them.

Like the industrial revolution, the digital one is an exciting idea. The gift or coincidence, depending on your orientation, of being alive in revolutionary times heightens the senses and the affections you're likely to feel for souvenirs of the experience. Just as that miniature Eiffel Tower pencil sharpener may identify you as someone who's been to Paris and back, so does your e-mail address make you a card-carrying digital revolutionary.

Glorious as it is, this is hardly the place to review Surman's complete history of cable television, but the parallels between even the rhetoric then and the rhetoric now will floor you if you're not already familiar with both stories. In 1970, *The Nation* even ran an article on the promise of cable tech called "The Wired Nation," and Surman points to numerous examples of the use of the "electronic highway" metaphor.

Bear with me a moment and take a look at just this one paragraph. "Some envisioned two-way, switched common carrier information networks on which anyone could say their piece. Others saw an international network of networks made up of cable systems from around the world. Still others imagined a new world of home shopping, home voting, home banking, facsimile newspapers that would 'roll off' a television set, movies-on-demand, electronic mail, interactive computer information services, and digital libraries. And because real two-way cable systems were actually up and running on a trial basis in a number of small American cities, many people believed that these services would be available within a few years. The cable revolution was a chance to grab hold of tomorrow today."

Sadly, the story ends with a few mega-companies buying up all the "mom and pop" cable outlets and transforming this democratizing, many-to-many medium into yet another entrenched few-to-many broadcasting model. "The techno-revolutionaries dreamed of a cabled utopia. All they got was a whole lot more television."

Now, all that being said, Surman wraps up by pointing out that the Net may very well indeed represent the first genuine opportunity to "break the loop," to collectively swerve out of the seemingly endless cycle of invention and cooptation of new technologies by the powerful and moneyed elite. The most promising aspect of the Net as a truly different sort of new communications medium is that people have been built into it since its beginning.

This is not a top-down technology. The essential nature of the Net wasn't intentionally conceived by anyone. After the merest semblance of a core was created, the rest just sort of happened. There were no test cases in Nielson-like households, no market surveys, or for that matter, any marketing efforts at all until very late in the game.

Online technology has more potential for realizing the dreams visionaries dreamt when they saw their first radio, their first telephone, or going way back, their first printing press. But that potential is threatened by the same market forces that have hijacked the hopes placed in the technologies that preceded the Net. Already, we're looking at the words we have to say to one another and wondering about their monetary value. What do we have that could be digitalized and sold to the highest bidder? And how much would we be willing to pay for somebody else's? And is the middleman's fee worth it, or is there a cheaper offer elsewhere?

Although his INET '96 paper is more dour than Surman's, William Birdsall of Dalhousie University is more succinct as he dissects what he calls the Ideology of Information Technology which "links the adoption of information technology with free-market values and the commodification of information." Speaking of which, the value of information itself as an instrument of social change on a global scale is called into question by Nils Zurawski of the University of Münster, especially when the content of that information is utterly ignored—"information as fetish" is a phrase that pops up, and is one that belongs in any time capsule we bury documenting the first half of the decade.

As to what will denote '96 and after, the final days of the 20th century—itself punctuating one hell of a millennium, crescendoing and decrescendoing with revolutions, counterrevolutions, and reformations— wouldn't it be fine if we could say of our times, This was when we started asking the questions that mattered: Who's served by our technologies? What are the values that last, that matter, and how do we apply our abilities and talents on a global, national, local, and individual scale to ensuring they win out?

And wouldn't it be even finer if we actually stumbled over a few of the answers, and then went so far as to put them to practical use? But don't be putting any money on that actually happening. No one else is.

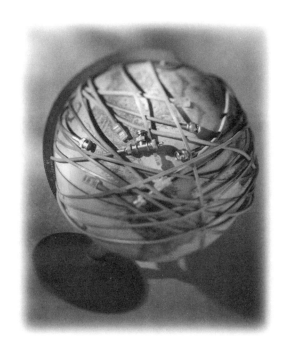

Con.txt: A Brief (and Opinionated) Net History

"The Net is nothing but an inert mass of metal, plastic and sand. We are the only living beings in cyberspace."
Richard Barbrook

Chapter One
Anarchy That Works

Every history ever written or told is to some extent revisionist, just as every fleeting moment of the present is prismatically fractured by individual perceptions of it. And every prediction of the future is bound to be wrong, either a little or a lot.

So take this little Net history as you should take every history—with more than a few grains of salt. This discussion sweeps quickly, almost irresponsibly so, over ground already well covered in books and articles great and small, from the Net's fuzzy genesis to just before the scene-stealing entrance of the Web in 1993.

It is a landscape currently being mapped in finite detail on probably one of the most interesting and appropriate of Net history projects, the Community Memory Discussion List on the History of Cyberspace. Sponsored by the Computer Professionals for Social Responsibility (CPSR) and moderated by writer David S. Bennahum, the mailing list connects the voices of those who were there when the first computers were linked, as well as those who wish they had been there, and those just interested in eavesdropping on the conversation. With a nicely resonant touch, the list has been named after the original Community Memory Project in San Francisco, dating back to the early 1970s. Many suspect that this project was "the world's first grass-roots electronic bulletin board," as the CPSR announcement puts it.

The Net, of course, precedes that Bulletin Board Service (BBS) and all others. It is worth noting, however, that almost immediately after the

core of what was to become the Net was in service, up popped the urge
to apply this new technology to form a community, to personalize and
humanize it. That urge manifested itself from the very beginning, when
the handful of supercomputers that were the original nodes of the Ur-Net
were soon being used to exchange personal messages, e-mail's ancestors.
This "extracurricular," personal use occurred more often than functions
specifically related to the Net's originally intended use—namely,
supercomputing along a sort of government-sponsored time-share
program.

A "look back" is in order here, lest the discussion jump into modern
waters without relevant review and credit being given to the rain that
made it all possible. Like all technologies, online tech is intricately rooted—
or wired—in the technologies that came before it. Every narrative
necessarily begins *in medias res*. If you tend to view the Net as just
another step in the development of telecommunications, therefore, you
go back to Alexander Graham Bell and start from there. In that case, the
first words in cyberspace were "Come here, Watson. I need you." How
human can you get?

Poetic as this scenario is, Bell's phone of 1876 was actually antedated
by the one developed 15 years before by one Philipp Reis, a German
physicist. And because the Net works by transmitting encoded information
along wires, how could you count the telegraph out? As early as 1858,
cable technology had advanced far enough to give the Atlantic cable a
try—it didn't really work until 1866, but once it did, it operated for nearly
100 years, providing a link between Europe and America a lot faster than
your typical 28.8 bps modem of today. And if you look up telegraphy in
your trusty encyclopedia, you find Greeks and Persians saying, "Howdy,"
with torches at around 500 B.C. Although this is really stretching the
point a bit, it does add an air of historical depth to the Net's fine art of
flaming.

If you look at the Net as essentially another aspect of computing, you
will start where most histories start—with ARPAnet. You picture a time
when what used to be the Soviet Union shook a complacent U.S. awake
with a tin can in the sky, Sputnik. Wars do wonders for the advancement
of technology, and the "cold" one was certainly no exception. The way to
get a technology advanced is to gather a lot of really smart people under
one roof and get them to simultaneously concentrate on a single project.
Of course, that takes some organization and money on the part of either
the government or private enterprise. That can of worms is opened later.

In this case, the funding and organization emanated from the only
body that had a stake in making certain that the Net would work—the

government. Then President Eisenhower sent out the call and created the Advanced Research Projects Agency, or ARPA. The first thing the agency did was get America's own satellite up and orbiting within a year and a half. Next, the agency shifted its collective focus onto computer networking. Here's where it gets interesting. ARPA was being funded with Defense Department money (and later even switched its name to DARPA to justify those funds, the D standing for the Ds in DoD). What with the Cold War in full swing and all, the military—specifically its think tank, the Rand Corporation—was concerned that if the war ever got "hot" and large chunks of the country were vaporized, those phone lines (not to mention considerable segments of the population) would be radioactive dust. And then the top brass would not be able to get in touch and carry on.

The solution goes like this. You're at point A and you've got a message you need to get to point Z. You write your message, which of course to the computer is nothing but a long string of zeros and ones (no matter how eloquent it looks to you on-screen). When you send it, it gets splintered off into little packets, little pellets shot out into the network. Each of these packets has an address written at the front of it: point Z. These things go bouncing around more or less in the direction of point Z, but not directly. On purpose. This is the beauty of the design. You will need some of the points B through Y, but not all of them, and it doesn't particularly matter which ones.

The packets don't need to zip in alphabetic order because ultimately, even if not directly, all the letters—or nodes of the Net—are connected to all the others. Think of the knots tying the strings of an actual net together (say, a fishing net). You can trace your finger along the strings and eventually connect any of the two knots. Even if you cut a couple of holes out of the net, you can just trace around them. The same principle applies to the Internet. Even if letters G, J, R, and S are bombed out, you can still get your message from point A to point Z.

Consider what the sci-fi writer Bruce Sterling noted in his own (very fine) *Short History of the Internet*, dating all the way back to 1993: The Net is probably one of the only technological innovations built with the assumption that it is going to take several serious hits, that it would "be unreliable at all times. It would be designed from the get-go to transcend its own unreliability."

Now for this to really work, each of the *nodes*—computers hooked to the Net—has to be more than just connected. It has got to have all the privileges of any other node. Because if you have any one machine acting as authority over any other, overseeing the traffic, nodding approval, and letting messages pass, and that happens to be the machine that gets blitzed, the system's out. Each and every node, therefore, must be capable of sending, receiving, and passing on data.

What's being described here is a model of anarchy that works. But it is a very controlled environment. These nodes all get along and work in perfect harmony for the following two reasons:

- TCP/IP
- No inherent intelligence

First, all these nodes speak the same language, a protocol called TCP/IP. That protocol, as Sterling puts it, is "strictly technical, not social or political." This is possible only because of the blatantly obvious second reason: The machines have no inherent intelligence of their own.

This amazing model works because it is a lot like that couple the Woody Allen character meets on the street in *Annie Hall*. He asks them why their relationship functions without ever hitting any bumps in the road, and they frankly reply that it is because neither of them has any thoughts or opinions of his or her own. Such is the Net—beautiful to look at, but dumb as a stick.

A serious mistake was made early on, however, when humans looked at that beautiful model of TCP/IP enhanced anarchy, saw it working, and assumed it could and would be metaphorically transferred to another sort of protocol—human behavior. The machines may be dumb, but they aren't greedy. They don't try to drive any other machines off the Net, and they're not out to dominate the marketplace. As Richard Barbrook, a professor at the Hypermedia Research Centre of the University of Westminster, London, has put it so well, "The Net is nothing but an inert mass of metal, plastic and sand. We are the only living beings in cyberspace."

And those living beings are not behaving themselves. You know, the usual little tricks. Hold on to that thought! This line of thinking is picked up again more than once later in this book.

Chapter Two

The Untelevised
R/evolution

Meanwhile, back on track. After the group of brilliant minds had been gathered, and after the symposiums had been held, the papers exchanged, and the method of solving the military's riddle had been decided on, the time had come to put the theories, experiments, and test runs to work. The time was 1969. The world was enraptured with Neil Armstrong's planting the first human footprint on the moon, thoroughly convinced that this footprint would grow to orbiting space colonies and generations of earthlings born and raised on Mars.

Few would have guessed that the conquering of outer space, the final frontier, would eventually be indefinitely postponed even as a group of researchers were virtually switching on a whole new frontier: Cyberspace. While most eyes were trained on the sky—or at least television's reproduction of it—the first nodes or "hosts" of the ARPAnet were quietly connected.

The Internet was born in a single moment at four locations: Stanford Research Institute, UCLA, UC Santa Barbara, and the University of Utah. Significantly, all of these college campuses were (and are) sites of a significant amount of government sponsored research. Just as significantly, all of these sites are in the western United States, three of the four in California (home to Silicon Valley and oodles of Cold War-era Defense

Rewired

Department dollars). Another couple of thoughts to file in the back of your mind for future reference.

Nuclear war may have been on the minds of the military sponsors, but the researchers, scientists, and engineers actually doing the nitty-gritty work that got the Net up and running had other concerns they considered more immediate and practical. To keep that advancement of technology momentum rolling, they needed as much computing power as they could get their hands on, and supercomputers could and still can take quite a bite out of a budget. So they were eager to embrace the ARPAnet as a way they could all access time on a supercomputer without everybody having to be in the same room with one.

A lot of the traffic flowing along the tiny Net soon had less to do with the research the military was interested in and more to do with whatever it was the researchers themselves were working on at the time. It wasn't long, as mentioned earlier, before even that had to share time with messages shooting along the wires that had nothing to do with science or technology whatsoever. Not even the white coats could resist the naturally human appeal of personal e-mail.

Then there were general announcements to be made. Rather than meticulously addressing the same message to each and every recipient, the ARPAnet crew invented the electronic mailing list. You could write your message once—"big meeting of brilliant minds on Tuesday"—and zap it automatically to several personal e-mailboxes with a single keystroke. Here too, the rules were soon bent to favor the ways real people wanted to use the technology. Bruce Sterling notes, "One of the first really big mailing-lists was 'SF-LOVERS,' for science fiction fans. Discussing science fiction on the network was not work-related and was frowned upon by many ARPANET computer administrators, but this didn't stop it from happening."

Throughout the 70s, ARPAnet quietly rumbled along, growing sturdier, its hosts multiplying, their computing powers becoming increasingly super. Even as late as 1981, however, there were still only 213 hosts. Even though this was quite a bit more than four, and what's more important, not all of them were in the U.S., this was not exactly the phenomenon that would be grabbing headlines in the 90s.

It was around 1979 that things really started hopping. Computer networking in general started taking off and a variety of nets scurried around their own territories using different protocols—and hence, were not linked to each other, much less ARPAnet. For one thing, the military took a liking to its baby, but it wasn't wild about having its internal messages running on the same lines as the ones used by research institutions, universities, and so on. In 1983, therefore, ARPAnet was actually split. There was the ARPAnet and the Milnet (Military Network), though gateways existed between them.

For the most part, however, the heads of the various networks were concentrating on ways of linking them all. The most interesting case of many is probably BITNET, created in 1981 to link the City University of New York and Yale. Interesting because it grew as fast in three years as ARPAnet had grown in more than ten. Universities piled on for reasons of shared interest, and because most of them ran IBM mainframes and the BITNET protocol was an IBM concoction.

"When the technology is credited for the actions of the people using it, not only is that inaccurate reporting… but the same two-edged sword can whip back the other way in a flash. Given an uninformed, fickle press, 'The Internet' can just as quickly become synonymous with child pornography, make-money-fast schemes, and credit card number crunchers as with a worldwide community and the savior of a moribund economy."

David Hudson

Chapter Three
Anarchy That Sort of Works and Sort of Doesn't

The other big story from 1979 is UseNet. Two graduate students at Duke University, Tom Truscott and Jim Ellis, and Steve Bellovin at the University of North Carolina developed some software for their Unix machines that would enable them to get word out to each other should anything happen of interest to Unix-types. (Unix machines are big, robust monsters favored by hardcore programmers.)

A couple of vital points about UseNet: It also grew incredibly fast, and new topics being discussed quickly and completely veered away from Unix and computing. Now there are thousands, maybe tens of thousands, of topics from the most mundane to the most sublime being hashed out by millions of people. E-mail may be the most personal form of human communication going on out there, but it was UseNet that presented the prospect of a genuine, worldwide community (as yet, unrealized). The reality of UseNet as it is remains a far cry from the ideal that some thought it might have been. And yet, its attraction was immediate and remarkable. Hence, a pause in this history lesson for a few immediate remarks.

It was, and of course still is, something of a giant BBS. Messages didn't zip from one mailbox to another, but were posted to an electronic board—a newsgroup. The same program that enables you to see what has been pinned up there enables you to read the posts and write your own.

UseNet stands for the Users' Network. Users created it, and for quite a while, they ran it. No government agency or private enterprise was behind it. A connection, or feed, could be had for the asking so long as you generally behaved yourself—or even better, helped someone else jump aboard. Again, another model for anarchy that works. Only this time, the model wasn't counting on the absolute unintelligence of machines, but rather, the good faith of its users. How long could it last?

Well, that's debatable. You will hear some say it still works just fine. And you will meet others with horror stories to tell. To back up, calling the content on UseNet "news" is a bit of a misnomer. What you find in each of the newsgroups is usually pretty chatty. In fact, unless you have an inordinate level of tolerance for a highly skewed signal-to-noise ratio, or you've stumbled over a newsgroup that you're interested in that happens to be moderated to a degree you can live with, or you've found that rare newsgroup that has got itself under control, you may find the whole experience too messy to trouble with.

Yet it is next to impossible to talk about what happens on UseNet in general terms. The virtues and vices of UseNet range as widely and to such extremes as human behavior itself. People have met and fallen in love there, found husbands and wives, and/or fed the fires of extramarital affairs there. There have been confrontations that have led to real-life courtroom dramas—cyberrape, cyberlibel, cyberstalking, cyber just about anything nasty you can do to a fellow human. When people talk about *flaming*, a term referring to the rabid verbal abuse usually directed from one person to another via the Net—a practice with such a long and rich tradition it is sometimes hard to tell whether it is being done in earnest or in sport—they are more often than not talking about UseNet.

At the same time, UseNet has brought out the best in people. That may sound schmaltzy, but let me tell you. I once took a summer job writing up little blurbs for a book on health-related Net resources (hey, it took care of a few outstanding bills). What I found on UseNet moved me in ways that information I found elsewhere never could have. When disease strikes, it strikes a whole family and their circle of friends, and few can cope without talking to someone who has been there before or is now dealing with the same terrifying challenges. I found online enclaves exchanging posts ranging from practical medical tips (that doctors just don't take the time to give or explain) to heart-crushing death watches in which an entire newsgroup would be there for the patient, the family, and friends (even if "only" virtually).

There are also the stories the press loves to pick up and run with. The one about the guy in the U.S. who saw a suicide note posted and got in touch with the poster's Internet Service Provider in Nijmegen, Holland. Dutch social workers naturally reached the depressed man in the nick of time. Film at eleven.

Certainly, these episodes aren't to be scoffed at, but there are two sides to this coin. For every online wedding or transcontinental rescue operation, there's a sweet newspaper clipping or television sound bite. These are just more drops in the overflowing cup of Internet hype that only does more to mystify the technology than to clarify it. When the technology is credited for the actions of the people using it, not only is that inaccurate reporting plain and simple (as well as being unfair to the genuine "heroes" of the story), but the same two-edged sword can whip back the other way in a flash. Given an uninformed, fickle press, "The Internet" can just as quickly become synonymous with child pornography, make-money-fast schemes, and credit card number crunchers as with a worldwide community and the savior of a moribund economy.

The last note about UseNet to play isn't really about UseNet at all, but about its distant relatives—the thousands of BBSs that sprouted mushroom-like all over the globe. The big, obvious difference between these and UseNet is that they weren't global, but localized. To get into most of them, you would set your modem to dial in to them directly. Choosing a BBS in your own area code, therefore, made solid financial sense. But this isn't the only reason. A BBS may be set up for users who share a particular interest or profession (doctors, artists, and so on), but the vast majority are meant to serve (or cash in on) a community defined by geography.

Locals gathered (and still do) as they would at a party, and the guest list was the usual mix of old friends and new folks in town. Conversation ranged from the movies showing at the cineplex to local politics to the weather. Some have compared these BBSs to local town meetings. But if meetings were this unruly, nothing would ever get done. A lot of hope has been placed in online technology as a harbinger for a new genuine democracy, but again, that hope is misplaced. The technology itself couldn't care less about democracy or any other flavor of politics. With apologies to James Carville: It's the people, stupid!

"The idea of haves and have-nots was beginning to take hold, and some of those concerned about the gap and its impact were taking their first steps toward doing something about it."

David Hudson

Chapter Four
Acronym City

BITNET, Janet, CSNET, UseNet, Milnet, and of course ARPAnet and countless other networks were teeming with life in the early 80s, and the life forms inhabiting each were looking enviously at those in nearly all the others. Gateways were erected to accommodate the natural desire to mix and mingle, translating the protocol of one so that it could be fed to another, and vice versa. Needless to say, it was getting chaotic.

It was time to come up with a way to enable everybody to get together with everybody else. Among those on the team that would come up with it was Vinton Cerf, sometimes referred to as the "Father of the Internet" (a bit personal, but that's it). Granted, Cerf had been elected as the first chairman of the Internetworking Working Group way back in 1972 and had been actively engaged at every step of the way, but to ball up the efforts of so many behind a single name is an oversimplification to which Cerf himself would readily object.

At any rate, the sought-after enabler was TCP/IP, the Esperanto of the "Internet"—a word first used in 1982 as an umbrella term for all the connected networks. Now here's where this discussion picks up speed (just as the Net itself did), skimming over all but a few dates and names, and focusing instead on just the significant events and pre-web applications that fed the Net's amazing growth before it really went boom.

Something like a second ARPAnet was created in 1986. By this time, the next generation of supercomputers was redefining "super" all over again, and the universities and research institutions were faced with the same old problem. They needed time on them, but couldn't afford to buy one of their own. The National Science Foundation, therefore, created NSFNET, which was faster and sturdier than ARPAnet. Guess what? It blossomed overnight as well.

Why they didn't just use ARPAnet in the first place is another long story. Suffice it to say, because it involved so much bureaucracy and red tape, it was easier and quicker just to build a new one. That, too, should be kept in mind before waxing too poetic on the benefits of government largeness. Nevertheless, it was another happy accident in Net history. NSFNET performed so splendidly that the old (but faithful) ARPAnet could retire in 1990 at the ripe age of 21. NSFNET was now the "backbone" of the Internet.

NSFNET was all well and good for the hotshot university and research types, but what about the other educational institutions (the community colleges and so forth)? Furthermore, because the taxpayers are indeed paying for all this anyway, what about the kids (the K–12 graders)? Providing these second-tier educational facilities, the public libraries, and others with the benefits of the new resource was the object of the High-Performance Computing Act of 1991 sponsored by that dashing young senator from Tennessee, Al Gore. The act created (ready for another one?) NREN, the National Research and Education Network.

The government wasn't the only body directing its attention to what would become an increasingly complex problem of access to the Net. Back in 1986, when NSFNET went online, the first freenet was set up by Case Western Reserve University in Cleveland for the Society for Public Access

Computing. The idea of haves and have-nots was beginning to take hold, and some of those concerned about the gap and its impact were taking their first steps toward doing something about it.

These were the waning years for the favorable light in which the government was cast in the eyes of what was then often referred to as the Net community. You don't hear much about them anymore, either. That comes up later as well.

Jumping ahead ever so briefly, NSFNET eventually went the way of ARPAnet in 1995. The government was officially out of the Internet business. Indeed, by that time, the Internet had truly become a business.

"...the obvious key to the hearts and minds of the masses was the interface. The more friendly and self-explanatory the interface, the more willing people who rarely spent time on a computer were to try it out."

David Hudson

Chapter Five

The Net Before It Got Webbed

Take a look at these numbers. In 1984, there were around one thousand Internet hosts. In 1987, ten thousand. In 1989, one hundred thousand. That's growth. Such growth is cause for brushing off the old and overused headline screamers "Phenomenal" and "Explosion." No wonder that when the mainstream media finally caught on to what was going on under its nose, it couldn't find superlatives super enough to convey it to those who hadn't yet heard. After numbers such as those got out, the Net didn't need the hype.

Anyone who has come online in just the last few years may very well wonder what people were doing on the Internet before there was a web. E-mail, sure. And some had heard of the newsgroups. But what did you actually do?

The answer lies in a plethora of unique applications, protocols, and just plain neat stuff to waste your evening hours away with, most of which is still up and running. This discussion avoids diving into the history or technical aspects of each of them, but a few warrant honorable mentions in any retelling of the Net's story, especially one that's meant to set the stage so that you can watch things fall off it in later chapters.

Where to begin, now that the shackles of chronology have been thrown off?

How about Internet Relay Chat (IRC)? Several versions of talk programs enable you to, that's right, "talk" with another person, which actually means write in short rapid spurts (but nevertheless "live"). Basically, it is a telephone conversation in which both parties act as his or her own stenographer. In these days of live audio Internet telephony, all that has become rather quaint. But at the time, it was exciting to be able to chat with people halfway around the world either for free or for next to nothing. That, however, was only half the thrill. The other half was that it was on your computer.

That half a thrill shouldn't be underestimated in any deconstruction of whatever it is that got so many people so terribly excited the first time they saw things popping up on their screens that they weren't putting up there themselves. Signals from the beyond, right there on their own personal computer. Exhilarating!

It didn't matter that a lot of what appeared there could have been had much easier offline—articles from some magazine and scanned copies of the classics (dotted with odd characters, typos, and Dadaesque punctuation). Part of the excitement was about the potential, where all this might lead. Part of it was about grabbing stuff for free, and part of it was the plain old American love of gadgetry—a love not necessarily shared by all cultures (as discussed later).

But the people-to-people connectivity, especially when it so seamlessly ignored geographical hurdles, was unique to this new technology. Few Internet tricks brought this into greater relief than IRC in 1988. IRC was talk on the wide open plain, where you could meet potentially anybody online at the same time you were on and chat away. There might be just the two of you, or there might be ten or twenty on a single channel. When the O. J. Simpson verdict was handed down, around two hundred people gathered on #oj. (The # stands for "channel.")

You will find IRC cast in some histories in a somewhat heroic role, getting news out during the Gulf War or when what used to be Yugoslavia unraveled. But mostly, it has been just people being people. Some of them meet regularly, others just wander through, and many just hide behind the mask of anonymity (out on the prowl). Some of them were (are) quite charming, and others really not.

During the Net's salad days, communication on BBSs, UseNet, IRC, or the various MUDs and MOOs (role-playing games) was mostly text-based. Thus a faceless veil combined with the immediacy of talk. This combination, either live or at least faster than the post office, brought out qualities in people even they themselves may not have been aware they had—good ones and bad ones, openly displayed to strangers.

Sherry Turkle, a psychologist and professor at MIT, has written one of the most popular and fascinating books on the online experience. *Life on the Screen: Identity in the Age of the Internet* dives into all this and comes back up with some intriguing theories on both the benefits and the dangers of the multiple selves that almost inevitably arise and introduce themselves when people go online. Turkle interviewed countless people, and one of them comes out with arguably the most telling line in the book when she says that online, "I feel more like who I wish I was."

That, too, must be factored into the attraction of the Net and its incredibly rapid growth—a subset of the main attraction: communication with other people.

Two or three other things to do on the pre-web Internet were not about that immediate communication, but they were always mentioned as part of the package when you tried to justify those hours spent online or when you tried to pull another friend aboard. Via FTP (File Transfer Protocol), you could download just about anything that could be digitized— texts, pictures, sounds, little video clips, screen savers, games, and software.

FTP is important in this context because it encouraged the incredible sharing mode into which early Net users fell to such an extent that it was almost (eerily) not quite human. Software, for example. Sure, many companies were releasing updates to software that you had already bought or demos for software they wanted you to buy. But the majority of the programs out there were either shareware (for which you were encouraged to pay a nominal fee, usually somewhere between $5.00 and $25.00) or freeware. Free! Just log on and take it.

Here too, of course, the motives behind a programmer's freely distributed work were not always as pure as the driven snow. It is no fun pointing that out, because they were surely purer than most motives you come across in the real world—that has to be stressed. But at the same time, it should be noted that the programmer would get his or her name around, the program serving as something of a résumé (equally useful to those who wrote it and those who read it).

And then in 1991, Mark MaCahill and his team at the University of Minnesota created Gopher. Gopher was, in MaCahill's words, "The first Internet application my mom can use." That pretty much sums up its importance. In many ways, it was a precursor to the web in that you could point your mouse to an item on a menu, click on it, and that item would pop up on-screen (usually after some hesitation). Gopher, in fact, generated a lot of excitement; so much so that when Tim Burners-Lee was trying to get attendees at a conference interested in an early demonstration of what was to become the web, he could barely drag anyone out of the demonstration of the then-current state of Gopher.

In many other ways, however, Gopher differs significantly from the web. Its structure was essentially hierarchical, meaning that you had a sort of "table of contents" way of navigating around the resources available. You could follow your nose for a while, but to get oriented, you might very well have to back out to a menu on a higher level. As Gopher grew more sophisticated, links became more intertwined, and you could feasibly "surf" just as freely in Gopherspace as on the web.

More importantly, although you could download pictures, sounds, or other nontextual files, they were never displayed on a single, cohesive "page" as they would be on the web. Gopher, in other words, never got pretty. And that, in terms of its capability to catch the eye of a non-techie user or coverage in the mainstream media, explains why it quickly lost out to the web as the Net's feature attraction.

Still, Gopher was a step (even if in another direction) toward putting a user-friendly interface on what were still most often referred to as resources. Those resources included scholarly papers, news, magazine articles, and what have you—textual goodies served up for free from all over the globe right to your screen. Quite a thrill! How long it would last was a matter of individual taste. When writer Dennis Woo wondered out loud on the conference board ("RE-sponse") at the "Rewired" site why what he used to download isn't what he downloads anymore, he tripped a few synapses in my own memory of the pre-web Internet.

Cheap thrills. They don't last.

Yes, I too remember my first days and weeks after getting hooked up—quite a surprise, actually, considering the state those weeks threw me into, what with no sleep and all. Henry James! Have I read that story? No. Download it!

Wow! A HyperCard version of *Heart of Darkness*! Sure, I've all but memorized it, but...a HyperCard!

You started filling your disk with the gems of world literature...and then what? How many did you actually read? Who sits down at his or her desk and stares into the monitor to read for pleasure?

You then moved on to the next thing: raiding those FTP sites for games, pictures (now I've got all these great pictures of Björk...now I can...what?), sound clips (come over here, dear, listen to this, it's from *2001*... That's great, honey. It's 3 a.m. We have the whole movie on video. Come to bed.)

And Gopher. And IRC! Did that for a week. Hi, how are you? I'm fine, how about you? Fine. Any horny women on this channel? Ugh.

Telnet. Libraries! Couple of nights reading files from the card catalogues. Fun for a while, but...next!

Next, of course, would be the web, and how long that will hold the public's interest is the subject of chapters to come.

Before wrapping up, it is important to mention the commercial online services. I have only had to deal with them personally for about a week or so each, so I could review them for a computer magazine. These commercial online services include America Online (AOL), CompuServe, Prodigy, Delphi, GEnie, and many others that have come and gone. To put it mildly, none of them are viewed all too favorably by hardcore "real Net" users. Some of the criticism is fair, but a lot of it is snobbishness plain and simple.

As of this writing, one of the points being debated is whether the web will kill them all off. Certainly only two have any real bankable hope at the moment: AOL and CompuServe. I would not bet money on Prodigy's survival one way or the other, because it, like any other proprietary service, is being forced to redefine itself as quickly as the Net evolves (and that's still pretty darn quick).

The point of bringing up the commercial online services in this historical fly-by review, however, is not to discuss business strategies and survival tactics. The services are important historically for a couple of reasons. Even if they didn't introduce it single-handedly, they did wonders for the idea of online time as a commodity. You pay by the hour. In return, you get e-mail (at first internal and later Net-wide), conferencing (BBS-like boards localized according to interest rather than geography), and eventually live chat. The services offered content.

Content. What a buzzword this would turn out to be. Sometimes the services paid content providers—magazines, newspapers, other media companies, or individual writers—to put some or all of their good stuff online to attract customers. Sometimes it worked the other way around. Content providers paid the services for distribution of their product. Either way, you, the user, didn't pay for the content itself. Instead, you paid for the time to access it, so the pressure was on to get in, get busy, and get back out.

Ideas have been floated for selling content by the bit (literally), both on the services and the Net itself. In some ways, it makes sense. You pay for the actual product you are there for. The provider has a tighter control on the supply and can see up close who wants what, so it can target its future products more accurately. But so far, none of these ideas has been really workable for a lot of reasons. Probably the overriding reason is that after people are actually faced with the decision to fork over a tangible amount of cash for a specific chunk of content, they usually won't.

The commercial services were a hothouse of clever approaches to the challenge of getting people online and keeping them there. Again, they were essentially big BBSs, but they sure didn't want to be seen that way. Likewise, BBSs—even those set up as money-making propositions—wouldn't want to be classified as commercial online services.

America Online sold the idea of just that: online access to the whole country. CompuServe, on the other hand, which soon became known as a businessperson's network, offered the world—but you paid accordingly. To give credit where credit is due, CompuServe was for the longest time one of the only ways anyone without hacker credentials could pick up his or her e-mail in just about any major city in Europe or the U.S., and even a few others outside the "first world" as well.

Ultimately, America Online would outpace CompuServe by concentrating on economy rather than business or first-class customers. Live chats with celebrities, big stadium-like events in which you would actually be assigned a certain seat on a certain row, regularly scheduled club meetings—all kinds of gimmicks were introduced that would later be picked up and exploited by other services, BBSs, and web sites, many of them ironically long-time critics of AOL's pandering to the masses.

The irony goes deeper than that. Maybe more than any other factor, the commercial online services brought non-technical types online in droves during the Net's pre-web days. For better or worse (and the truth is probably a bit of both), they were the ones doing the marketing of the online experience, while many on the Internet (certainly not everyone, but a considerable crowd) resisted popular acceptance of what they considered to be their own underground toy. "Newbies" were shunned.

Besides the marketing campaigns—the most infamous example of which has got to be AOL's mass distribution of disks with the software and a few hours of free trial time online—the commercial services showed developers what worked, what clicked with the masses. And the obvious key to the hearts and minds of the masses was the interface. The more friendly and self-explanatory the interface, the more willing people who rarely spent time on a computer were to try it out. Certainly the Macintosh had already proven the crucial importance of user-friendliness, and by adhering closely to this simple principle, AOL came out on top.

Remember that while millions were already on the Internet before 1993, many were accessing it at work or through a university or some other nifty institution. Those at home had a tremendous amount of configuring to do. You had to get your hands on each individual program to handle e-mail, read UseNet, download files via FTP, explore

Gopherspace, and so on. And each one of these programs took time to master.

The commercial services offered access to at least their own quarantined realms of cyberspace via a single program designed for people who had no idea what they were getting into. Just type in a few numbers, click here, click there, and you were off. And if you ran into trouble, the product support people would take you by the hand back into the fold. On the Net, you were pretty much on your own.

Finally, while the commercial services were marketing the online experience, they were playing an instrumental role in the ultimate evolution of the online experience into a marketplace. Several vital turning points occurred in Net history, and the year 1991 is one of them. Gopher was one, of course. But two more major events took place that year. First, the National Science Foundation lifted the ban on commercial use of NSFNET. The very backbone of the Net was now open for business.

Next, after having worked with the idea for eleven years, Tim Berners-Lee, working at the CERN lab in Geneva, Switzerland, sent a little message to the UseNet newsgroup alt.hypertext: the first computer code of what would become the World Wide Web. Within a few years, the web will have, for all practical purposes, all but swallowed the Net whole.

Net history is chock full of revealing lessons. As long as that history keeps unfurling as quickly as it has (and there are no signs of it letting up), it is easy to let these lessons fade into the dust clouds left behind. Moving ahead, however, a bit of perspective can help you determine whether what's going down is really a revolution or just business as usual.

References

Aboba, Bernard. *The Online User's Encyclopedia*, Addison-Wesley, November 1993, ISBN 0-201-62214-9.

Cerf, Vinton. As told to Bernard Aboba, "How the Internet Came to Be."
gopher://gopher.isoc.org:70/00/internet/history/how.internet.came.to.be

Community Memory Discussion List on the History of Cyberspace.
http://www.reach.com/matrix/community-memory.html

Engst, Adam. *Internet Starter Kit for Macintosh*, Third Edition, Chapter 4, "The Internet Beanstalk."
http://www.mcp.com/hayden/iskm/iskm3/pt1/cho4/cho4.html

Gromov, Gregory R. "The Roads and Crossroads of Internet's History."
http://www.internetvalley.com/intval.html

PBS, "The History of the Internet."
http://www.pbs.org/internet/history/

Rewired "RE-sponse" Page.
http://www.rewried.com/Board

Sterling, Bruce. "Short History of the Internet," *The Magazine of Fantasy and Science Fiction*, February 1993.
http://www.forthnet.gr/forthnet/isoc/short.history.of.internet

Turkle, Sherry. *Life on the Screen: Identity in the Age of the Internet*, Simon & Schuster, 1995, p. 179.

Part II:

Triumph of the Web

"The key to what will eventually make the web stand apart from print or broadcast media is, in a word, interactivity—not with abstracts, but with people."
David Hudson

Chapter Six
The Rise and Fall of the Web

In the last few decades, a handful of guys have shot a few holes of golf on the moon; a president has been blown away in broad daylight; political spheres of influence, of which there used to be two, have shattered into entropic chaos; an epidemic has broken out claiming victims in geometrically increasing numbers, and there doesn't seem to be a thing we can do about it. Even the end of history itself has been announced. Before all the reviews of the book bearing the news were out, however, troops from twenty-eight nations were lining up in the desert to carry out the United Nations' first war effort.

Still, to hear some people tell it, none of these blips on history's radar screen shine as brightly as the advent of the Internet and its proud centerpiece, the World Wide Web. The web has been said to represent second or third waves washing over civilization, leaving it waterlogged and bloated with information—a multi-functional new medium that will eat up all the old media before this millennium is out, or even "the ultimate habitat for the human mind," according to the statement that kicked off Ars Electronica '96, one of Europe's most renowned arts festivals.

Granted, anyone launching a browser for the first time can't help but be overcome by the web's wow factor. It seems the whole world has been digitalized and put online in an easy-to-use, graphically stimulating mutant cross between a slick magazine and very slow television. You can read articles, books, stories, poetry, medical reports, and scholarly papers; play games; chat; scan up-to-the-minute maps warning you of freeway traffic jams or maps tracking the weather. You can use the web as a telephone, listen to live music, or navigate three-dimensional environments. And of course, there's lots and lots of advertising to wade through.

If features such as the latest news on traffic and the weather sound all too familiar, the reason is that the web has spent much of its infancy imitating previously existing media. Starting with print, the lives of all the media before it are passing before the web's eyes. The key to what will eventually make the web stand apart from print or broadcast media is, in a word, interactivity—not with abstracts, but with people. Long before the advent of the web, the "Internet" represented access to potentially just about any and everything that can be expressed in a series of 0s and 1s, and a wide open route for your own feedback—a chance to do the publishing and broadcasting yourself.

The Internet, that broad umbrella term for all those networks brought up in the previous chapter, had been a two-way street for years before the web was a sparkle in the eye of Tim Berners-Lee. But as long as one had to master at least a handful of separate programs (one each for e-mail, Gopher, FTP, Telnet, and so on), none of them—with the possible exception of Gopher, a hierarchically structured network not as freely navigable as the web—would be anywhere near as easy to comprehend or use as a web browser. Actual activity on the Net had been limited to the technically inclined or those who had the time and the gumption to learn.

Marc Andreessen's realization of Mosaic, based on the work of Berners-Lee and the hypertext theorists before him, is generally recognized as the beginning of the web as it is now known. Mosaic, the first web browser to win over the Net masses, was released in 1993 and made freely accessible to the public. The adjective "phenomenal," so often overused in this industry, is genuinely applicable to the (here comes another one) "explosion" in the growth of the web after Mosaic appeared on the scene. Starting with next to nothing, the rates of the web's growth (quoted in the press) hovering around tens of thousands of percent over ridiculously short periods of time were no real surprise. Nonetheless, after the basic structure had been established by the end of 1993, 1994's total growth rate of 1,758 percent was astounding.

Before focusing on what then happened on the web itself, we should note that this growth was attracting new people to the Internet as a whole. Many of those had been hesitant to go online as long as it entailed reading and studying book-length starter kits and spending hours tweaking IP addresses, unstuffing and unzipping bundles of new software, and so forth. Yes, the Net had been growing anyway, but as news of the user-friendly web got out in a word-of-mouth campaign any self-respecting CEO would kill for, Net accounts started selling like hotcakes. Most of the commercial online services were also doing fairly well for themselves on their own. After each of them in rapid succession began announcing that you could access the web via their interface, however, they began to really take off.

The web's population was in the mere thousands (measured in sites). Each site was the work of a "webmaster"—a sort of sci-fi tainted term that has unfortunately stuck. The web was a mixed bag of a few powerful figures towering over a landscape relatively sparsely populated by the rest. "Home pages" were devoted for the most part to résumés—not the most exciting reading in real life, much less so online after you've waited for the eight-by-ten glossy of Joe the Pharmacologist to download—or to the banal: a pet dog, a couple of jokes, a bit of random silliness. And nearly all of them featured the inevitable "Hot List," links to, for the most part, the genuinely interesting sites featured on everybody else's Hot List.

There's a reason we call web pages "pages," besides the fact that they resemble nothing else more closely than the pages of a book or a magazine. The origins of the web are based on the idea of hypertext—not hyperspace, hypersound, or hyperanything else. Most links from one page to the next are still underlined words, and clicking on these links is very much like following a number to a footnote in a book, looking up a cross-referenced passage, or even being referred by one book to another entirely.

Designers, software companies, and the like are working hard to break the hold of the page. The race is on among the major players to introduce a more engaging web, where clicking means entering a world in which everything you see is clickable again: the light switches in a room, the fire in the fireplace, and (most intriguingly) the door to the next room...or the next world. Add more animation, more sound, sharper image quality, and you have something very close to a web that acts more like an interface to the real world than one that acts like a giant loose-leaf folder. At present, but not for long, the web is dominated by those entities that must naturally feel most at home in an environment that promises to absorb all the qualities of all the media that have existed before it. So far, however, the web has succeeded in completely subsuming just one, the print media.

After the web hit the headlines of the mainstream media and after millions of new browsers stumbled out into its twisted labyrinth of links, the wow factor diminished. After jumping from Hot List to Hot List for a while, the average browser began to realize that all the hype trumpeting the web was actually about its potential and not so much about what it actually had to offer, even as people kept pouring on. (An especially noteworthy moment in 1995: America Online released its then three million subscribers out onto the web in one fell swoop).

Whenever the Internet was featured on a front page, a cover story, or one of those human interest spots on the nightly news, accompanying images were naturally called for. Almost without exception, these images would be screen shots from the web. You could argue that an e-mail program such as Eudora is a more useful application than a web browser, but it's not nearly as sexy. The look of a web page was immediately comprehensible to those accustomed to taking in a magazine or a television news program. Gopher, another point-and-click information retriever, has never made the cover of anything. But the web has been everywhere. Further, its star power is great enough to pull many of those associated with it into the spotlight as well. The White House has had an e-mail address for years, but when it hit the web, the cameras rolled. When it is announced that someone or something has just gone online, the public has by now a clear image of what that means, and importantly, what that online presence probably looks like—even if their television monitor is not glowing with a shot of a computer monitor.

1995 was not only the year the Internet became a household word, it was also the year that all the Net's important players realized that the web was to be the center of any further development in online technology. No one with enough money to use to make more money was going to sit around and let this boom boom without him. Wall Street fell just as deeply, if not more, in love with the Net and its star, the web, as the public had. One of the most remarkable stories among the flood of public offerings related to all the newly formed companies occurred when Netscape went public, an event preceded by its own ad campaign carried out on its home page—"Welcome to Netscape," the very page preprogrammed to open once the browser is launched. Theoretically (but only theoretically), millions were treated to information that in other venues could have been grounds for an accusation of insider trading. That aside, demand for stock was so great that the number of shares made available the day before they went on sale had to be doubled. The very next day, at the ripe old age of twenty-four, Mark Andreessen was a multimillionaire.

The gold rush was on. There was that pair of college kids at Stanford who had started to draw up a hierarchical directory of the web during their free time. "Yahoo!" pretty much summed up the spirit with which they went about constructing their pages of links. In 1995, rumor spread that someone had offered them twelve million dollars to buy them out, but that they'd turned it down. Eventually, they too went public. The value of that company also skyrocketed absurdly for a while there.

But the most interesting story of 1995, because of its long-term implications, can be told in the series of stories that made for different sets of headlines throughout the year. That would be the story of Microsoft and its dance with the web. 1995 began with the hype machine for Windows 95 already in gear, but not even Microsoft could keep the media's eye focused on it as an operating system. Instead, all attention centered on one little button that appeared after it was installed: MSN, Microsoft Network.

Other commercial online services cried foul. Demos at various conventions didn't ease their fears in the least. Anyone on MSN could drag-and-drop an URL into an e-mail message, send the message to a friend on the network, and that friend could click on it and be there. You could be looking at a page on the network from Encarta, its online encyclopedia, for example, click and be out on the web, click again and come back. The eerie effect was of a seamless connection between MSN and the web itself. To someone on MSN, it looked as if the whole Internet was owned and run by Microsoft. It wouldn't be the last time.

But fears did begin to subside when a combination of factors came together to put MSN in perspective. First, Windows 95 was catching a lot of flack as an operating system, and all the smoke and mirrors of MSN's mystique couldn't cover the flaws the critics were highlighting. Interestingly, at about the same time, the nearly reclusive Bill Gates stepped out into the public eye. Suddenly he was everywhere. Just as suddenly, he became the computer industry's first genuinely universally recognizable celebrity. He golfed with the President and gave interviews on prime time television. (Of course, he had just made a deal with the NBC network but that's another story...).

Microsoft rounded out 1995 with a big press conference announcing, in the words of Gates himself, that the sleeping giant had wakened. Microsoft wouldn't be working on any application, any new system, anything at all without the Internet in mind. At the same conference, Microsoft announced, among other things, that it would license Sun Microsystems' JavaScript. That one license alone denoted that Microsoft had a lot of battles on a lot of fronts going on at the same time if it wanted to realize its plans for web domination. Microsoft had been working on its own script for its own little applets, so it came off as if it were giving in to Java, although at the same time, Netscape had beat them to the licensing of JavaScript long before. The Netscape and Microsoft browser wars were on.

But for all that, at some point in 1996, the hype peaked and the backlash began to roll. It didn't come in the form of bad press from the established media, much of which is still enamored of anything tagged "cyber." Instead, it came for the most part from the disillusioned websters themselves. At first glance, the medium seemed so slick and easy—how did it turn out to be such hard work to do it right, to get people to come, look and click, and above all, to make any money? Especially when there's supposedly so much of the stuff being thrown at it?

Wired magazine's flirtation with the demise of the web in its "Great Web Wipeout" story was something of a preemptive strike. In case you missed the story, the article was a parody of just the sort of thing you could expect from *Time* magazine if the big shakedown finally rolls around. Now that the story has been pre-written and ridiculed, the constituency *Wired* has jurisdiction over already has one up on the vultures of older media who would be thrilled to come swooping in on the carcass of the web were it to start really stinking. But they don't even know it's dead yet. Or dying. Or just going through growing pains, depending on your point of view. But the offline media will catch on after the shakedown quakes, and it will indeed wipe out more than a few major sites. "Major" being defined as those set up by some company or joint venture with the money to blanket webspace in clickable banners, hire a sizable staff, buy some serious serving equipment—in other words, a lot of money. Which hasn't been coming back lately.

Why not? You'd think that with the whole world as your potential market you would have to be doing something really stupid not to be raking in the advertising or subscription revenues.

But think about it. When was the last time you went out on the web and stayed for more than an hour? Or as long as an hour? How many sites do you really check regularly? The truth of the matter is, there may be millions of people around the world with web access, but there isn't that much accessing going on. It still takes too long for a single page to ripple down the screen, and the mechanics of it all are still too clumsy. For many, online time is still just too expensive.

But you know, it's not all about money either. The identity crisis the web is going through would be happening right about now even if the big guns had kept their money in their baggy pockets from the start. The dirty little secret at the root of what many were calling "the death of the web" throughout 1996 is that, excepting the merest fraction of what's out there so far, the web is boring. There's still a lot more interesting content offline than on. That can change, of course, but not as quickly as the hype had it pictured, and almost certainly not quickly enough to head the shakedown off at the pass. The term shakedown doesn't necessarily mean the end of the web itself, just a selection of its sites.

While some Net watchers quibbled over the "35 Million People On Internet/Online In First Quarter 1996" that headlined IntelliQuest's announcement of its survey, others such as John Evan Frook at *Interactive Age* leapt onto a whole set of numbers further down the page. Because that's where the real story was. As Frook notes, people may still be pouring online in droves "at work, home and school, but most of the masses are just not satisfied with the experience." That's putting it nicely. Take a look at IntelliQuest's percentages this way: More than four out of five people online would rather be watching TV.

And maybe that's what they were doing. Of that supposed 35 million that had sunk a couple of thousand dollars into an online kit, only two and a half million actually lit up that modem for more than twenty hours a week. In contrast, a majority of the over 250 million folks in the U.S. will burn up twenty hours in front of the tube in a couple of days.

Not satisfied? The web was boring people out of their skulls.

Frook's article is naturally aimed at an audience of webmasters, and his bottom line goes something like: Gosh, fellas, we've got to make our content more compelling. Maybe. IntelliQuest president Brian Sharples says the problem is "time management" (leave it to a manager). That is, web designers tend to try to impress their employees, themselves, or each other with graphics and toys, but all users really want is to get in, grab the goods, and get back out. So Sharples recommends cutting down the time required to get at what people are there for. Well, that might help.

But here's what may be the most telling figure in the whole survey: Four out of five onliners don't surf.

Not only would that partly explain the sudden ubiquity of URLs advertised offline, it ought to be tripping alarms among those counting on the web to sell PCs and their accessories, ads, online accounts, and so on—in other words, to finance the information age. Links, hypertext, and freewheeling non-hierarchical browsing are, after all, supposed to be what the web is all about: the surfable landscape. My hunch is that it is a pretty cool experience when people try it out at first, but it is a quick, cheap thrill that fades almost overnight. No one browses a magazine stand twenty hours a week; and there, the pages swish by a lot faster.

IntelliQuest also asked participants to rate sites according to a set of categories such as news, hobbies, personal interest, and so on. Web sites rated lowest as entertainment. So the few people that do venture out aren't necessarily enjoying it. It makes you wonder what all those millions of people are doing online in the first place. Granted, IntelliQuest counted everybody—people with direct Net access, people on the commercial online services, BBSs, everybody. Hence the figure nearly triples anybody else's. So what are they doing out there? They're e-mailing each other.

And loving it. Plain old, low-tech, ASCII e-mail is the clear favorite of all online applications: the thrill that lasts. The implications are obvious. People are far more interested in each other than they are in "information." Until human interaction is a part of the definition of interactivity, people just aren't interested. As we'll see, companies large and small have caught on to that formula, and several models applying it are now being put forward.

Simple e-mail, though, is a greeting card, a phone call, a business transaction, a love letter, a message left on an answering machine, a postcard, the bearer of good and bad tidings, words that matter—personally. When a plane is shot out of the sky or a bomb goes off at a crowded venue, folks will certainly check CNN for the footage, for confirmation that this has actually happened. But that footage can only be looped so many times before a professional news organization has served its purpose. The next step is to pick up the phone or chat online. Who knows how much private e-mail flew related to TWA Flight 800, but 350 people were talking to each other about it on a mailing list within a matter of days.

Where does all this leave the web? Nowhere until it gets human. Which is precisely the project the major players see ahead of them. Celebrity futurist Paul Saffo, who once called the web an "information mausoleum," later told the *Washington Post* that the web will be "the hottest salon venue on the planet. We're not going to surf in cyberspace, we're going to hang out on it."

Maybe what he has in mind are all these 3D chat environments or the playing fields where we actually gather to play with each other. In the summer of 1996, Intel CEO Andy Grove announced that his company had found a way to do all that at 28.8 bps, and that we should be enjoying this new phase of multimedia sometime in 1997. Microsoft predicted it would take several years. Anyone who hopes to see the web survive the current dissatisfaction of its users is also hoping to see a radically different web sooner rather than later.

Early in 1997, the going thing was "push media," a wide open term referring to what basically amounts to broadcasting via the Net. The success of PointCast the year before had caught the attention of the financiers. The company flashed news headlines, stock quotes, and the like on the monitor after you "tuned in." The end result was that you no longer had to go to the trouble of clicking for what you wanted. Although PointCast was wildly successful, many technology pundits didn't like the general idea. The whole point of the web, they were saying, is the freedom to do the selecting and exploring on your own. Push media was turning the web into television, and there's certainly already enough of that.

The cover of the March 1997 issue of *Wired* magazine featured an eerie blue hand and a clever "special bulletin" that set the story on push media going right then and there; you didn't even have to lift a finger to start reading. As Scott Rosenberg pointed out at *Salon* magazine's 21st, although the story was bylined by *Wired*'s editors, they neglected to mention that Wired Ventures itself was launching a few push media services. "Not too long ago *Wired* was telling us that the Web was great because it took power away from big-media dinosaurs and put it in the hands of the little guy," Rosenberg wrote. "Now *Wired*'s saying 'good riddance' to the Web. What it's really kissing off is its own credibility."

Wired's credibility is the subject of another section of this book, but what's interesting in this context is that just a few years after the web appeared to be the ultimate destination for all the media that preceded it, suddenly reports of its death didn't look all that wildly exaggerated.

In the long run, the hype that accompanied the web's inception did a lot of damage to the morale of both the websters and the pool of viewers they're chasing so desperately. All the talk of "the world at your fingertips" or of making everyone's voice heard on a level playing field raised expectations too unreasonably. When Joe or Joanna User took the Christmas computer out of the box, secured an ISP, finally figured out how to get it all set to go, and launched that browser for the first time, he or she felt deserving of nothing less than revelation.

The letdown has been preprogrammed all along. After the novelty has worn off ("Hey, I just downloaded Hamlet!"), the realization sets in: Dressing up content in a new form does not make the content itself new. And a lot of it is better suited for books to curl up with, newspapers to fold and unfold on the subway, and live video that doesn't jerk or require more time to download than to see. When Wall Street loses faith, when advertisers start insisting on real (as opposed to virtual) viewers, when just a few more sites are built to which nobody comes, there will be some serious rewiring going on indeed.

"There is a certain romance to technologies gone by... But as that romance fades to mere nostalgia, eventually we all have to let go. The dilemma facing more people than we usually care to admit is how to let go when you can't afford to grab the next lifeline to the present, much less the future."

David Hudson

Chapter Seven
From Friendly Interface to Storefront Window

"You *gotta* upgrade (I suggest via my ten-year-old Mac Plus)," says nessie. "nessie" is the userid (user name) of one online personality sporting proudly marginal interests. He's talking to an online friend, from his clunker to hers. She's been complaining of late, albeit just a bit, about lag time, about her lack of web access (their conversation is taking place on a free online service), about not being able to see all the wow stuff people keep telling her about. Trapped in a text-only land of two dimensions, she feels blind, or at least struck with a severe case of tunnel vision in an increasingly graphically enhanced, multidimensional, extrasensory world.

What's remarkable about her entrapment is that it has had absolutely no bearing whatsoever on her ability to more than effectively communicate who she is and what she has to say to the rest of the crowd.

The mighty "Queen of Norway," as she invariably signs her posts—after some unique adverb and her full name— commands respect and inspires affection across the board. In short, she's a star. An icky word, but there's no way around it. It was probably never her intention to become one, but there she is. Furthermore, she got there on your standard set of wings: that old standby, the written word.

But the limitations of getting that word across to us, the adoring rabble, and having ours bounce back through her thin wires are beginning to get on her nerves. nessie has even gone so far as to suggest we all chip in and buy her a new computer. Few takers there, unfortunately.

Well, she can at least check this store he knows about "for a deal on a good used computer. Last time I was there they had 286s w/100meg HDs, loaded with software for $100. That was six months ago. My friend Homeless Harry, the World's Greatest Dumpster Diver has been pulling - working- 286s and Ethernet nodes out of West Berkeley dumpsters for over a year. He -gave- my late bro Clance a dozen just to experiment on. I'm not sure what Clance's widow did with them, last time I was over there they were looking dismantled and piled chest high in the living room. She's probably made the guts into sculpture by now, but I could check if you like."

Life in the trenches of the digital revolution is no bed of roses. But it goes on, even on the tightest of budgets. nessie says, "But if you're gonna actually break down and pay money, you want a 386 minimum, which really you can get free if you scrounge components and stick 'em together yourself. (Help IS available.) Somebody offered me a couple 386 boards for nothing just last night. I told her to give 'em to my SO who should really have her own computer. EVERYBODY should have their own computer. You already have the keyboard and monitor. So BUILD a 386. It ain't rocket science, believe me. The difference between using a computer and assembling one is like the difference between playing with handcuffs and playing with rope. Handcuffs cost forty bucks and work the first time. Rope costs six bucks and takes some practice. Got it? Then go for it. It's -well- within your capabilities."

Potentially, this may be true for everyone, but speaking for myself, at present, I'm lucky if I can get a plug into a socket without burning the house down. And the sheer idea of actually putting one of these mysterious machines together by hand blows a major mental fuse. But nessie is an inspiration. If I had the time, it would undoubtably do me a lot of good; it would take some of the fear and mystery out of the future for all of us.

If we had the time. There's the rub. Chasing down this spanking new age and all its time-saving gadgets seems to be an increasingly time-consuming job itself. So instead of tinkering, we upgrade.

For nessie's friend, the star of the board, "a Plus (and especially an SE30) would be like going from hobbling on crutches to driving a Chevy. It ain't a Ferrari, but the spare parts are free, and it sure as all hell beats walking, especially uphill. Black and white ain't color, but it does LOTS more than radio, to say nothing of the telegraph. Besides, there are people in this world (trust me on this) who actually PREFER Fredricks of Hollywood to Victoria's Secret. For one thing a rip here and there and a torn strap can actually ADD to the Fredricks's esthetic (if you have an imagination, that is) and the other hundred bucks is still in your purse (which NEVER hurts)."

There is a certain romance to technologies gone by, to the used and abused. But as that romance fades to mere nostalgia, eventually we all have to let go. The dilemma facing more people than we usually care to admit is how to let go when you can't afford to grab the next lifeline to the present, much less the future.

That's the downside. The other side looks like this. You can still, for a little while longer, make considerable headway in this world—even one as fleeting and all but imaginary as the one we wince and call cyberspace—with a decent command of the word and the barest machine to get it out. It is a lot harder, of course, and no, it isn't fair. But it is possible. For now.

The constant onslaught of new bells and whistles from the bell and whistle makers is, ultimately, probably a good thing. The process is part of the progress.

What isn't always such a good thing is the immediate adoption of any new bell or whistle by a slew of web sites just because it is new. Many sites are starting to get better about providing alternative versions of themselves, the jazzed up version for jazzed up browsers and the economy class version. But those sites that go jazz only are making marginalization of browsers on a budget a de facto state of affairs, not a choice. When TV went color, it was immediately decided that those with black-and-white sets could in no way be shut out. But how many can afford to double their RAM or the speed of their modem every few months just to keep up?

Of course, many would argue that all this is a sort of romantic pining for the days when everything about the Net was free and the hierarchy determined by money had not yet been installed online. That would be before 1991 when the rules were loosened, allowing for commerce to transpire on the Net, replacing the "gift economy" with the one we're more used to dealing with in the offline world. Interestingly, according to Tim Berners-Lee, had this shift occurred before he came up with the code that makes the web work, there might not have been a web, at least not the sort of web we have now. "The thing that the Web has given the world is interoperability," he says. "Interoperability is something that has just never happened on such a scale. And if that broke, that would be a big shame. The thing spread largely because I didn't make World Wide Web Incorporated in 1991. If I had done it in 1991, it would have been just another hypertext product. All the big manufacturers would have come out with lookalikes."

In other words, he had to give it away to save it. "[T]he fact that the specs were open and there was an open process discussing them was why people adopted it so fast. They could reorganize their entire activity around the World Wide Web because they knew that it wasn't based on some model where World Wide Web Incorporated could suddenly turn on the licensing and say, 'All right, next year everything is the same as last year but 3,000 bucks a pop.'"

And the product that the web now peddles, most of it in some form of publishing, is as intangible as thin air. To the consumer, most of it is still just as free of charge. But for the publisher, even for the publisher of the tiniest webzine, it is hardly free. Fun maybe, but not free. It takes time and work, and we all know what that translates into.

The giddy "information wants to be free" days of the Net are long gone. Call it information, call it intellectual property, call it whatever you like, it comes with a price. A price we'll either pay outright or indirectly—that is, by agreeing to look at some ads. We can argue about whether that is good or bad or really necessary. For now, though, let's face facts and get on with it. As writer Paulina Borsook remarked, "I may be nauseated by the commercialization of the Web, but there ain't nothing going to stop it."

So what might the effects of commercialization actually turn out to be? "Is commercialization of the 'net really going to remove the 'many-to-many' communications model that is so valuable?" asks *Infoworld* reporter Jim Balderston. "I am not sure that the invasion of the telcos and massive ISPs and corporate Web sites is going to kill off the anarchy of the Net; I suspect it is just going to drive it underground." Responding to the ideas put forward at the "Rewired" web site and in the introduction of this book, Balderston wonders, "Are we going to see in the age of 'The New Sobriety' different gradients of Net users? Those that know the less-traveled byways and routes versus those that cruise along on the well-lit, elevated toll roads of the Information $uperhighway?"

The results of commercialization may not be absolute. But who wants to be driven underground? Will political activists, aficionados of any particular strain of literature, art, music, and so on, or medical personnel, botanists, historians, or just plain anybody have the resources in terms of both time and money to learn how to tunnel to what they're after? Which isn't always more information—access to each other is just as vital, if not more so.

The development of a stratified Net population, of "different gradients" of users is already well under way. Although a lot of attention has been justifiably focused on the rift between "the haves and the have-nots,"—those with and without access at all—not enough has been directed at the virtual class system people run up against after they do get online. The barriers are manifest not only in the challenge posed by working around the glut of corporate-ssponsored mainstream viewpoints, but also in the blind drive to upgrade the means of communication.

What we're most likely witnessing is the rapid evolution of the Net into an online mirror of the real world—really nice in some spots, pretty horrible in others. A nice quotation comes from the many pages of web writer Justin Hall. He asks, "[S]o if you put together tci, surfwatch and at&t/what kind of internet would that be?" The brand names are probably grabbed at random, but the gist of the question is clear. And the answer, it seems, *is* pretty much the Internet we're gonna get.

"...advertising seems to fly in the face of two of the more fundamental aspects of the Net. First, choice and freedom of movement are constants of the online experience. Secondly, unedited content and a variety of opinions and perspectives on the same topic are always just a click away."

Andrew Sullivan

Chapter Eight
Follow the Money

"Now that much of the present Internet is privately owned and most future development will be by private telecom giants, the operative concept will be that of the shopping mall." This on-target metaphor was suggested by Carl Guderian at the "Rewired" site.

"In the mall, expenses are for construction or leases and security, and if the shops that rent space there aren't selling they close and the mall doesn't profit. An Internet that charges by the minute to download software to a diskless network computer is a mall with a cover charge."

Guderian is referring here to the NC, or network computer, which we'll get to in a moment. Whether or not the NC takes off or is made redundant by WebTV, the effect is the same. "Folks who lurk on the Internet and don't buy anything will still bring in a few bucks to the Internet provider, much as mall rats loiter in the malls and spend a few bucks at the food court. Such rabble are tolerated as long as they don't scare away the legitimate shoppers. In fact, the more colorful mall rats may add color and funkiness to an otherwise bland shopping environment (the 'Renaissance Faire' effect)."

It's stratification, just as it occurs in the real world, only sterilized. Further, the prize feature of all online technology—interactivity—is diminished. When the idea of the $500 network computer was first floated, many scoffed. Others, such as technology and business writer George Gilder, declared it the future of the Net. Five hundred dollars, half a grand. This is not the pocket change of the masses. But assume that they eventually fall in price like Walkmans and pocket calculators—that is, after everyone who has $500 to spare shells it out, the cup is passed again and again for steadily decreasing amounts until the number hits rock bottom (cost plus a reasonable profit).

The logic behind these toys supposedly has to do with separating the functions your basic PC is now performing. If people want computers so that they can get on the Internet, why make them buy machines that do that plus spreadsheets, word processing, desktop publishing, the whole number-crunching, RAM-hungry rigmarole? Why not just give them their e-mail and their online magazines if that's all they want?

That's the nice way of looking at it.

Here's another way of looking at it. Even if the Internet were the only thing you came to a computer for, how would you compose the business correspondence, the e-mail, or the pages that will secure your place on the level playing field the web is supposed to represent if there's no software on the thing except a web browser, or whatever equivalent the future has in store? Where's the ware? Behold, the access-only machine solution: You rent it.

At a dollar an hour. Online. Wyse Technology, for example, is prepared to rent out whatever you need to "cruise the Internet" or do anything else you can do with what normally comes as standard equipment with any PC worthy of the name.

The *Wall Street Journal* quoted a Zona Research analyst: "This is something that will generate a lot of interest in the software community."

You bet it will. For a handful of clever companies, the access-only machine is the gift that keeps on giving.

It is encouraging to see the new web-accessible television sets come equipped with keyboard-like infrared remotes. If the computer and the television must merge, merging with it the cable, broadcast, and ISPs, at least the bare minimum of interactivity is being respected and recognized for what it's worth. Still, the road to the merging of the media has had its amusing pit stops.

First, we should note that a very primitive form of interactivity via the TV set has already been around for a while. If you don't like what you see on the screen in much of Europe, for example, you simply hit the text button on the remote control. A menu appears. World headlines, perhaps, are on page 101. You have to punch in 1-0-1, and then comes the second level menu, the headlines and their respective page numbers, and so on.

Videotext has been around in Germany for well over a decade, but no one has ever talked about "surfing" it. The idea would not occur to anyone not only because surfing is hardly a cultural highlight of Mitteleuropa, but also because Videotext has a Gopher-like hierarchical structure. It is clunky and quite unsexy—little blocky letters and logos made of video bricks. But on the up side, it is relatively fast, convenient, and usually up-to-date. Elementary as it is, Videotext is online technology brought into the home via cable or satellite just as several companies would have us eventually receive the web. They are scurrying around even now making alliances, doing lunches, and tinkering with set-top boxes and key cards.

No single committee oversees the project. This is the free market at work here, so of course there is a lot of redundancy, plenty of start ups and fall downs, and a constant flurry of press releases and quotable bites about the wide-open future, interactivity, and so on. It has all got a Keystone Cops sort of hilarity to it. But one way or another, with the web and TV reaching out for each other the way they are, yearning for that final quivering embrace, it does look like it will happen.

But where does the money come from at the moment? A few sites with readerships that can afford it, such as the *Wall Street Journal*, are charging admission. But few have hopes for the subscription model working out on the web. Not that many print publications could survive on their subscription revenue, for one thing, and for another, there's just too much "free" material out there for consumers to turn to.

The respectable web publication *Salon* has depended on its sponsors, such as Borders Bookstores and Apple Computers, to carry on. The sponsorship model, or what Howard Rheingold calls "the PBS model," is nice revenue if you can get it, but it's tough going. You need a track record, a business plan, and all those other pesky components of the old way of running a publication—which isn't what new media are supposed to be about. We will see soon enough if there is such a thing as new media when it comes time to pay for it.

The most common source of revenue, obviously, is advertising. Here too, it is a lot tougher going than it was when web euphoria was at its peak. Advertisers are growing savvier of just how the web works—indeed, just how few people are actually out there surfing it, seeing their ads, and clicking on them. "No matter how many articles on the meaninglessness of 'hits' run in *Webweek*, *AdAge*, *Wired*, *Information Week*, or any other general Internet publication, hit-counts are continually brandished as the principal sign of site activity. And it's not just marketers doing the brandishing, but 'Webmasters' as well."

Andrew Sullivan knows about this sort of thing because he's a webmaster himself with quite a few sites under his belt, not to mention a couple of semesters studying economics.

"That marketers inflate the slightest signs of online life into evidence of super-human activity has never surprised me. But the reaction of those who peer into the log files, see the unique DNS entries, and know that their activity is relatively consistent—that is, the reaction of system administrators—never ceases to baffle me."

Here's a story that demonstrates how perceptions of the web market and real economics can be a disastrous mix.

"One wide-eyed, Web-possessed marketer was crushed to hear me describe how his site, which was pulling a hair-raising 4,000 hits per day, was actually being viewed by about thirty-five to one hundred different pairs of eyeballs. And out of these hundred or so possible viewers, only thirty-five accounted for substantial activity. He was completely unaware that each time his home page was called up, that single access accounted for twenty-three of the precious 4,000 hits." So how could he have been so naive? "His trusty Webmaster had never deemed it necessary to correct his fantastic association of hits with users. And for good reason. The Webmaster himself accounted for nearly 40 percent of site activity, while the company's staff accounted for an additional 20 percent. The marketer's bubble was burst and there was silence on the other end of the phone as the realization sank in that the company had spent nearly $100,000 to service under a hundred people."

Seems downright irresponsible of the webmaster not to pass hard realities of the return on this substantial investment along to his boss. "It's not hard to see why this particular Webmaster was reluctant to deliver the sobering news behind the low number of unique DNS entries, the effect of a twenty-three hit home page, and the probable meaning behind such consistent hit counts. If he had, he'd probably have been out of a job."

You'd think, having sunk that much money into the project, the guy would pull out of the web. But no, the confidence that an online presence is a foothold on the future still hasn't waned with many.

"The marketer's reaction to this situation is one I see being repeated en masse—he immediately felt the need to increase promotional efforts, go after new ways of creating an 'exciting' site, offer free stuff, change the content daily, and advertise, advertise, advertise! I suggested they place nude pictures on their home page and become a distribution point for some popular software item, but they wanted to create a content site."

This facetious suggestion is rooted in a telling truth. Indeed, sex sells, as it always has, online or off. And software is hot out there, which says a lot about the demographics still pervasive on the Net. But if you're on the web to make money, the tactics advocated in many a magazine or how-to Net book need to be taken with a grain of salt. Those books and magazines are out to sell the future of the web as a viable marketplace; their own existence depends on that eventual transformation actually happening, hopefully sooner rather than later.

"The motives of an administrator who could very well offer realistic activity estimates but doesn't are clear. But the role of the marketer is a bit more complex. Beneath the issue of hits on the web lies another, deeper point about advertising and its relationship to the market. You see, we actually have very little solid evidence to go on when it comes to figuring out what it is that makes a person buy or how effective marketing is in changing consumer behavior. Marketing is a big Ouija board and everyone, on some level, knows it (assuming that no one really believes the accuracy of media audits).

"In my opinion," Sullivan continues, "successful marketing campaigns are little more than a combination of a rising trend and an aggressive marketing approach. So much is left to chance that the respective roles of the trend and the marketing in getting people to drink a certain kind of gin in their martinis is hard to differentiate. After all, if there were a direct relationship between media presence and the popularity or success of a product, there would be many, many more people on the web."

He's got an example to back up this point as well.

"Recently a friend of mine in charge of online marketing at a major media company experimented with advertising on one of the hot search engines which receives an estimated 1 million 'visitors' per day. He essentially bought a word, the name of the city in which his company is located. So anyone interested in that particular city would see his ad and a direct link to his site. The venture produced about 6 additional 'visitors' per day."

Ouch.

"The irony is that this engine already drives a significant portion of the site's activity, and the promo was expected to at least double it. So, the search engine alone generates high-volume, but advertising was ineffective in attracting additional activity. In fact, this is not at all surprising, as advertising seems to fly in the face of two of the more fundamental aspects of the Net. First, choice and freedom of movement are constants of the online experience. Secondly, unedited content and a variety of opinions and perspectives on the same topic are always just a click away."

Again, the Net flies in the face of traditional means of generating income. And vice versa. One of the two ways will eventually win out. Place your bets where you will.

"Creating our individual pathways to content watering holes is one of the more enjoyable features of being there. And the idea that someone could, for a fee, alter or control that path seems to defeat the very force of the medium."

Andrew Sullivan does not believe advertising on the web is futile. Otherwise, he and his company, eLine Productions, wouldn't be in the business. But he reminds us that the medium is young and poses challenges to old ways of thinking when it comes to trying to make a buck out there.

"The problem is that the models of advertising we're most accustomed to break down on the Net. In the land of traditional media, we're accustomed to free TV, free radio, and free print publications in exchange for allowing Coke, Pepsi, Bud, and Coors to publicly fight over our consumer habits. In essence, because the price of admission to the media would otherwise be too high, we are willing to forgo uncensored access to information to avoid assuming the cost of production and delivery. On the Web, however, the costs of production and delivery are far less, and the idea of 'access to the market' is non-existent, since it's the market that accesses you!"

So what might actually work?

"If Prodigy had been really smart," for example, "they would have launched as an entirely free, commercially driven online service." Instead, like most other online services, Prodigy is now a glorified ISP, its prospects hardly glorious at all. "And if Pepsi really wanted to capture the attention of the online market, they would have struck a deal with a national ISP to enable the exchange of Pepsi points for online time. But neither were that smart. And the online biz still awaits the first true success story of a major mainstream marketing campaign that worked."

There will be a lot of trial and error before we come to the point at which pictures of naked babes or free software demos are no longer the only revenue-generating draw on the web. There is hope. Amazon.com, for example, essentially an online bookstore that capitalizes on the genuine appeal of online technology by inviting people to gather and discuss the books it sells, looks as if it is going to make it. Even if Borders Books drives it off the Net (hardly a done deal), Amazon will have proven for a while at least that an innovative model just might work. But it doesn't take too much deliberation to come to the conclusion that the ultimate survivors will be those who can afford this rough-and-tumble period of experimentation.

Chapter Nine

The Fittest

Imagine checking into a hotel room overlooking Times Square right now and putting money down on it day after day just so you can be sure to be there for the big bash on the night of December 31, 1999. Granted, you can't, because all the rooms with a view have already been reserved. But there's a metaphorical link and a couple of defining dissimilarities between the lucky rich holding on to their reservation numbers and the hopeful rich holding on to their for-profit web sites.

Both parties are betting on splashy payoffs on their investments. Both are aware that they are going to have to wait a while. But among the differences, two stand out. One, only the lucky are guaranteed a good time, and two, only the hopeful have to keep financing their front row seats should the fireworks ever go off. But, with few exceptions, they keep on keepin' on, waiting for the lights to start flashing.

Andrew Sullivan has nailed several reasons why they haven't yet. In sum, most placing their bets on the web have placed them on content as opposed to human interaction.

"Despite the fundamental elegance of the Net to unify niche communities into formidable groups, despite the mantric chanting of Net critics who emphasize dialogue over databases, despite the brutally honest tales that log files are telling about users' minimal interest in second-tier content, despite a recurring theme of content-driven sites peaking and leveling off in activity, despite the hard evidence that little content currently available on the Net is remotely relevant to the audience, despite all this, traditional content providers continue to heap their hay onto the overloaded web wagon in hopes of generating those golden hits that land the big green."

First, you can't blame them. As a medium, the web cried out to be used for the tasteful presentation of a swath of text and a few illustrations. No wonder magazines said to themselves, well, this is easy, we've been churning out this stuff for decades. Just feed it to the server and sell it again. What a shock when so few showed up to buy.

But traditional content providers, who were among the many to hype the web over all other Net applications in their own pages, forgot that what the web does is not why people rushed onto the Net in the first place. The thrill lay in meeting people they wouldn't have otherwise met (UseNet, IRC), a cheaper, faster way to exchange mail with people they already knew (e-mail), and free stuff (FTP).

So, as Andrew notes, big-time access providers such as Microsoft and AOL are changing gears. They're shifting down. They're going after funky, offbeat, Gen X—in a word, alternative—content as a means, not an end. An article on Pavement (the band, not the asphalt), for example, is dangled as bait. The name catches the eye, the eye reads, ho hum, but lo, there's a link to a chat area where other people who bit the bait are discussing the last concert, the next CD, and a lot else that has zilch to do with either music or streets. Doesn't matter, especially in the access providers' view, so long as they keep talking.

On one level, they're on the right track.

"Despite its facility for seamless global discourse," Andrew Sullivan continues, "the Internet and telecommunications' real contribution will be its ability to make local connections. It's quickly becoming the singles bar of the 90s, driven by the buzz that the person you're chatting with may very well live down the block. In a world where religion, bars, and singles groups are all dead zones for viable mates, online communications are becoming a sort of 'church of technology,' the new Sunday meeting place that's safe for the modern paranoid. So, the web seems to be coming full circle. Right back to the models of the BBS and topical newsgroups that started the whole Internet buzz in the first place and, irony of ironies, the groups leading this retro charge are the biggest, most depersonalized entities in the online arena."

Of course, they can afford to shift strategies as often as they need to. In the case of AOL's Digital Cities or Microsoft's CityScape, the new approach is to treat content as packaging, not product. And because the market for the product is relatively young the ideal package is alternative content. Of course, this takes a fair amount of cash and time to squander and for one to be aware enough of what's going on around them to be online. One of the places they went shopping for it to resell it was the 1996 annual convention of the Association of Alternative Newsweeklies in Salt Lake City. "The tragedy for the Alternative Press is that while they spend thousands to get their content into the forefront of the online scramble of new-world publishing, the big players are spending millions and using alternative content as a mere backdrop for building online communities right under the noses of these local papers. And the fact that the boys from Redmond are seeking deals with these local publishers plays right into the egos of the smaller content providers, as this justifies their feelings about the value and importance of their content. But again, the value here is not the content, but the context which brings users together."

Andrew Sullivan sees more than a little irony in the situation. "While AOL has excelled in building chaos online, whether they have the chemistry to shape test-tube communities is an unknown. For Microsoft, the question, as usual, will be whether they are willing to spend the cash to do it. Currently, they haven't a clue as to how many or what kind of resources it takes to build, maintain, and grow niche and local online environments."

The question is why the alternative press hasn't been successful with the sites they have built for themselves. Why haven't they applied the community model? "The reason that alternatives (and publishers in general) are falling for the content myth is that they are stuck in traditional models of 'table of contents,' brand recognition, and distribution, and have serious problems exploring their value beyond these categories. They view the Net as but another point of distribution for their 'product,' never realizing that most of the models that fostered success in print are out the window in the online environment, and that most of their value in going online has little to do with their content and a lot to do with their position within a local context. And that position is their unique ability to collect dialogue. These papers have serious contacts and are uniquely positioned to reflect the flavor of a particular area—but none of their success online will be tied to their content."

The overriding point in terms of what it all means for the web is that it is being forced to reinvent the wheel. A look at most attempts at web chat and conferencing reveals a web dreadfully uncomfortable, bending over backward to try to do things it was not designed to do. Not all that long ago, it either threw up its hands altogether and tossed the baton to a Telnet application or reminded you to reload often, which in essence was a reminder that nothing on the web was either live or genuinely interactive. There is hope, however, for the web as a decent gathering place where we can all carry on with what we were doing before the web came along (as you will see in the final chapter on communities). As Andrew puts it, "Watching the web don the gown of a distributed BBS is like watching your parents' clothes come back into style: even technology is hip in cycles."

Too much has been invested in rounding us all up and herding us onto the web. Now that we're here, the web will be bent until it breaks, giving us what the investors think we want. So eventually, maybe sooner, maybe later, the web will be doing most or all of what we want out of online technology, and we'll probably be doing what it wants, too. In the meantime, the hopeful have secured their block of real estate in cyberspace, their room with a view, pay rent on it, and wait.

Andrew Sullivan has another piece of bad news for them while they wait. The market has flattened. Just about everybody who is going to go online is there. "Either almost all of the people who will be getting wired are wired, or the fragmentation of destination points on the web is seriously outnumbering new users—the publishing version of too many chefs, not enough cooks."

He draws these conclusions from watching the logs of several large sites and chatting with his fellow systems administrators. "The story is almost always the same. There is an initial lag upon launch, a surge in activity when advertising, word of mouth and database registration kicks in, and then a stabling in activity after a few months. Even the big name sites have a problem attracting new users." Perhaps there are fewer new users—no question, when you have a phenomenal growth rate spoken of in exponential terms. It has to start leveling off at some point. When services are built on the assumption that the original growth rate would be maintained, it is hard to feel sorry for them when they start feeling the pinch of the natural evolution of a curve. But have we peaked out or is the problem, as noted earlier, that people just are not enticed by what they see to come back and look again? Regardless of whether the party grows in mere numbers or not, Andrew's right about why the hosts are running around rearranging the furniture. Here, they see us up, milling about, chatting, flirting, dancing. And they thought we would be happy to just sit around and read.

So local is the way to go, it has been decided, and that is where the big guns are aiming. It has been especially interesting watching Microsoft shift gears again and again in a rapid succession of moves to maintain the Internet strategy CEO Bill Gates announced at the end of 1995. By now, just about everyone has come to understand that Microsoft wants to take over the world. Not that Bill Gates has made any effort to cover up his intentions. On the contrary, the only question that remains at this point is, Will he succeed? Few doubt it.

But at this crucial point in the game (okay, there have been few points that haven't been crucial in the last couple of years), too many are jumping to conclusions, throwing in the towel way too soon. Here's a small example, one of many: *The Wall Street Journal* ran an article in the late summer of 1996 about CityScape ("Microsoft's On-Line Plan Puts Newspapers in Highanxiety.com"), Redmond's version of the "Go local!" craze. People don't want the world on a platter (though that was the thrust of Net hype not all that long ago), they want restaurant listings, classified ads, movie show times, and so on.

Although everybody was doing it, Yahoo!, @Home, TCI, AOL, and so on, not everybody is Microsoft. When Microsoft jumps in a game that has already been going on a while, number one, that is often the first you will hear about it from the old media, and two, panic spreads like brushfire coast to coast (and hops over to London, the first international city targeted by CityScape). You get quotations like this one from the *WSJ* article: "The smart publishers are going to team up with Microsoft. You can't ignore them. If publishers won't play ball with them, they'll do it on their own." That's the sound of the CEO of Media News Group throwing in his towel.

Microsoft swooped into local markets like Reconstructionist carpetbaggers and threatened newspaper publishers with big fat wads of cash. Sell us your soul or we'll run you out of town. It had editors and publishers in a tizzy, and over at "Editor & Publisher Interactive" site, they went on about it for weeks. Columnist Steve Outing kept his head levelest in terms of what it all meant, but he still jumped to the conclusion that all any newspaper could do was pick one of its suitors and tie the knot. Of course, he's also a consultant for Microsoft.

If you're shopping for content and willing to hustle, there is no easier target these days than a newspaper. They're struggling, to put it nicely—cost of ink and all that. A lot of former two- and three-paper towns are now one-paper towns. Outing perceptively pointed out that if Microsoft, AOL, and one of the other "goin' local" ventures aims at your town armed with $2 million each (according to Cox Enterprise's Peter Winter, this is the average start-up budget for each local market), you as a publisher are staring down the barrel of $6 million worth of competition.

That is one way of looking at it. It is an impressive equation, but it overlooks a few vital factors. Who says that one guy's $2 million isn't ignoring the local paper, but instead, is aimed squarely at another guy's

$2 million whose own $2 million is split, covering the $2 million on his left and the $2 million on his right, while the third guy... It all makes the last scene in *Reservoir Dogs* look like Geometry 101.

Furthermore, while the online guys are shooting it out, how much of the local paper's readership decides that 25 to 50 cents a day is too much to spend when, for a mere two or three thousand dollars (cost of a computer et al), plus the $15 to $20 a month for an ISP, they can get their restaurant listings for *free*?

Of course, this in turn ignores the probability that online restaurant listings are an inevitability in every home one way or another eventually— via cable TV, telephone service, ATM print-outs, whatever. This is what Microsoft and the others are banking on. Which brings up the other factor. If you (the publisher) don't sell your innards to Microsoft, do you really think the software company is going to hire a team of reporters (not to mention the restaurant critic) to cover your town like the CEO said they would in the *WSJ* article? And even if they did, would their coverage be better than yours? Even within the newspaper business, does *USA Today* cover Dallas better than the *Dallas Morning News*? Does *New Times*-owned *SF Weekly* cover San Francisco better than the homegrown *The San Francisco Bay Guardian*?

When you look a bit closer at just one of the many fronts on which Microsoft is advancing its grand plan, several questions emerge, buoyed by sheer common sense. But there is hardly time to look at any one front. The very day before the *WSJ* article, MSNBC was launched. On the heels of Microsoft's online magazine *Slate*. And so on.

Microsoft is coming at us full force, pounding the tiny window of media coverage with one major headline-grabber after another. Raw momentum, propelled by the hyped-up announcement of the Internet strategy, is the company's greatest strength. Few, however, have stopped to wonder whether it isn't also its greatest weakness. Few question whether what looks like strategic Blitzkrieg isn't actually a desperate move to cover all the bases because the company doesn't know what's going to fly any more than anyone else.

There is little point in rehashing here all the pies Microsoft has its fingers in. After *Business Week* had run down the list in its cover story on Microsoft, it reported on the telling event that transpired the night before the big press event during which Bill Gates would announce that Microsoft, at the end of 1995, had finally stumbled over the Net. Someone pointed out that the presentation is too fuzzy, and Gates fired back, "I just want them to get that we're hard-core about the Internet!"

That's all. What else counts? Certainly not the specifics. The part about adjusting the business the company had been in for well over a decade before it discovered the Net makes sense. From then on, Windows and all other Microsoft software would be Net-ready. Fine.

The riskier and far more costly aspects of the new strategy involve the geek company's seemingly aimless transformation into a hip hypermedia center. Microsoft, following just about everybody else's lead, perceives the web as a publishing medium. Or maybe it's a broadcast medium. Better spread out. The web is a magazine? Hire a hotshot editor. WebTV? Buy a network. Movies? How much is Spielberg going for these days?

Each of these purchases make for great press, sound, and video bites. Which in turn create the image of Microsoft the Steamroller, paving the Infobahn from Redmond via the White House to Atlanta, terrifying the natives into submission along the way. Webzines quaked before *Slate*. *HotWired*'s Jon Katz couldn't get over it, racking up at least five or six columns on it. But who has wondered whether it is all worth the bother? Who has actually clicked on these monsters and not found too much glitz, too much trouble, or just plain too much? Who has wondered whether the strategy so far might not be working?

"We will find ourselves standing in the one shade beyond nuts the day the web goes fully audio-visual, maybe even slaps on another dimension, and there we will be, full circle. No longer a medium, the web will just be."

David Hudson

Chapter Ten
Down with the Web

As the drum rolled prior to the debut of Microsoft's Slate, an online magazine edited by Michael Kinsley, the jealous webgods were hopping all over Kinsley's case because he had been so uncouth as to publicly dis the state of web journalism long before he'd tried his hand at it himself. In essence, the editors of other prominent webzines, HotWired, Feed, Salon, and so on—all of which had been struggling to attain and maintain at least an air of professionalism—would have had him put up or shut up. You would think that after Slate arrived, after there was a there there, the Slate-bashing would really take off in earnest. But it didn't. For the most part, members of the web publication club were uncharacteristically tame as they gave Slate the once-over- lightly treatment.

Not that there wasn't anything to bitch about. For one thing, *Slate* was a browser buster—specifically, a Netscape buster. After a deluge of e-mail about *Slate* crashing the Navigator, the house techie claimed the kinks in the code were ironed out, but nevertheless urged readers not to venture in armed with anything less brawny than Netscape 2.0, or of course, Microsoft's Internet Explorer 2.0. He bemusedly brushed off accusations that Microsoft would even entertain the notion of using *Slate* as something of a Trojan horse in its ongoing war with Netscape. Who, Microsoft? Play dirty? Please.

Whether such tactics were beneath its host, *Slate* still assumes a tie-and-jacket, basic-black-and-pearls readership. Surely you're not coming in dressed in anything but 28.8 (at the very least) and 16 MB of RAM? Twice, *Slate* brought my system to its knees, the equivalent of being told that no more tables are available, terribly sorry, and then, after insisting on service, being asked by the manager in a polite yet firm tone of voice whether I was absolutely certain that I had made reservations.

It is disturbing to see Kinsley, whose opinion pieces I've followed faithfully even unto *Time*, Mr. "...and from the Left" himself, heading such a technically, and therefore economically, elitist operation. Because I so often like what he says and the way he says it, I tend to give Kinsley the benefit of the doubt. He has been quite open about not knowing the first thing about how the Net or its web actually works, and when I picture it being demonstrated to him for the first time, I don't see him on a three-year-old PowerBook like mine.

But for all the admittedly really dumb things he said before, he at least got acquainted with what he was talking about; Kinsley had several valid points to make about web journalism before jumping into the fray himself. In sum, he said it stank. That's what sparked the fury of all those editors and writers. But gosh, it's all water under the bridge now.

Steven Johnson, editor of *Feed*, ran quite a nice piece skewering both *New Yorker* writer Ken Auletta and Kinsley. But guess who was caught chatting up "Mike" just after *Slate's* launch in May 1996? Steve!— and, Gary Wolf of *HotWired* and Marisa Bowe, who edits *Word*. There was a big "we're all in this thing together" pow-wow at *Feed*, and there was no question as to who the guest of honor was.

So what was up? First came the Great Kinsley Barbecue, next it was a scene straight out of the movie *Freaks*: "One of us! One of us!..." The second take on Kinsley and his *Slate* was no doubt the result of it suddenly dawning on these editors and writers that Kinsley had brought respectability to what, up to *Slate's* arrival, celebrated in the offline press, had been a pretty Rodney Dangerfieldish profession. Before Kinsley came aboard, you couldn't say the words "web" and "journalism" in one breath without razing high brows. But with the clout of Microsoft behind him and the résumé he had composed before *Slate*, Kinsley may very well be the one to make the accusation of respectability stick to web journalism.

The web's dire straits have not so much been reflected on the web itself in the magazines that had a life before they went online or in those started by writers and editors who had a life in magazines before they started writing for the web as they have in web publications that grew up there. The predominant culture among these web-grown platforms for mouthing off for nearly free has been...well, "celebratory" would not be the word for it.

The primary example would have to be *Suck*. You don't go to *Suck* for hard news or soft illumination. You go for the 'tude. Which is usually...well, the name says it all. "Suck" is a noun, a verb, transitive and intransitive, the monosyllabic fountainhead of many a verbal phrase, the progenitor of many a www.oneword.com, a great name for a site in a decade in which the angry and cynical are rewarded with hits, ratings, money, and votes. In a sense, the web and *Suck* were a perfect fit. Every weekday, *Suck*, bought out by *Wired* in 1996, delivers a single page: an op-ed with a twist of bile. Essentially, the machine runs on a single joke. Within each piece, individual phrases are highlighted, often not very nice ones, linking you to whoever the writers are up to dissing that day. The irony is, it has become almost point of honor for web publishers to have been *Suck*'d at least once (and yes, *Rewired* has been— by name, mind you!); it's far worthier than being chosen "Cool Site of the Day."

Even if occasionally monotonous, the writing is usually at least fun and sometimes sharp, and the site has had quite an influence over the shape and design of many others. But now that *Suck* has become something of an institution, you can't help but wonder if the joke hasn't backfired.

Way back in the 80s, I found my tongue, stuck it off to the side of my cheek, and wrote up an eight-part "short" story about a performance artist who sent out invitations to come and watch him live his life for a full week. He wouldn't be doing anything particularly noteworthy, just carrying on. As the story opens, we find him waking the first morning to find that people have actually come to watch. This stab at art was not, alas, to remain conceptual. Nor was the story.

The twist: As the six or seven of us who were indeed performance artists at the time were gathered at the printers watching the premiere edition of our tiny Euro arts review roll off the presses, I picked up a "real" paper, skimmed, and found... That's right, a report on a performance artist who had invited people... My heart sank, and then flew. Okay, so I had lost the bite of originality, but in its place, I now had the weight of verisimilitude.

The lesson: The world is always just one shade more nuts than you think.

Having had this lesson verified many times over in the decade that has followed, it not only comes as no surprise that people are putting their lives online, but it doesn't faze me in the least that they're reporting that people are actually showing up to watch. I'm thinking of sites such as Justin, perhaps the Ur-confessional site (the original online diary), Geek Cereal, or Rebecca Eisenberg's "Read Me!"

What does surprise me is that I get a real kick out of it. And that is what counts. After a day, sometimes a day and a night of ingesting information and spitting it back out in columns and articles, I'm ready for dessert. Who really cares whether it is voyeuristic on the part of the clicker or exhibitionistic on the part of the clickee? Fun's fun.

Had the web come along at another point in history (it wouldn't, but if it had), would this be going on? Medieval monks spent their time copying the standards despite the example of Augustine who had made it pretty big with his *Confessions*. On the other hand, for all the hardcore info shows on cable, people seem to prefer, en masse, a television sitcom about nothing.

We will find ourselves standing in the one shade beyond nuts the day the web goes fully audio-visual, maybe even slaps on another dimension, and there we will be, full circle. No longer a medium, the web will just be. No filters, no shades—wearable webcams and webmics aimed at other wearable webcams and webmics.

All that work, time, and effort, not to mention the persistent and pesky analysis, just to have the thing become so ubiquitous and get so good at what it does, it disappears? Who needs that? What makes some of these diaries work is the distance between a thought and its expression, the experience and its display. This distance is shortened with each new plug-in, and with it, that recollection in tranquillity Wordsworth was talking up way back when.

Not a serious problem. The written word will still be around. Funny, as mere representation gets easier and easier, books are selling more than ever. Clearly, it is not simple nostalgia for the old media. As Nicholson Baker has shown, especially in his earlier novels, the mundane can be made into a thing of beauty. But it is hard work.

New media flipped the old Keatsean adage on its head. When it was tough to get at the truth, that is, when it was scarce, truth all but equaled beauty. Now that it is so cheap, what we may end up with is more a case of truth versus beauty.

Chapter Eleven

State d'Art

Toward the end of her review of *Can You Digit?*, an exhibition at the Postmasters Gallery in New York City's Soho district, Regina Cornwell, writing for the web publication TalkBack!, suddenly blurts out, "To artists I'd pose these questions: Why the obsession with the computer and its bags of tricks? Technicians do what you're doing, but they do it better." That's the whammy question. She follows up with lots more, including:

"Why does emulating rather than criticizing the mass- and multi-media pass muster these days? When will we see more artists finding new themes and ideas made possible through the computer, its interactivity, and its telecommunications potential, rather than repeating a tired round of concerns about technology and media itself?"

Well. Several answers to the several questions implicit in just these three questions suggest themselves. Peter Plagens might have summed them all up pretty well toward the end of his remarks made at a recent gathering of his fellow art critics: "Talk about something immutable in art—it's the ol' 90 percent ratio." Otherwise known as Sturgeon's Law, the axiom Plagens is referring to posits that 10 percent of all art at any given moment is worth a look. The other 90 percent stinks. When Joseph Beuys said, "Everyone is an artist," he didn't mean that everyone is a good one.

As for the obsession question, historian Eric Hobsbawm suggests an answer, or at least a precedent, noting that throughout the twentieth century, "The forces determining what happened within the arts, or whatever old-fashioned observers would have called by that name, were overwhelmingly exogenous. As might have been expected in an era of extraordinary techno-scientific revolution, they were predominantly technological."

In 1959, C. P. Snow delivered his famous lecture, "The Two Cultures and the Scientific Revolution," asserting that an unbridgeable chasm was yawning ever wider between artists and scientists. Not that they didn't respect each other—though if you read between the lines, you can tell Snow thought they didn't—most importantly, they didn't understand each other. They lived in separate worlds and supposedly just plain didn't get the point of whatever it was that was going on in the other's camp.

Snow was either overstating his case to make a point or prophetizing a true split that burst through to popular culture throughout the 60s when artists took on countercultural roles as renegades and vagabonds who distrusted the men in the white coats who served the military industrial complex and its dirty little wars, its threat of the Big One, its pollution of the environment, and so on. But clearly, at some point, the two sides kissed and made up. One of the more remarkable aspects of the Net in all its rapidly evolving manifestations is that from its beginnings, it has attracted a disproportionate number of scouts from both camps. Currently, they seem to be tripping over each other's paths even more frequently than they have since Leonardo embodied the best of both worlds by refusing to distinguish between them. The Net surely is not solely responsible for bridges Snow was afraid would never be built, but it has played a vital role.

New media artists in particular are naturally given to tossing around ideas about the potential of genetic algorithms and the like as artworks, and a Virtual Humans Conference will gather equal parts animators who went to art school and programmers with computer science degrees. A previous chapter of this book devoted considerable attention to several meeting grounds, of which Ars Electronica is only one example. At Ars Electronica, refereed by philosophers, artists and scientists exchange their findings, sit on the same panels, put their heads together, and try to figure out where everyone is going.

There is yet another answer to Regina Cornwell's question. Ever since the idea of the avant-garde set in, well over a century ago, artists have been trapped in the endless. "Avant-garde" is not spoken out loud any more, but it is still the insatiable modus operandi of art production. To attract even the briefest moment of cultural attention, to score at least a footnote in the art history books, artists are compelled to scrounge the not-done-yet.

Artists crave to chalk up a first: first canvas painted in the artist's own blood, first spark-plug sculpture, and first whatever. Getting there first has become even more important as this exhausted century wears on and on and on and the crowd to which artists play becomes almost impossible to shock—the original intention of the avant-garde; its raison d'être long gone, it persists as mere mechanism.

It comes as no surprise, therefore, to find artists all over the Net today. They could be found there even in its salad days, experimenting with the new medium, challenging preconceptions even before they had time to jell, calling into question the standards by which...and so on, and so on. All that good "pomo stuff" is alive and well on the Net, even as online technology may be ushering in whatever it is that will follow postmodernism (and it had damn sure better not be called post-postmodernism!).

Clearly, repurposed art—that done up first in one medium and then scanned into the new—is not the focus of this discussion. Digitalized Cézannes are scorned by new media artists. ASCII art—little images composed of the typographical elements of your basic e-mail program—was the graffiti of the pre-web days. Now that the web is here, however, ASCII art is just as passé. The web's stab at handling multimedia online all but begs for creative play. The web site as art. Many have risen to the challenge. Only a few have conquered it. Yep, that ol' 90 percent ratio.

The challenge is more daunting than you might think at first. You would imagine that a medium that can handle text, graphics, animation, sound, and what-not—all layerable in frames and floating windows, and so on—would be more than enough for an artist to work with. If it were not for the hurdle of bandwidth, you would be right. But it is no fun staring at an abstract image on your computer screen while waiting for a 400 K sound clip to trickle in and accompany it. (I'll do a lot for art's sake, but not that.)

The far greater challenge lies in overcoming the technological limitations of re-reproduction. The number of times an image is composed, decomposed, and recomposed on its way from an artist's palette, electronic or not, to somebody's 15-inch monitor may or may not be relevant. In practical terms alone, it doesn't matter at all—like text, digital images are just a series of zeroes and ones. Get them right, and you've got yourself a perfect copy each and every time. Same with sound. Visually, however, 256 colors is a damn finite range, not to mention the loss of real resolution and texture (qualities pinched in the compression of sound as well). A CD-quality symphony is still a bit much for a set of twisted copper wires to bear.

If something seems vaporous about an image on a computer monitor, new media artists can be grateful that so much groundwork had been laid before them in an effort to excuse the physical presence of an artwork from actual existence. Conceptual art informs new media art by necessity. Consider what happens when you open the URL http://www.jodi.org. The screen fills with letters, numbers, and other typographical symbols such as the ones that scroll on the faces of computers in old science fiction movies when they are thinking madly about something. As it turns out, here it is just one lengthy blinking link. You go in, the index is next. It is quieter in there, but it too starts with a bit of code-like print-out-looking lines, as if quoting from a chat that one computer has been having with another—maybe your own with some server somewhere else in the world.

Then the menu, and this is a quote:

```
/100CC                /betalab
   |                      |
   |_message.HQX       |_Flock
   |_Reflector         |_W147PPP
   |_Surgery           |_HAVOCS
   |_Nemo              |_Re:Machines
   |_NewsArm           |_YourPage
   |_Txt               |_Manual
   |_Top100            |_AU.RAIN
                       |_ZAPP:01:04
```

More than that, by the way, the following is the closest thing to a signature I found anywhere:

Connected to//www.jodi.org Heemskerk(#1267) Paesmans(#496)

After a while, it sinks in that each menu item is something like a separate room at an exhibition; as far as I know, there are no links from any one item to any other, and only a few of them will take you back to the front. "message.HQX" was blinking, and I entered via that door first. It is very pretty in there, but it didn't take long to decide to move my self-guided tour along to the second item, "Reflector."

First, the background rolls down. Essentially, it is a collage, snippets from the interface that has not changed all that much since Steve Jobs and his crew introduced the Macintosh over ten years ago. After the background is all there, you see that it is comprised of layers of windows looking a bit perhaps like the clutter on your own desktop when you are multitasking, but cut up in impossible ways. That is, it overlaps so that the effect is really only slightly more cluttered. Over this background come rectangles with corner-to-corner Xs, looking like the spaces in passports where you're to place your photo.

And indeed, photos come in when you click on the squares, photos snapped during a CU See Me session, a primitive form of Net video conferencing—hardly a surprise, this is "Reflector," after all, an IP address you connect to to run such a session. At any rate, it was here that for some reason I thought: Rauschenberg. An extremely clean, almost sanitized, electric Robert Rauschenberg. Let me leap to say that I seriously doubt Rauschenberg even wisped briefly through the minds of Jodi's creators, but he wisped through mine—it was the collage thing, touched up with noise.

The differences, of course, make the point interesting. Picasso and Braque did some cutting and pasting before Rauschenberg came along, and they used the materials that were mighty contemporary for their time: newspaper clippings, cigarette packages, and so on—items so contemporary that from the distance of the present, they seem atmospheric, historical, or quaint.

Further, compared to Rauschenberg's cutting and pasting, they seemed to have made a fairly neat job of it, "outrageous" as the very idea was at the time. Rauschenberg was messier, but he did work in messier, noisier times. The next thought was only natural: When has enough time gone by for the context to have changed enough, how essentially different must a set of materials be, and above all, how "other" must another set of signs be from those used in artworks of a previous period before you declare a stop to one period and the dawn of the next? Declare the line between, say, modernism and postmodernism? And postmodernism and...what?

At the time, you probably can't. Ezra Pound was forever declaring the dawns of new ages right there and then, and that rapid fire succession of brave new worlds seems laughable now that Vorticism or Imagism are not the household words he was certain that they would be. To give credit where credit is due, however, he did almost inadvertently orchestrate the overall arc of modernism itself, a combined effort of a flock of movements within it.

Take the first page of "Reflector" (it does lead on to others) and set it next to your basic Rauschenberg creation with, say, a JFK, some more photo-rubbings, some money, and a lot of paint washed together—first of all, you can't. "Reflector" doesn't actually exist in physical space. The first vital difference.

If you could, however, and you can in your mind (not a minor point), the cleanliness of "Reflector" leaps out at you, even with its snapshots of disorderly geek living rooms framed and set off by windows within windows. The Rauschenberg is dripping with the liquid memory of its time; "Reflector" hacks off into pixeled rectangles of a ghostly land where there are only two dimensions and none of those 256 colors are really real.

If that last bit comes off like a value judgment in Rauschenberg's favor, it is not meant to be; all in all, Jodi is an absolute blast. Each of these "rooms" explores a different function that the web is capable of and makes a stab at doing a piece on every single one worth your attention—now and maybe even later. "Surgery" may be the silliest, running a search on some naughty words. (Granted, it may be a bit of grandstanding for free speech, but the Net has already got more than enough of that.) "Flock" is one of the nicest works out there. A very simple shot of a pigeon with web-form dots laid out over it and a clock; choose a dot, click on it, and you have submitted a form taking you to another pigeon, the clock denoting another time zone. That pigeon may or may not have been photographed on another continent, but the concept is a complete and beautiful whole.

What makes me wonder whether all this represents just another movement within the post-modern period or the inklings of another era just now breaking might be best illustrated with yet another compare-and-contrast. This one may be a bit more fair. Pick a music video, any music video. Pick the one showing right now on MTV as you're reading this. It also does not exist in the physical world (though, as opposed to the works of Jodi, many of the materials that went into making it do). It also lives in a box. Unlike Jodi to an extent, however, it is calling on you to complete ideas it suggests in 8-frame cuts with your life-long experience in, one, the actual physical world, and two, watching movies and TV.

That video playing right now, which to some is the pinnacle of post-modern art, has a couple of decades of television and an entire century's worth of movies to jostle, reshuffle, and regurgitate back to you to the beat. Jodi has...what? Four years? This entire site, a web art project primarily about the web, and by extension, the Net and all of online technology (okay, so more years than four). It fulfills the post-modern criteria of self-referral so well that it has very little material to call on. In terms of experience, it can count on only a passing acquaintance that any of its viewers has yet with the new medium.

But this is precisely the challenge a few artists who had established themselves long before there was a web to play with have greeted full force. Jenny Holzer serves as an example of a successful crossover. Douglas Davis, on the other hand, exemplifies the artist's version of the typical mistake many make in their initial ventures out on to the web—namely, the assumption that just being there is enough.

Holzer's artworks are usually characterized as quickies—snappy content aimed at a fast-paced world with no time for ornament, much less for allegory or ambiguity. But I would not be the first to point out that this just is not so. Sticking to just the Truisms that she's most famous for, there's the context to consider. Holzer wants art to be out there, and although you will find her work in galleries and museums, you will also run across it on Times Square, on a Las Vegas marquee (PROTECT ME FROM WHAT I WANT, perhaps her most well-known Truism), on pencils, T-shirts, baseball caps, and so on. And now, for a while now actually, on the web.

The web is just about perfect for Holzer's work. It is an awful place for painters, but if you are primarily concerned with flashing text at people as they surf on by, if you have always had a thing for the most recent technological innovations in communication (in Holzer's case, LED displays and even a venture into virtual reality), you could hardly do better anywhere else.

Besides just getting your art out on the web—whether in the name of raising the general consciousness of all art or promoting your own career—you can one-up any Keith Haring or Barbara Kruger by getting your audience to reach in and mingle with it, even vote on it.

If you stick to the basics, the web is also a relatively easy medium to master. Over time, however, it has been interesting to watch a pretty neat thing going on at Adaweb, the site where Holzer's work resides with that of other New York artists. It is getting harder and harder to tell where the Jenny Holzer pages end and the rest of Adaweb begins. As she told *Wired*, "There really is an artificial line between someone who is a real artist and someone who's writing the software for the stuff."

She evidently gets a lot of help from the Ada crew, and it makes the visit a lot more fun. Your browser gets force-fed with images that splash over text and then disappear. You are ushered on to the next page without having so much as thought of clicking yet. And again, without being conscious of it, you may realize after a while that you are not looking at a Holzer any more. You're somewhere else, very Holzerish maybe (there seems to have been a mutual influence thing happening at Ada), but definitely somewhere else.

But when you're in Holzerspace, you can click from one Truism to another, vote on the ones you like, or submit a form admitting which ones you actually believe. Some of these Truisms are pretty straightforward (FATHERS OFTEN USE TOO MUCH FORCE), others aren't (CONFUSING

YOURSELF IS A WAY TO STAY HONEST). But like aphorisms—those related but more structurally balanced one-liners—nearly all of them seem easily passed over at first glance, though, to the thoughtful surfer, they may throw a bump in the wave.

Jenny Holzer has remarked that if Andy Warhol were alive today, he would be so into cyberspace that he would never come out. Although I don't doubt that for a moment, it is still hard to picture Warhol sitting at a desk, his ashen face glowing in the screenlight. There was a lot of geek in Andy; he spent a lot of time alone, he adored TV, talked on the phone for hours, but there's a big chunk of geek missing from him as well. He wasn't a tinkerer, a hands-on, DIY kind of guy.

You wonder what sort of web site Andy Warhol would have come up with. I would have loved for him to have risen to the challenge. Certainly it would have been more than a storefront site from which to sell silver pillow balloons, Brillo boxes, and silk screens. And without a doubt, it would have made a lot more imaginative use of the web than the one that a museum in Pittsburgh has put up in his name. Maybe you would have been able to click somewhere and launch a bot to go out and find the most prevalent image on the web, bring it back, squiggle a few day-glo lines strategically, sign it "Andy Warhol," and drop it on your hard disk. He might have liked that. Of course, he would have had to find a way to get you to pay for it.

What really would have irked him, though, is that the web has not produced the sort of image he would have been after. Nothing like a sudden take on a historic moment printed and reprinted in newspapers and magazines and eventually in textbooks, etching itself indelibly on what was once a collective consciousness. No official portraits to recast over slabs of glorious, unreal color. And nothing like the clips recycled every half-hour on CNN and MTV. Nothing everyone has looked at regardless of whether he or she wanted to. Nothing, in other words, that resonates. Guess Andy knew when to go. He was just too fabulous for these times.

Douglas Davis, however, is still with us. Davis is no stranger to the art world. By the standards of anyone's definition of new media art, however, he is still on getting-to-know-you terms with the web, where his "Breaking Out (of the Virtual Closet)" is currently on display. Plans are to keep it there, too, until the millennium closes. I'm afraid we won't have to wait until 1999 for it to fade in revelation or even relevance.

Open the URL and you are met with a poster-like image, Davis behind a video camera, out of focus, calling you in. "COME CLOSER. GET INTO THE LENS. LET ME SEE YOU. WE ARE ABOUT TO CREATE

TOGETHER..." Now, if that is not "icky" enough for you, there is more: "But not yet, please. Wait just a few pages...hold out your hand there...yes, I think I got it...your fingers...hand in hand..."

And one would have thought John Perry Barlow was drenching cyberspace in post-hippie romanticism. Granted, the gist of most of Davis's work throughout the last couple of decades has been about countering the bad rap technology was getting as he was launching his artistic career. In the days when, for example, the front page image was shot (1973), there was a point to arguing that technology was not an impersonal threat to humanity, but rather, could be put to intimate use.

In his heyday, Davis would link galleries in various parts of the world for live performances that would prove you could whisper sweet nothings to somebody a hemisphere away. And lo, technology made it all possible. It seems almost embarrassing to have to remark, though, that since then, the point has long since lost its thrust.

Davis's web come-on could not be more superfluous; yes, he and some of the artists he has worked with (Nam June Paik among them) helped focus attention on television as a two-way medium when it wasn't generally perceived as accessible territory, but even the most unwired out there knows that the very crux of this whole online thing is about person-to-person communication via the Net's inherent many-to-many model. The question of whether it stays that way would make the stuff of a far more interesting project at the moment.

And yet, as many of the previous pages go on about, the web in its present form is not exactly the ideal manifestation of online technology for many-to-many communication. Some art, in other words, especially art that depends on collaboration and interactivity, would be best served by other Net applications. Some artists have tried their hands at such projects: text-based MOOs and MUDs, Dada e-mail lists, or some combination of the Internet and another medium—usually live performance, such as "Net Game - An American Dialogue" by Michael and Deena Weinstein, the text of which (all about the Net, by the way, a virtual orgy of self-reflexivity) was published by CTHEORY. Director George Coates staged a show in San Francisco in 1995 and called for people to submit text via the Net, but the results were no more artistically innovative than the projected sub-titles at an opera.

On December 30, 1994, the artist Brad Brace posted the first digitalized photo of his "12hr-ISBN-JPEG Project." They are still coming along, one every twelve hours, and he plans to keep it up for a total of seven years. The "hypermodern photos, perfect trans-avant-garde memes for the nineties," are uploaded onto several FTP servers, and are available by e-mail and on at least two newsgroups. Although Brace maintains a web site (which features other works as well), for this project in particular, he seems primarily interested in making the most of low-tech connectivity, getting his art out and people involved with it.

You can join a mailing list to discuss the "authentic gritty greyscale" images and participants are encouraged to "view them, re-post 'em, save 'em, trade 'em, print 'em, even publish them." Not only are the pre-web modes of networking being celebrated here, the free movement of ideas and overall ethical spirit of the Net's early days are as well.

English artist Heath Bunting encourages much of the same attitude in his work, and get this, he does it on the web. Very few of the very many pages on his site exceed 3 K, and for that alone, Bunting deserves some sort of grant from somebody. Even when images do come into play, most have been reduced to a minimum of bits for a maximum of impact. Stark black and whites. There is even a nice show called, appropriately enough, "Velocity," which pushes shots snapped from the streets in rapid fire order. It is a web slide show that, unlike so many others, actually hits the speed for which the feature was built.

Even better, the ultra-reduced resolution serves the work. Seemingly at random, "markings"—streets outlined by the white stripes of curbs and arrows against a black blacker than asphalt—are mixed with "tags"— most probably negatives of street graffiti. The dashes, curves, and slashes start looking an awful lot alike and add up to a swiftly moving portrait of another term for "speed," with the word "city" in it. Bunting is more well-known, however, for his mixed use of the web and other telecommunications media. He is concerned with setting up networks of communication that would not exist if the technology he calls on for help were only used in the way in which they were intended. Bunting's primary materials are the public telephone, the fax machine, e-mail, your basic snail mail (postcards, and so on), and a few unsurprisingly surprising media such as the signs held up at Tokyo subway stations with people's names on them.

Bunting then uses the web as an interface between browsers and these other media to create private networks among friends, acquaintances, and total strangers. You can fill out forms to call someone up, send a postcard, or write an e-mail with a message that has already been sketched out for you. Take the Tokyo subway sign project, for example. Bunting introduces the idea behind it with these words:

"When i arrived at the airport there were lots of people holding up sings with peoples names on them. there was not one for me, this made me a little sad." Notice how Bunting cloaks the mischievousness of this project with a faux innocence exempting him from any claims for damages that may incur. The language, complete with misspellings, run-ons, and the lack of caps, sets a tone that says, these are not prank calls, kids, let's see what happens without anybody getting hurt. And the audience follows, the messengers and the messengees. The idea here is that you can fill out the web form with a messenge for somebody at a specified subway station in Tokyo; a sign will be held up for them, and the message delivered. You can check the results, and the one right at the top...

> "to: the suited man
> station: shinjuku
> from: Goeff in Derby
> message: Im sorry about yesterday, perhaps we can try again. Do you think you are doing the right thing?"

...jibes in every way with the Bunting's announcement of the project. The timbre of the language is naive, the situation absurd, but the message delivered is not. There is a picture of a primly dressed woman passing the message along to the first suited man that came along. I doubt he thought too much of the incident, though at the same time, I'd bet it was the most unexpected thing to happen to him all that week. I would love to think that he went home and sat down and thought to himself, "Am I doing the right thing?"

But even assuming that he forgot all about it five minutes later, the incident is recorded and posted for all the world to see. Some guy in Derby reached out and touched some guy in Tokyo. Even with all the e-mail, telephony, and online networking in all its many forms, this would never have happened if Heath Bunting hadn't introduced a wrinkle in fabric of the technology. This technology is supposed to help us bank and shop faster, get the things that need to be said by those that need to say them to those to whom they need to be said faster, easier, and with as few wrinkles as possible. With a sly wink, Heath Bunting reminds us of the vital human need of the unexpected.

The unexpected is difficult to attain when you have only a handful of variables with which to deal. Andreas Troeger, a German artist living and working in New York City, originally set up his site, "Zero Tolerance," in 1994 on a PowerBook using the simple but popular MacHTTP; sometimes I wonder just how many sites of historic note (Justin Hall's, for example) got started this way. Troeger began as many artists did. He scanned in images, documentation, and so on from the projects he had been doing before he plugged his laptop into the network, and then laid them out in a somewhat presentable form, and hoped people would drop by and have a look at them.

Anyone who did could sort through stills from his videos, download audio clips, or read the screenplay to his short sci-fi film. As the writer of that screenplay, I was enthralled, naturally. My first page on the web! My work and my name, up there for all the world to see. Of course, not much of the world did bother to read a screenplay online or even pretend they had by clicking on that particular URL.

That didn't stop me, though, from expanding my presence on the site with poetry and other textual self-indulgences—even going so far as to lean over the keyboard of my own PowerBook and read my poems into the little microphone, and then send over the recordings for Andreas to place on the site. Thus went my venture into multimedia. "Zero Tolerance" is a terrific site; there is a handful of intriguing artists at work there, and I continue to score the fewest hits of any of them. By far.

In the meantime, Andreas has gone on to do web and other work with Nam June Paik, video artist Paul Garrin (Media Filter), and the 235 Media group. He also edited the film *Synthetic Pleasures*, and sees to his own solo film and video work. In the fall of 1995, he introduced OnLine TV, his first to have been conceived for the web itself. Somewhere in New York, a video camera is still directed out on to a busy intersection, and every 60 seconds it feeds an image to the ZT server. After you are logged on, you can adjust the frequency of loads according to however smoothly your own connection is going at the moment. After that, there is little else to do but sit back and watch the streets flow. Cars, people. Rain, snow, no weather at all.

Naturally, the question arises, Why? It's hardly "TV" as we know and either love or hate it. The barest minimum of conscious effort has been applied to do any actual programming. And in terms of being on the forefront of web technology, for whatever that may be worth artistically, well, yes, at present, this is as live as live video gets via the sort of connection the vast majority of us have. At the same time, we are also aware that the web is on the verge of some sort of melt into TV, and that page-by-page animation is going to look like the Lumiere brothers standing next to Stanley Kubrick. As if to emphasize that it is precisely the sense of wonder that greeted the first Lumiere films (also the result of "merely" pointing a camera at something somewhat interesting and letting it roll) that he's after—no more and no less—Troeger flew to Munich in the spring of 1996 to set up a sort of client station at the Gallery on Lothringerstrasse, quite a respectable address in the Munich art scene. There, you could wander in and see the goings on at the New York City street corner projected onto a wall and ponder the means by which those images got up there. Or you could ponder Troeger's choice of content.

After all, video cameras have been set up on the street corners of a few American cities, most probably quite earnestly intended as instruments of law and order, yet chilling nonetheless for all the obvious reasons.

We've grown accustomed to the live images of "history in the making" on broadcast television, the ultimate one-to-many medium. The Net has been all about making many-to-many communication as live as possible. Its earliest and simplest forms were pretty excellent at it, too. Getting the web to perform as well has been one of the toughest technical challenges in all the Net's development. How do you get what's essentially a call-and-response method of data transfer to come alive?

But how live is live? In an interview conducted in February 1996, futurist Paul Saffo remarked, "The web as we know it today is dead. It's dead in two ways: because it's going to mutate into something else very quickly and be unrecognizable within 12 months, and secondly, it's dead because all it's got on it is dead information... It's a big information mausoleum." "Dead" was the buzzword throughout the first half of 1996 when it came to talking about the web. The word is still hot enough that even *Word*, the webzine, refers to its back issues as Dead Word. The articles are still there, and the text might seem as lively to anyone reading as it did on the day it was put up, but in the current lingo of the happening crowd, it's finished, over, passed on. As the John Cleese character in the Monty Python Parrot Sketch might put it, "This is an ex-Word."

Notice the two very separate definitions of the web's demise according to Saffo. The first relates merely to the technical aspects of the state of the web. Saffo goes on to talk about the animation Java will bring to life on-screen and the 3D chat applications that will enable surfing in groups through virtual spaces so that the web will no longer seem like such a lonely place. All sorts of other innovations are also in store to resuscitate the global corpse.

Fine. It is the second definition that I find fairly alarming. And not just because some futurist has uttered it, but because I'm running across the general idea again and again out there. It is as if once a bit of content is created, be it text, an image, a swath of music, or any other form of content that can be digitalized, once it goes up, it's over—as if the creator has lost all personal investment in the creation and no one is going to get a thing out of it any more.

I wonder whether some of the Net savvy critics giving voice to this view remember that at several moments in art history since the advent of modernism, views a hair's breadth away from this position were all the rage. Action painting, the happenings, and a lot of the performance art that followed come to mind. I doubt that they are thinking in process-over-product terms, but in a sense, the call for animation—for bringing the web to life to make it relevant at all—runs along the same lines.

If you go out looking for art on the web, you will find a lot of it, of course. And although you could categorize it in other ways, you can also pretty much cut it down the middle according to this criterion: alive and dead. The work you find on a site such as "Razorfish" serves as an example of alive art, the sort of browser-jamming, up-to-the-second work online connectivity is supposed to be all about. The "Razorfish" front page buzzes with blue dots dividing up like living cells, logos sweeping in over other logos, "orange alerts," and most tellingly, a clock that tells you not just the hour and the minute, but the very second at which you're taking all this in.

Examples of dead art abound at one of the web's most popular art sites, the "Web Museum"—which appropriately enough used to be called "Le Louvre," until Le real Louvre got upset about it. Appropriate because throughout this century, Le Louvre (the real 3D institution in Paris) has, for many artists, stood for all that is dead in art. At the "Web Museum," most of the artists featured are indeed quite dead and have gone on to art heaven, more commonly referred to as the pantheon. Yet on an average week, the "Web Museum" claims to have over 200,000 visitors to whom it delivers over 10 million documents. So how dead is dead art really? Popularity is certainly no argument for quality or relevancy, but it surely counts as a consideration.

Still, most artists concerned with coming up with relevant art that speaks to the present, maybe even with the hope of making a mark on the future, are not out to compete with Rembrandt. In literature, Harold Bloom made a mark of his own when he wrote about "the anxiety of influence," the fear live writers have of The Great Dead who seem all too present when staring at a blank page. Artists, on the other hand, seem far less anxious, even less respectful of their forbears. Postmodernism, in fact, turned dead art into a playground through which artists romp, cutting and pasting, quoting and alluding to at will, fully aware of the signifying value of works that history has declared "masterpieces."

The key element in defining the difference between alive and dead art is neither truth nor beauty, but time. And online technology is all about crunching time to the "diamond-pointed Now." The experience of art happening this very moment, or any other kind of "information" for that matter, is such a visceral rush, it becomes an addiction. Look at the news junkies who, the moment something blows up, start flipping between CNN and the networks for the deepest scoop on what just happened. One of the hyped-up promises inherent in online technology is its potential to write all of history, including art history, not in the present perfect tense ("has just happened"), but in the present continuous ("is happening").

To illustrate, let me back up to the fall of the Berlin Wall and the "reunification" of Germany. I was involved with a performance art group at the time, and on a couple of different occasions, we incorporated Germany's most-watched news program, the Tagesschau, "live," into a series of performances. Because we were addressing the capitalist buyout of what used to be East Germany, and because we could pretty much count on the day's news dealing with the details of that overall development, we usually wound up with some fairly nice resonance between the television monitor and what we were doing, live and in-person, on stage or in the gallery.

Alive, up-to-the-moment art, you'd think, but not any more. After all, the Tagesschau might be being broadcast live, but its news would be hours—hours!—old. It had been gathered, selected, edited, and then simply presented from the studio. By Saffo's standards, we were interacting with dead information. Ultimately, you can cut the time between a news event—or the creation of a work of art—and its delivery and reception down only so much. That object (news item, art work) does not become "live," or in Saffo's eyes, alive, until the receiver reaches in and begins to manipulate it on his or her own.

We end up with forms on the web enabling you to vote on the sort of paintings you want painted, or exhibits in which you download pictures, twist them according to your own twisted desires, and upload them again, and so on. It is called interactivity, and those who are addicted to it, who came up with this dead or alive distinction, might as well be called "Now" junkies.

Where does this leave dead art? Frankly, I can still dig it. Years ago, I downloaded a Michelangelo, and it still serves as my "desktop pict"— the background to all I do on my laptop, on or offline. Besides the quirky functions of dead art such as these (in sum, wallpaper), the distinction leaves dead art in the museum, which rings eerily with Saffo's "mausoleum." However you pronounce it, these institutions, be they downtown or on the web, still have a place in the now, and maybe the future as well. As Glenn Lowry, director of the Museum of Modern Art in New York, remarked, "We're living in such a speeded-up world that information is transmitted globally in nanoseconds. Perhaps the key role of museums in the future is to create ways to slow things down."

Speeded-up or slowed down, museums are catching on to new media art. In the fall of 1996, the exhibition "alt.youth.media" opened at the

New Museum of Contemporary Art, almost simultaneously with the "Mediascape" exhibition at the Soho Guggenheim. As Ellen Tepfer reported to the Rhizome list, "The entire season-opening weekend in the New York Soho art world seemed saturated by an interest in the 'cyber' arts." Space Untitled Gallery lined up some monitors and presented art works on CD-ROM and the web.

All very exciting, all very now, and yet, I'm ready for new media art not confined to a box. It doesn't thrill me to walk into a gallery and be handed a mouse any more. Of course some wonderful things are being done inside the machines, but more and more, I'm wondering whether we won't be able to turn that inside out.

I am not talking about the many cybernetic body art scenes, Survival Research Laboratories, or any other mechanical, hydraulic, motorized modernist-posing-as-pomo man-machine noise. New media art has already raised a fresh batch of far more relevant issues—the value of information, its dissemination, access to it, timeliness, perception in an age of realized virtuality—that seem difficult to extract from a very enclosed web of connectivity.

So back to Regina Cornwell's whammy question. Why the obsession with computers? The cynical answer would address marketability. Computers are hot, so art on or with computers must be hot, too (though not everywhere). The ideal answer would address new tools and a new public for creative expression. The realists, however, will just keep an eye out for that one out of ten site that will be worth the click.

References

The Andy Warhol Museum.
http://www.clpgh.org/warhol/

Amazon.com.
.http://www.amazon.com

Association of Alternative Newsweeklies.
http://aan.eline.com

Auletta, Ken. "The RIeducation of Michael Kinsley," *The New Yorker*, May 13, 1996.
http://www.enews.com/magazines/new_yorker/archive/960513-001.html

Berners-Lee, Tim. As quoted by WebMaster, October 1996, eLine Productions.
http://www.eline.com

Brace, Brad. Brace, "The 12hr-ISBN-JPEG Project."
http://www.teleport.com/bbrace/12hr-isbn-jpeg.html

Bunting, Heath.
http://www.cybercafe.org
http://www.irrational.org

Caruso, Denise. "Microsoft Morphs into a Media Company," *Wired* 4.06.
http://www.hotwired.com/wired/4.06/features/microsoft.html

Cohen, Jodi B. InfoBytes, *Editor and Publisher Interactive*.
http://www.mediainfo.com/ephome/news/newshtm/bytes/bytes.htm

Cornwell, Regina. "Letter from New York: Cyber-art in SoHo Galleries", *TalkBack!*, Issue #2.
http://math.lehman.cuny.edu:80/tb/sceneletter3.html

Davis, Douglas. "Breaking Out (of the Virtual Closet)."
http://math240.lehman.cuny.edu/art/

Drudge Report.
http://www.lainet.com/drudge

"Faster Pussycat! Click! Click!", *Suck*, August 6, 1996.
http://www.suck.com/daily/dynatables/96/08/06

Frook, John Evan. Interactive Age.
http://techweb.cmp.com/ia/iad_web_/newsnow/july22-26/july25/july25-3.htm

Geek Cereal.
http://www.geekcereal.com

Hobsbawm, Age of Extremes, p. 501.

Holzer, Jenny, on Adaweb.
http://adaweb.com/adaweb/project/one.html

IntelliQuest, "35 Million People On Internet/Online In First Quarter 1996."
http://www.intelliquest.com/release13.htm

Jodi.
http://www.jodi.com

Johnson, Steve. Filter, *Feed*, May 1996.
http://www.feedmag.com/96.05_filter.htm

Justin.
http://www.links.net

Katz, Jon. "The Once and Future Kinsley," *Media Rant*.
http://www.netizen.com/netizen/96/29/index1a.html

Lowry, Glenn. As interviewed by Robert Atkins, "Scene & Heard: Sound Bytes,"",
TalkBack!, Issue No. 1.
http://math240.lehman.cuny.edu/talkback/Talk_html/Scene_Heard-1.html

Meeks, Brock. *Cyberwire Dispatch*, November 11, 1995.
http://cyberwerks.com:70/oh/cyberwire/cwd/cwd.95.11.21.html

"Mid-Hype Crisis," *Suck*, August 5, 1996.
http://www.suck.com/daily/dynatables/96/08/05

Nee, Eric. "Paul Saffo: An Interview,", *Upside*, February 1996.
http://www.upside.com/print/feb96/qa.saffo.html

Outing, Steve. "Back to the Future of the Internet," Stop the Presses, *Editor and
Publisher Interactive*.
http://www.mediainfo.com:4900/ephome/news/newshtm/stop/stop626.htm

Outing, Steve. "Playing With the Competition vs. Fighting It," Stop the Presses, *Editor and Publisher Interactive*.

http://www.mediainfo.com/ephome/news/newshtm/stop/stop717.htm

Plagens, Peter. "Art Criticism and the Vanishing Public: In Search of Some Interesting Reading,", *Artnet Magazine*, June 24, 1996.

http://www.artnet.com/plagens6-21-96.html

Razorfish.

http://www.razorfish.com

Rebecca.

http://www.cyborganic.com/People/rebecca

Rebello, Kathy. "Inside Microsoft," *Business Week*, July 15, 1996.

http://www.businessweek.com/1996/29/b34841.htm

Rhizome Internet.

http://www.rhizome.com

Rosenberg, Scott. "Wired gets pushy,", 21st, Salon Magazine, February 13, 1997.

Slate.

http://www.slate.com

Slate's Technical Help.

http://www.slate.com/Email/Current/Email.asp#SlateTech

Time, Techwatch, August 12, 1996.

http://pathfinder.com/time/magazine/domestic/1996/960812/business.html

Troeger, Andreas. Zero Tolerance.

http://Zero.Tolerance.org

Virtual Humans Conference.

http://www.crg.cs.nott.ac.uk/dns/conf/vr/vh96.txt

Web Museum (several locations, here's one).

http://www.fhi-berlin.mpg.de/wm/

Weinstein, Michael and Deena. "Net Game—An American Dialogue."

http://www.ctheory.com/ga1.12-net_game.html

"Wiring the Fourth Estate," *Feed*, June 1996.

http://www.feedmag.com/96.06dialog/96.06dialog1.html

Word.

http://www.word.com

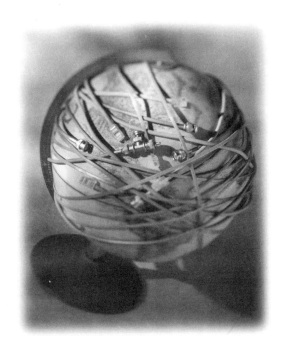

Part III:

Utopia and Its Discontents

"...the Internet, virtual reality, cyber-this, and cyber-that present yet another possible future even more promising or more threatening precisely because for most it is an invisible one."

David Hudson

Chapter Twelve
The Engines of Change

"On or about December 1910, human nature changed." Virginia Woolf had the puckish audacity to set this shocker to paper in 1924. Her fellow Moderns may have squabbled about the actual date, but most of them essentially agreed with Ms. Woolf. There was no century quite like the twentieth. And now, as we're about to wrap it up, many are claiming that it is happening all over again. Two major shifts in human nature in one century?

Radical as that may seem at first glance, consider that those who do a lot of thinking about the arts, philosophy, or cultural studies pretty much take the idea for granted. Careers have been made defining the two shifts of the twentieth century, each with its own name, modernism and postmodernism—each blocked off with a set of dates that invariably varies according to the slant and vision of each interpreter.

The dates of the century itself slide the scales of individual perception. Eric Hobsbawm titles his history *Age of Extremes: The Short Twentieth Century, 1914–1991*. For Hobsbawm, humanity jolts four years after the quake Virginia Woolf felt, but five years before the one Paul Johnson sees in his *Modern Times*, the very first sentence of which reads, "The modern world began on 29 May 1919 when photographs of a solar eclipse, taken on the island of Principe off West Africa and at Sobral in Brazil, confirmed the truth of a new theory of the universe."

For Johnson, the modern world is an invention. Science made it. But switch back to Hobsbawm: "By 1914 virtually everything that can take shelter under the broad and rather undefined canopy of 'modernism' was already in place: cubism; expressionism; futurism; pure abstraction in painting; functionalism and flight from ornament in architecture; the abandonment of tonality in music; the break with tradition in literature." (pages 178–179) Hmm. Now the twentieth century sounds more like a work of art than a science project.

Surely the century has gone the way it has guided by the innovations in both the arts and sciences, even if the artists and scientists themselves haven't crossed paths all that often until more recently. *Leonardo*, a publication from MIT Press, was founded in 1968 as a reaction, a hopeful stab at mending the damage done by the art versus science arguments that were all the rage a few decades ago, and its relevance hasn't faded one iota since.

An afternoon spent paging through a copy not too long ago tripped a couple of synapses and sent me stumbling over a memory of the night I decided that all the dabbling I had done in the arts had not been for nought. As the late 70s became the early 80s, James Burke had a book and later a PBS series called *Connections*. It considered the great turning points in human history, particularly the scientific and technological advances. Burke was full of fascinating observations on the unexpected ways one thing can lead to another.

The Chinese invented fireworks, for example. It was Europe, however—naturally—that came up with the idea of taking the powder out and sticking it in guns instead. Such is the way the course of history, as the cliché goes, gets altered. Imagine how far the European colonists of any continent but their own would have gotten without gunpowder.

At the time, Burke's series made for a terrific excuse to watch TV rather than study for exams. At the very end of the last episode, he had a little speech that shook me to my bones. He even began by warning that what he was about to say would disturb and upset a lot of people, and he wasn't kidding. In sum, he said that the Michaelangelos and the Van Goghs of the world hadn't really made much of a lasting change in civilization. The real movers and shakers of the world have been the Galileos and Einsteins. It was the ultimate swipe at art from an old adversary, science.

I jumped in my VW Bug and raced across the UT Austin campus to a friend who was firing pots in a kiln, and panicked (ah, college days), told him about this dark night of the soul Burke had tossed me into. He didn't have a lot to say outright to console me, but he did manage to pose the right questions. Answering them, I managed to calm myself, my faith in art (and hence, my life) reconfirmed.

I had reminded myself that history, the evolution of culture, was propelled by neither art nor science alone, but by the dialogue between them. Philosophers love to point out that all of Western civilization would never have got off the ground if it weren't for those pesky dreamers posing one seemingly ridiculous question after another. But without empiricism, there would have been no scientific method, and hence, for better or worse, no "civilization."

Oversimplification aside, the profound impact of the dialogue is more readily recognized by its artsy side than its geek side. Would chaos theory, as just one of many examples, have occurred to any scientist without the subliminal groundwork laid by the modernists? Would modernism have come about if it weren't for the industrial revolution of the nineteenth century? Nope and nope.

For all the agents of modernism Hobsbawm assigns to the arts, he also notes, "No period in history has been more penetrated by and more dependent on the natural sciences than the twentieth century. Yet no period, since Galileo's recantation, has been less at ease with it." (page 522)

Some greet yet another theory of the origin of the universe or yet another "ism" to attach to the tail end of art history with open arms, while others thumb their noses and run away. Others have mixed feelings. It is exciting, enthralling, but that doesn't necessarily mean we're "at ease with it." I think Hobsbawm is right. Every century preceding the twentieth has had its leaps and bounds, but none as many as ours, and certainly not as many that have so radically altered the physical space in which we live.

After the industrial revolution, skyscrapers, airplanes, and telephones both exhilarated and frightened more immediately than, say, a cathedral that could take a few decades or centuries to get up. Reactions to these changes were accordingly more emotional and more extreme. And while utopias and anti-utopias have come and gone before, we have been more wildly speculative in this century than in probably any other (visions of cataclysm based solely on religion aside).

Now the Internet, virtual reality, cyber-this, and cyber-that present yet another possible future even more promising or more threatening precisely because for most it is an invisible one. This is a change that is hard to keep an eye on. Further, the language seems so strange, sometimes as if it were meant to be that way so that only those who understand what is going on in the wires twisting through our homes will have control over it.

Rewired

It is probably not a good idea to generalize about these things. What's life, though, without the occasional risk? Here goes: Among the many, many factors defining the differences between those who embrace change—the automobile, abstract expressionism—and those who resist it, the chance anyone stands to profit financially from it is certainly one. Only one, mind you, but it is one factor that counts. We should keep this in mind as we review the various interpretations of what online technology means to us now and what it has in store for us in the future.

Chapter Thirteen

One World

In the summer of 1994, I checked into an ongoing event called Serious Chiller Lounge in Munich. The particular night I was there, techno throbbed, people were "netsurfing" (still an exhilarating word at the time) on terminals set up throughout the dark, post-industrial warehouse, Japanese animation rolled on dozens of monitors, "smart" drinks were served, performances performed. There was a live linkup with William S. Burroughs, and afterward, an aimless discussion that got a bit nasty when it became clear that this was not the crowd for the talkshow format.

But after the formalities were tossed, the mood lightened and I managed to corner R. U. Sirius, a founding editor of *Mondo 2000*, a publication that was all the rage at the time, highly appreciated as an alternative to *Wired* because its focus was more on the cultural than on the business side of Net-related issues. Already something of a celebrity in the hub of the scene at the time, San Francisco, R. U. Sirius was brought to mainstream attention when he was featured in *Time*'s gloss on the cyberpunk "movement."

Referring to the Virginia Woolf quote, I asked him whether he thought it was happening again. Was human nature itself changing? His immediate, "Yes," radiated with enthusiasm. "What it means to be a human being is definitely changing. We're having the opportunity to live beyond the limits of biology. We're doing that through technology, and to an extent, we're doing that through media communications. We're evolving a global brain that actually starts thinking and processing information so fast that it feeds back into the system and starts resolving problems." Such as? "Biology and material wealth, gravity and time..." Big ones, in other words.

Notice the idea of biology as a problem. While all of us there in the Lounge were still undeniably human and the various goings on were rather primitive stabs in the dark at something else (mere gestures really), the urge to jump-start evolution was palpably real. Although some have always recognized nature's superior "intelligence," at the same time, they have felt that its eat-or-be-eaten system of values stinks and that we could come up with a better one, a better way of being. Tinkering with ourselves, we have usually taken the outside-in approach, great political or social schemes to improve humankind as a whole. Or we have redecorated our environment (those skyscrapers, and so forth). This time, our attention is focused on our insides, on the essential human formula.

After all, many would suggest, what is so great about human nature as it is? Tune into CNN for a while: People hacking each other to pieces, ethnic strife, crime, overpopulation—anyone could write this list. Many see something screwy and horrible in the DNA code. Should we wait a few hundred thousand years for Mom Nature to work the bugs out of the system? Besides, how good at it is she, really? Take evolution. Haven't the really mean bastards always come out on top? No, we know what we want, let's go for it. That is the whole point of civilization, remember?

This line of thinking, this view of ourselves versus the world around us, has been around almost as long as we have. We have even gone so far as to anthropomorphize nature as a single Being or host of beings, some of them benign, some jealous, and some just barely a notch above us at all. And each time a new technology or set of technologies is introduced, there is a revival of such ideas, sometimes bordering on the religious yet again. The advent of online technology has been no exception.

R. U. Sirius (a.k.a. Ken Goffman) figures prominently in the first chapter of Mark Dery's *Escape Velocity*, a fine book on the hopes and misgivings surrounding technology in "cyberculture." While sketching out the background to some of the more utopian rhetoric floated throughout the early and mid 90s, Dery points to Sirius as a special case in that, as the name implies, R. U. Sirius isn't quite (at least not 100 percent of the time).

More in the theoretical than in the practical sense, Sirius plays the role of culture jammer, as defined by Dery in a previous book on the social phenomenon of *Culture Jamming*. Practical, foot-soldier-type culture jammers rearrange billboards (for example, "Tropical Blend. The Savage Tan" becomes "Typical Blend. Sex in Ads"), run pirate radio stations, or hack their way on to web servers to deface the home pages of the powers-that-be. Sure, some call it vandalism, but "culture jammers are Groucho Marxists," Dery notes; most of their work is harmless and a lot of it—not all of it—is rather clever. They are comedians, and comedy, when it is good, can be as serious as serious gets.

Though Sirius would probably slough off the culture jammer label as he would any label, he is right up there with the best of them, tossing out contradictory, inflammatory, or intentionally ridiculous yet irresistibly thought-provoking ideas all in the same breath. It would be hard to pin down what a guy who writes books with titles such as *How to Mutate and Take Over the World* really thinks deep down in his heart of hearts, but a general drift does seem detectable from that night in the Serious Chiller Lounge in 1994 to an interview for *CTheory* in 1996.

In 1994, with the volume of the media hype focused on the Internet turned up to eleven, with anybody who was anybody declaring that the new technology would have an immense impact on just about everything, the only way to jam the culture was to go beyond mainstream superlatives. Yes, human nature itself was changing, we were escaping ourselves. It was just a matter of how soon we would be something entirely different from this old worn out model, homo sapiens, how fast we could pull it off. If "escape velocity" sounds like rocket science, it should. That is where the term comes from, but it is actually a fairly simple concept in its original context: "...the speed at which a body—a spacecraft, for instance—overcomes the gravitational pull of another body, such as the Earth."

"Cyberians" accelerated the connotative thrust of the term to such an extent that it split off in a variety of directions, but all of them basically fall into two general categories: the escape of the mind from the body into some futuristic computer hardware, and the emergence of a single global mind born of interconnected electronic networks. Both clearly depend on a single metaphor. The mind is a computer. We are what we think. The more we think, the more we are. So just as two heads are better than one, after you link two or more computers in a network, you have yourself a smarter mind. Keep on linking, and you have one helluva smart thinking machine, maybe even smarter than your run-of-the-mill human, and eventually, as you add more and more thinking modules, smarter than all of us put together.

There are so many holes in this construct it is hard to know where to begin airing them all out. Details aside, the greatest chasm to leap is the central mind-computer metaphor, and we'll deal with that when we take a look at the Extropians in Chapter 15, "Utopia in Extremis." Here, we should move right along to one of the more significant aspects of the metaphor, its extension in these two fundamentally opposite directions.

One leads to the ultimate preservation of the self. Your mind escapes your doomed body and sits out eternity on some hard disk. Hence you, if you are indeed your mind, live on and on, having abandoned the corporeal sinking ship to the worms. The other direction is all about the dissolution of the self, maybe even all of humanity into something just as immortal but more deserving of immortality than humans are—a global mind, thinking faster, better thoughts than any one of us could possibly handle on our own.

Proponents of both views pride themselves on a grasp of the big picture, an understanding of evolution as an on-going process and the surely prescient acknowledgment that we are not nature's last word on anything. At the same time, both want a hand in helping nature finish its sentence. Appropriately enough, the politics and cultural backgrounds of the two groups casting their lots with each of these opposing visions of the future are just as diametrically opposed. The self-preservationists, headed up by the Extroprians, are radical conservatives, most of them having been weaned on Reaganomics. The one-world folks, on the other hand, tend to stem either from the 60s or the aftermath of that cultural quake.

Ironically, because much of the rebellion (or rather, many of the various rebellions) that took place in the 60s were political in nature, the one-worlders are less overtly political. At times, in fact, you might suspect that the global mind represents a welcome escape from politics altogether. "[I]dentity, politics, and ethics have long turned liquid," R. U. Sirius posits in an interview with Jon Lebkowsky for *CTheory*. "It seems that what we have, at least among the sort of hip technophile population, is an experimental attitude. An experimental attitude is one of not knowing, otherwise it's not really experimental."

It is a good attitude, especially if it is as self-aware as Sirius describes it. "I'm anti-utopian. I don't believe in totalizing philosophies or perfect happy endings. But it could be helluva lot better than it is now." The tone is a lot healthier than it was back when he was telling me about "a global brain that actually starts thinking and processing information so fast that it feeds back into the system and starts resolving problems."

Which isn't to say his bright eyes have dimmed. If anything, they have become sharper. A month after the *CTheory* interview, he told Net critic Pit Schultz, "The possibility for cyborg liberation—for an interpenetration between humans and machines, artificial life forms, nanotechnology ad infinitum—in a way that wildly expands human freedoms—to jump like a kangaroo, see like a bee, live a million years, change sexes, get ripped on drugs without physical deterioration—all of these things look to be becoming possible. But what I see in front of me is not a people being vitalized and dynamic. What I see is people diligently working on the machines that will replace them."

Again, it is hard to tell what he is getting at here exactly, but that makes him so damnably and uniquely lovable and refreshing among the deadly serious of the escape artists. If he is talking jobs, he is a diagnostician of the highest order; if he's talking cultural evolution, well, that only leads one to wonder about the philosophical groundwork that makes this leap of faith possible. Who laid it? According to Dery, we can look to two prime suspects, Marshall McLuhan and Pierre Teilhard de Chardin.

As Dery told the Boston *Phoenix*, "[McLuhan's] ideas cast a powerful spell on fringe computer culture, where they have acquired a New Age aura. For the ravers, zippies, and other members of cyberdelic culture who believe they are neurons in an emergent global meta-mind, he is the medium's messenger." A play on the McLuhan dictum that has worked its way into popular vernacular: "The medium is the message."

McLuhan's other contribution to pop culture is the idea of the "global village," usually understood to refer to the worldwide interconnectedness of electronic media eventually leading to the actual realization of the congruent Walt Disney dictum, "It's a small world, after all." The bits of McLuhan that didn't quite make it to mainstream consciousness but nonetheless seeped into 60s counterculture and 90s cyberculture have to do with the village's psychic convergence. The media critic made no bones about going all mystical on us, telling *Playboy* magazine in 1969 that from electronic media would emerge a "universality of consciousness," linking this new man to "the mystical body of Christ."

Which brings us to the theologian Teilhard de Chardin. When, in February 1996, Dery was the featured guest at "Club Wired," an online get-together utilizing live chat, someone wondered out loud, "Why is Teilhard de Chardin being mentioned left and right, right now? It's kind of annoying." To which Dery replied, "It is annoying, isn't it? ...[E]specially given the rotten foundations on which his proto-New Age metaphysics was built—Lamarckian evolution, no less. De Chardin's attempt to reconcile deism with Darwinian evolution obviously strikes a responsive chord in an age of angel contactees, near-death tunnel vision, and techno-eschatological rhapsodies."

Dery's sentiments regarding the theologian's ideas and influence ought to be clear enough, but in *Escape Velocity* he's a shade more respectful as he outlines Teilhard de Chardin's version of the convergence (it preceded McLuhan's) which would lead to an "Omega Point," a state of "ultra-humanity," resulting from the revelation of religious truths by science.

De Chardin's has indeed been the name to drop among "unrepentant techno-transcendentalist[s]" such as John Perry Barlow, and Dery quotes him dropping it over the phone as he expounds on the creation, the "hardwiring" of "the collective organism of the human mind in one coherent simultaneous thing." Barlow is a significant bridge between the cosmic 60s and the cyber 90s. The two most famous features of his résumé are Grateful Dead lyricist and co-founder of the Electronic Frontier Foundation, which has played a mightily important role in the history of civil rights online (however ungratefully some contemporary Net personalities might regard the organization today).

Before setting both feet firmly back on the ground again, we would do well to catch up to the present state of the global mind theory. To do that, we have to add one more factor to the mix: Memetics. It complicates matters somewhat in that it is tough at times connecting the dots to figure out just exactly what one theory has to do with the other. My own suspicion is two-fold. First, both theories are just too cool for any self-respecting cyberian to have to do without one or the other. And a healthy mind can forge just about any sort of synthesis out of two or more hot ideas.

Second, they both lean on the hippest metaphor around these days. Whether your pet project is artsy or technological, if you can cast it in language derived from biology, you have already got half a hit on your hands. But you must be careful. Evidently, the temptation to get carried away with your metaphor, to forget that it is indeed just a metaphor and not an honest-to-goodness equation, is too tough for many otherwise admirable minds to resist.

An example of a biological metaphor that works because it knows its place is Brian Eno's generative music. When you buy "Generative Music" by Brian Eno, you don't get a CD. You get a floppy disk and you stick it in your computer, maybe play with a few parameters—that is, factors affecting the music you will be hearing, or maybe you just leave it alone, and set it in motion. Each time you listen, you hear a unique piece of music. Because there are over 150 parameters to play with, chances that the piece generated on one day is identical to that of another day are very, very slim indeed.

As Eno described it in an interview with John Alderman, "I'm setting a set of probabilistic rules which describes a series of envelopes with which the music can form itself." Okay, that's the lofty version, but here's what he means: "Imagine that you had to make a human being. You could either do that by creating that creature molecule by molecule or you could put a sperm and an egg together. I'm building the seed, planting it in the computer and letting it grow."

So even though Eno and Alderman go on to chat about "organisms in your computer," and algorithms reminiscent in their complexity of genetic algorithms, neither lose sight of the fact that what they are talking about is music. Neither would even consider claiming that what is going on between the speakers is life itself.

Yet this is precisely the claim on which more than a few utopian visions of the future are based. All we need do is set technology, often online technology specifically, in motion and we can become gods.

"[The] essence of cybernectics is just that the mind can only exist because it interacts, via the body, with the outside world. The development of a 'global mind' emerging from the networks does not contradict this idea, since any network that is worth mentioning still connects to the real world via sensors and effectors of some kind."

Francis Heylighen

Chapter Fourteen
That Memesis Thesis

The week-long Ars Electronica Festival '96 officially opened on Monday, September 2, in Linz, Austria, but artistic director Gerfried Stocker and the seemingly omnipresent Euro Net critic Geert Lovink had the bright idea of getting the symposium going as early as April.

"To start a discussion so many months in advance," moderator Lovink noted in a half-time compilation passed on to the nettime mailing list, "was an attempt to break down the old consensus of the pioneers and show that media-art festivals, like Ars Electronica, from now on should be more than just a trade fair for computer-related art concepts. The Net seemed to be a perfect tool to vitalize the static form of conference presentations."

So when everyone rolled into Linz from round the world, the hair was already flying. Via the AEC symposium mailing list, hardcore scientists, hardcore artists, and those who fancy themselves somewhere in between had been hashing it out over Stocker's opening statement, "Memesis—the Future of Evolution," which, as more than one participant in the discussion remarked, seemed to have been designed to provoke.

Get this. "Human evolution is fundamentally intertwined with technological development; the two cannot be considered apart from one another. ...[G]enes that are not able to cope with this reality will not survive the next millennium." And that's just for starters.

From there we move quickly to an almost telepathic definition of "meme," but there is a concise paragraph to be found on a collectively written database called, appropriately enough, the "Jargon File" from which these succinct sentences are taken: "meme /meem/ n. An idea considered as a replicator, esp. with the connotation that memes parasitize people into propagating them much as viruses do. Used esp. in the phrase 'meme complex' denoting a group of mutually supporting memes that form an organized belief system, such as a religion."

A most relevant example. Because with the flick of a phrase, Stocker's Memesis takes us "[f]rom the 'bio-adapter' of language as a proto-meme to the 'infosphere' of global networks as the ultimate habitat for the human mind."

Whoa-ho! Ever get that sinking "omigod, my genes are doomed" feeling? I've tried to follow the links from self-replicating strands of DNA through memes to this idea that we're all, as Mark Dery has put it in that Boston *Phoenix* interview, "neurons in an emergent global meta-mind," but I keep running into that old Error 404, common sense.

Again, it seems that two trains of thought are on two separate tracks that somehow end up colliding. And it is a mess. Dery, remember, has very helpfully traced the route of one of those trains, the one headed toward the global mind. So far it has passed through Teilhard de Chardin's notion of humankind evolving toward a mystical "Omega Point," and Marshall McLuhan plugging the apparatus of the electronic media into it. Okay. I get it. I don't buy it, but I do see and understand the line of thinking.

Now, on the other track, the meme track, we can go straight to the source, Richard Dawkins. His 1975 book *The Selfish Gene* got this train moving. Here, we're privileged in that we get to see the famed scientist's mind at work: "I think that a new kind of replicator has recently emerged on this very planet. ...We need a name for the new replicator, a noun which conveys the idea of a unit of cultural transmission, or a unit of imitation." He settles on an abbreviation of the Greek word *mimeme*: meme—in part because it sounds like "gene."

"Examples of memes are tunes, ideas, catch-phrases, clothes fashions, ways of making pots or of building arches. Just as genes propagate themselves in the gene pool by leading from body to body via sperm or eggs, so memes propagate themselves in the meme pool by leaping from brain to brain via a process which, in the broad sense, can be called imitation." Okay.

Imitation. Nothing particularly spectacular there. We used to call it "the spread of ideas." If you want to give the process a cool monosyllabic handle, if you want to go as far as to make a science out of it (memetics) and classify the way ideas get spread into seven separate modes, as

Aaron Lynch has done in his book *Thought Contagion* —quantity parental, efficiency parental, proselytic, preservational, adversative, cognitive, and motivational modes—fine.

Where's the link between cultural evolution and actual, physiological human evolution? When is it exactly that ideas catapult us out of our bodies and into the telephone lines? This is the part I don't get.

Nevertheless, as we peer on, we may actually see the train jump its tracks and slam head-on catastrophically into the on-coming global mind. Dawkins, it seems, bought hook, line, and sinker into the fallacy of his colleague, N. K. Humphrey, who wrote in an earlier draft of the infamous last chapter of *The Selfish Gene*, "...memes should be regarded as living structures, not just metaphorically but technically. When you plant a fertile meme in my mind you literally parasitize my brain, turning it into a vehicle for the meme's propagation in just the way that a virus may parasitize the genetic mechanism of a host cell."

Whoops. Key words here are "literally" and "technically," as opposed to "metaphorically." I'm not certain that I have ever been exposed to such unscientific thinking in a scientist. Whatever happened to good old-fashioned empiricism? Scientific method and all that? Has anyone anywhere actually documented a fertile meme parasitizing the grey stuff of a human brain?

Again, we are back at that leap of faith from the physical to the non-physical. How we long to believe! But no one has been able to establish any real connection between the two worlds other than faith. No one in artificial intelligence, no Extropian, no McLuhanite, no cybernaut—in short, to get from here to there, your ticket is mystical mumbo-jumbo or nothing.

David Bennahum has written a marvelous piece on Norbert Wiener, author of the 1948 book *Cybernetics*, and J. C. R. Licklider, a junior faculty member who sat in on Wiener's salon-like sessions at MIT. Wiener was fascinated with the idea of the computer as a mechanical brain, as so many of us are evidently, but the difference between Wiener and the rest of us is that he was in a position to do something about it. He directed loads of funds and resources into research on that ever elusive connection between the biological and mechanical thinking machines.

It was Licklider who perceived that the real use of the computer was as a tool for humans, not as a replacement. Licklider was the one to redirect ARPA resources toward networking, who shifted focus to the *Man-Computer Symbiosis* (his 1960 book) and away from what he called the "asinine projects" Wiener had initiated. As Bennahum notes, had he not done so, there might not have been an Internet. Bennahum's article amounts to nothing less than a well-drawn portrait of the beneficial, effective spread of a good idea. Maybe that is why he named his own regularly appearing column "MEME."

Poignantly, the Ars Electronica Festival was actually blessed on opening night by both a Catholic priest and a Protestant pastor. Fair's fair, I suppose. Afterward, the audience was led in a collective recital of the Lord's Prayer, "obviously becoming impatient while waiting for the buffet that followed the gathering," as journalist and media consultant Boris Groendahl reported to the Rhizome mailing list.

If on the first take religion seems out of place at an electronic arts festival, keep in mind that whether we are to fill in for God ourselves or to unite in His cosmic body, Net culture has long been charged with techno-transcendentalist visions of heavenly utopias. Nevertheless, it evidently didn't take long for participants of the symposium the following morning to bring it all back down to earth, or at least to a level we can get a grip on in the here and now. If you must obsess on the future, make your vision palatable to the most practical among us like Joe Engelbert—robotics pundit of MIT—has. Listening to Engelbert, Groendahl was reminded "of a big, heavy, glossy Time-Life book called *The Future* I enjoyed when I was a child."

Imagine robots doing the coal mining, the nuclear waste clean-ups, the dishes, the laundry... Imagine the *Jetsons*. According to Engelbert, we can look forward to a twenty-hour work week. "The fact that, at least in Germany, everybody is talking about the prolongation of the working day came to [Groendahl's] mind, but apparently not to Engelbert's."

Groendahl may have been bumming out on reality, but Niko Waesche, who also wrote to subscribers of the Rhizome list, was kicking back and taking in the show for what it was. He even filled Rhizomers in on what the panelists were wearing. Richard Dawkins himself was there in a suit. Richard Barbrook, a professor at the Hypermedia Research Centre at the University of Westminster, London, wore "what one could term trendy London working-class fashion" complete with "matching accent."

Most fun of all, evidently, was Mark Dery, "who was a riot. The American cultural critic burst out without pity for the poor German translator into a deluge of complex, poetic formulations comparing the Unabomber with the readers and editors of *Wired* magazine." Exactly what "the visions of an elitist Libertarian technocratic regime active in the *Wired* crowd" may have had to do with the topic at hand—Memesis—is hard to decipher at first glance, but it clearly made for great theater.

Yet like religion, politics does have more to do with the Memesis theory than robots do. This is what Richard Barbrook had been arguing throughout the online symposium that preceded the live one in an essay only a Londoner would dare entitle, "Never Mind the Cyberbollocks...," but most effectively, I think, in his initial critique of Gerfried Stocker's opening statement.

Behind the "bio-babble," Barbrook argues, lies an implicit social agenda by conscious or unconscious design. Let's go back briefly to that "Jargon File" definition: "Use of the term [meme] connotes acceptance of the idea that in humans (and presumably other tool- and language-using sophonts) cultural evolution by selection of adaptive ideas has superseded biological evolution by selection of hereditary traits." In short, memes are understood as agents of cultural evolution, which in turn, is to take over natural evolution's role as the prime determinant in the future development of humankind.

But Barbrook reminds us that nasty things happen "when natural evolution is used to explain social development. In this century, millions of people were shoved into gas chambers because it was believed that they possessed 'genes that are not able to cope' as the Memesis statement puts it." Goodness. Isn't Barbrook pushing it a bit? Francis Heylighen, a systems researcher at the Free University of Brussels, writes the most level-headed "[D]efense of 'Memesis'" of the bunch and calls Barbrook on this one: "Hitler was a Christian, so religion leads to the gas chambers. Stalin was an atheist, so atheism leads to extermination, etc. The fact that some people at some point have misused an idea does not in any way prove that that idea is wrong or evil."

So instead of guilt by association, we must look to historical fact. Which terrifyingly shows Barbrook to be dead right. For whatever genuine reason, Hitler despised the Jews (and competing theories abound). By damning the Jews as an inferior race, he used a bastardized interpretation of natural evolution to officially justify his intentions to exterminate them. This would be hideous enough if there were the slightest shred of evidence supporting any sort of real linkage between natural and cultural evolution in any terms other than the metaphorical. But there is none. As utterly amazing as we are, we still cannot do what nature does.

In all fairness, for Heylighen is nothing if not fair, the defense of the Memesis statement ultimately rests on the wildly expansive use of the biological metaphor to prop up elitist social behavior in the name of a brighter and better humankind of our own making. Heylighen remarks that the "essence of cybernetics is just that the mind can only exist because it interacts, via the body, with the outside world. The development of a 'global mind' emerging from the networks does not contradict this idea, since any network that is worth mentioning still connects to the real world via sensors and effectors of some kind."

Hook up as many sensors as you like, you won't get that network to think on its own. What a frightfully vital role language plays in every human endeavor. If you can't grasp the difference between a metaphor and an actual, verifiable equivalency, you run into one bloody mess after another. And Barbrook's history lesson reassures us that Hitler's mess wasn't and won't be the last. "Following the defeat of fascism, the biological metaphor is now more often used to revive an earlier illegitimate use of Darwinian theory for political purposes: Social Darwinism. As championed by Herbert Spencer, this theory claimed that unregulated market competition between private property owners was a natural phenomenon rather than a social one."

So Dery wasn't all that off-topic after all, was he? *Wired* editor Louis Rossetto, after all, claims in the interview later in this book that he believes that this literal "brains connecting to brains" idea is "the real digital revolution." Dery and Barbrook were interviewed as a pair by Willem van Weelden, and when Barbrook asserts that "what Kevin Kelly, *Wired* magazine and the Extropians and other leaders of this Memes cult are doing...is basically recycling Herbert Spencer's Social Darwinism," Dery couldn't agree more.

Ever word-happy, Dery adds that "the Spencerian theory was every bit as popular with the monopoly capitalists of his day as the neo-biological downsized demassified decentralized theories of Kevin Kelly are with corporate managerial theorists such as Peter Drucker and Tom Peters... The dissolution of the body politic in sort of a flesh-eating viral fashion into a puddle of atomized cellular units protoplasmically going their own separate ways on the one hand echoes delirious excesses of Deleuzian theory at its most outermost bounds, and the other hand, the American militia movement at this moment, which also embraces very much the notion of micro-political resistance."

Bubbling up from the bio-babbling brook are voices so opposed to any form of coordinated human effort that they would go to the extremes of a guy Barbrook points to who "even opposed the installation of municipal sewerage systems to prevent cholera and other diseases as an obstruction of the natural laws of the market!" Well, surely only those who deserved to would have died anyway. Natural selection, don't you know.

Chapter Fifteen
Utopia in Extremis

In July 1996, Chris Winter of British Telecom's Artificial Life team told tech reporters about the chip he was working on. He called it the "soul catcher." The idea is to stick it in your brain, hook it up to your optical nerve and other strategic points in the grey coils, and then go about your business. The chip will record the sights, smells, sounds, and maybe even other sensual paraphernalia of your daily life so that they can be stored on a disk and played back at dinner parties, family reunions, whatever.

Evidently not one given to modesty, Winter claimed he was cooking up "immortality in the truest sense." Hardly. What he was cooking up was a 21st century home video. You the consumer, in the meantime, will eventually grow old and die just like everybody else. Nevertheless, British Telecom considered the next generation's camcorder worth an initial $50 million investment.

Let's hope it will be as thrilling as *Brainstorm*. Remember that movie? Natalie Wood's last, unfortunately, but the real landmark of the film was its high concept. Experiences are recorded on a sort of gold foil tape (how analog), and when played back on a cute little headset, voilá, you are there, reliving the moment in 3D sense-o-round as real as real can be. Because after all, life is what the brain perceives it to be, right? The truth is, we don't know, but the idea is a great premise for a sci-fi adventure flick.

I watched the movie the night it opened in Austin, gritting my teeth for an hour and a half because I had just turned in a final draft to my screenwriting class at the University of Texas. I had had a guy wandering through holographic videos of his father's memories, unaware that they were being generated live by the old man's brain as he lay in a coma in... But I digress. Needless to say, there is a lot more to it than that, but nevermind. Then came Wim Wenders's *Until the End of the World* in which a family records its memories on video, sort of like Winter's chip but without the actual penetration into the brain. Well, you can't touch Wim Wenders. I locked my little science project away in a drawer for good.

The fallacy on which all these movies are based (and there are many more) is the assumption that whatever it is in us that is "experiencing" our experiences—and for lack of a better word, we call it consciousness—it is simplistic enough to be captured on tape or disk, when in fact, no one has the vaguest idea yet what consciousness actually is, where it is (the brain may or may not be "the seat of consciousness"), or how it works. Or even if "works" is an appropriate verb for it. Maybe it just "is."

Who knows? The point is, no one does. So for now, the idea of a protocol that jostles human and technological code is the stuff of dreams and movies.

But try telling that to the Extropians. If "Extroprianism" is a new one on you, here's the "ism" in a nutshell: Humans are terrific and all, but we can do better. Let's throw off these biological shackles, leave meatspace (a semi-grotesque term tossed around online referring to real life—the opposite of cyberspace), and "upload" our true selves—our minds—onto a machine where we can live forever and ever.

Now, I remember running across a few mentions of scientists working on biochips back in the early 80s, and this was pretty exciting news to the wide-eyed college kid I was at the time. Not much thrills like the prospect of immortality.

I also remember bumping into references to the Extropians on the Net several years later and thinking, How can this idea still be around? After all, hasn't just about anybody involved with either artificial intelligence or the study of consciousness—with the significant exception of Daniel Dennett who claims to have "explained" consciousness—renounced the idea of consciousness as mere data?

Few ought to be as up on this as Roger Penrose, a prize-winning Oxford professor who has collaborated with the likes of Stephen Hawking. He pretty much nails the elusive nature of consciousness and the scientific pursuit of it in his book *The Emperor's New Mind*:

"Is it not 'obvious' that mere computation cannot evoke pleasure or pain; that it cannot perceive poetry or the beauty of an evening sky or the magic of sounds; that it cannot hope or love or despair; that it cannot have a genuine autonomous purpose? Yet science seems to have driven us to accept that we are all merely small parts of a world governed in full detail (even if perhaps ultimately just probabilistically) by very precise mathematical laws. Our brains themselves, which seem to control all our actions, are also ruled by these same precise laws. The picture has emerged that all this precise physical activity is, in effect, nothing more than the acting out of some vast (perhaps probabilistic) computation—and, hence our brains and our minds are to be understood solely in terms of such computations. Perhaps when computations become extraordinarily complicated they can begin to take on the more poetic or subjective qualities that we associate with the term 'mind'. Yet it is hard to avoid an uncomfortable feeling that there must always be something missing from such a picture."

Or, as David Chalmers, a professor of philosophy at the University of California at Santa Cruz, puts it a bit less eloquently but more succinctly, "The more we think about computers, the more we realize how strange consciousness is."

From August 12 through August 16, 1996, Max More, President of Extropy Institute and editor of *EXTROPY*, traded volleys with writer Paulina Borsook on a set of pages *Wired* magazine maintains on its web site ("HotWired") for week-long debates called, appropriately enough, Brain Tennis. More argued the Extroprian point of view, obviously, and Borsook took up the task of speaking up for all humanity—and that in a forum not particularly known for its humanity fans.

So I made my way over and followed the links Max More put forward, read up on the Extropian Principles, the FAQ (Frequently Asked Questions About Extropians), and other articles, and then came back to catch up on how the crowd was taking to the showdown. "HotWired" members are encouraged to post their thoughts on anything at the site via a conferencing system called Threads. I even tossed in a post myself, but I was more interested in who else might have been attracted to the subject of the debate and what they would be saying about it.

I was looking for clues that maybe someone had run across the missing link between humans and machines and I simply hadn't heard about it. But I couldn't find it. What I found instead was a lot of legitimate hope that all the work being done in fields as widely varied as nanotechnology, cryonics, memetics, and so on, and so forth, would somehow all jell in a way that makes "uploading" actually possible.

Although I agreed with Paulina Borsook's argument that death is a defining characteristic of what it is to be human, at the same time, I respected the impulse behind Max More's hypothesis that it doesn't have to be that way forever. But I'm afraid I wasn't convinced then and have yet to be convinced now that it is going to work. Ever.

Still, if it does some day—and even Roger Penrose leaves that door open, though he seems to feel that that day would be way, way off in the future—if it does, it had better be good. If I were ever to "go over," I would want to take more than my consciousness with me.

Interestingly, none of the posts I had seen (until mine) brought up sex except in passing. Interesting because it informs so much of our essential being as well as the social construct we move around in. Well, I for one would miss it. Granted, I guess we would have the option of jolting our pleasure zones at will, but somehow, it is just not the same.

One post to Threads brought up Wim Wenders's *Wings of Desire*, which I obviously thought was a wonderful idea. The film follows two angels as they hover among the mortals of Berlin. They are able to listen in on people's thoughts and even have some vague sort of supernatural influence on them on rare occasions, but for the most part, they are invisible guests of the planet Earth. They also have the option of crossing over to mortality if they wish, and one of them is thinking very seriously about it. Peter Falk, in fact, plays one who has done it. He is mortal in every sense but one: He can sense the presence of his former colleagues.

There's a marvelous scene in which Falk picks up on the vibes of the doubting angel and tempts him with the prospect of taking that leap—with a pleasure as simple as a cigar. The angel's expression is perfect. He doesn't desire the cigar, he's an angel, freed from desire. Above all that, he desires the desire.

Want, need, challenge, pleasure, pain—with all that gone, I just can't see that whatever there is of us that would make that cross over to the machines would be "us" at all any more. Seems to me that there is a denial of all the embarrassing bits of human nature going on in the Extropian proposition, one that goes back to Plato's insistence that the mind and the body really ought not to have that much to do with each other, and runs right on through two millennia of Christianity after Paul. The way down that road leads to collective psychosis.

It is no fun shooting down utopias (unless they blatantly beg for it, of course!), and I doubt Paulina Borsook enjoyed doing so. For one thing, it puts you in the position of defending the status quo, which in turn, makes you an easy target in forums such as Brain Tennis. Who wants to argue death's case?

By now it should be clear that I seriously doubt that the whole "uploading" thing is really possible. Furthermore, if the Extroprians were all about that and that alone, they would be fairly innocuous. But there is something cultish about them as a group, and as with all true believers, they walk their dogma in neighborhoods far and away from their original home turf. You get to point five of Max More's Extropian Principles and suddenly you are knee-deep in the principles of the free markets:

"The free market allows complex institutions to develop, encourages innovation, rewards individual initiative, cultivates personal responsibility, fosters diversity, and decentralizes power."

Okay, but how did we get here from there? What would we as "transhumans" (their terminology for the in-betweeners on their way to becoming "posthumans," a term which should be chillingly clear enough on its own) care about capitalism in its most extreme form, or for that matter, any "ism" at all? We are sitting in some machine somewhere without need for food, sex, shelter, or any other commodity. Who gives a rat's bit about money any more, much less the economic system it worms its way around in?

But they do. The Extropian FAQ is loaded with a lot more on anything but the science of "uploading" than "uploading" itself. In fact, you don't even get to "uploading" until Question 14. Two possible explanations for this linkage of bad science and bad politics come to mind. One, the Extroprians have a thing for whatever buzzwords happen to be hot at the moment. Here's a modest list from another Extropian page:

"Extropian interests include transhumanism, futurist philosophy, life extension, cryonics, robotics and artificial intelligence, smart drugs, intelligence-intensifying technologies, personality uploading, and other practical applications of neuroscience, artificial life, nanocomputers and molecular nanotechnology, memetics (ideas as replicating agents), experimental free communities in space, on the oceans, and in the information ocean, effective thinking, information filtering, life management, self-transformative psychology, spontaneous order (free markets, neural networks, evolutionary processes, genetic algorithms, etc), cryptography and other privacy technologies, electronic markets, digital cash, critical analysis of environmentalism, and explorations of the ultimate limits of physics, among other things."

No, please, stop right there. Please.

So when it comes to politics, they will naturally embrace the going thing for today's technoid elitist: libertarianism. I'm surprised they haven't found a hipper name for it, but in the FAQ, it is just plain old "libertarianism."

The second possible explanation that comes to mind is that they seriously believe that this "uploading" is actually going to occur within their own lifetimes. Now, it is a stretch, but if you try hard and picture this happening to you, a transfer of your mind stuff on to some hard disk somewhere, you will naturally want it done right—under proper supervision, with state-of-the-art equipment, white coats, top of the line all the way.

And now I see where the economics fit in. Naturally, there are not enough resources in the solar system to pay for the uploading of 5 or 6 billion people. Decisions are going to have to be made. And the selection may not be all that natural unless you have previously plugged your trusty social Darwinism into the system.

This is one big budget production that I want no part of. If it has to be made, I would rather see it on video.

Chapter Sixteen

Luddite Lite

Few go on to quote what Virginia Woolf wrote immediately after she had grabbed attention with the declaration that not only had human nature changed, but that she could date that change to the very month it happened. The words that follow, however, are worth a look. "All human relations shifted— those between masters and servants, husbands and wives, parents and children. And when human relations change there is at the same time a change in religion, conduct, politics, and literature."

The key word here is "conduct." She was saying that we behaved differently; we did not all wake up one morning in December 1910 with three arms. Yes, there was a shift in the way we dealt with each other as the hierarchical social structure continued a collapse begun with the rise of commerce, and yes, the ways in which we went about seeing to our daily business changed; mostly, they sped up.

Speed, in fact, may have been the only real surprise, for the forms of change in the Modern period had long before been predetermined. You might argue that the more radical the proclamation of essential change, the more rooted it is in an ignorance of history. Granted, computers are changing our lives, but are they changing us? Our ability to crunch bigger numbers faster means we can now walk around with our offices tucked under our arms, but aren't we still writing the same dumb memos to each other?

Whether we fear or embrace any new technological development, the extremity of our reaction is directly proportionate to the inability to recognize that it is merely an extension of what was already there. One way of looking at the Internet, after all, is as just another fancy way of using the telephone. Isn't e-mail just faster, cheaper letter writing? Isn't downloading a picture, a music clip, something to read, or a piece of software easier and more convenient than fighting traffic all the way to the store and back?

Surely consolidation and speed are just improvements on a previously existing way of getting things done. Genetic engineering? You can cut out an appendix or maybe eventually program the body so as not to have one in the first place. The point is getting rid of the thing, does it matter whether you slice or splice? Virtual reality, interactive web sites, CD-ROMs, isn't it all just another way of watching TV? Hundreds, maybe thousands or even millions of channels broadcasting in all three dimensions are still no match for the sensory overload of a subway ride or a stroll in the woods. And all these projected species of cyborgs are just healthy signs that the age-old art of prosthetics is doing just fine. It's still us here. We still fall in love, struggle to make a living, kill each other, laugh, eat, and all those other wonderful and horrible things we do that make us human.

So where's the threat? If human nature itself, as opposed to human behavior, has not changed, what's wrong with the convenience technology offers? If there is little or no scientific evidence that some Extroprian will extract the mind from the body anytime soon, or that we will all melt into some single cosmic body, what's to worry (if indeed you find those prospects worrisome)?

Yet some do worry. A lot. Take the high school teacher in England who is fighting against the infiltration of computers into his classroom, despite the direction of the school's administration and the ridicule of his fellow faculty members. That teacher pictures himself "struggling in this world to make some sense of what I regard as madness and absurdity around me. Part of that madness—an ominously growing part—resides in computers. I reject modern society; I see only bleak visions of the future—a future in which human beings finally sever themselves from their age-old realities, and certainties, by computerised machinery and global networks."

This teacher's name is Peter Quince and early in 1996 he exchanged several hand-written letters with Stephen L. Talbott, author of a book *The Future Does Not Compute: Transcending the Machines in Our Midst.* With Quince's permission, Talbott released excerpts from their correspondence to the Net in an online publication Talbott edits, "NETFUTURE: Technology and Human Responsibility for the Future." The irony was not lost on Quince. But he actually greeted the opportunity to respond to critics and supporters alike, provided, of course, they write to him via old-fashioned snail mail.

"Part of my problem...as a citizen, as a father, as a teacher, lies in resisting the inexorable, one might say fascistic, pressures of modern high technology. What can I do?" Anyone who feels this strongly is indeed in a bit of a bind. The Amish at least can quarantine themselves off on large swaths of the landscape, warding off the seemingly persistent efforts of technology to penetrate their sanctum. Further, they have each other to lean on, their values reflected in every individual of their society.

Going it alone in the very country that served as a launching pad for the industrial revolution can't be easy, and now, with the digital revolutionaries planting computers in cars, banks, schools, and just about any household appliance that can stand one, it is all the tougher. "Computers draw us away from ourselves, rip out the centre, seek to replace the rhythms of nature (primordially learnt) with the synthetic rhythms of endless arid streams of electronic pulses. This seems to me nonsensical. And yet I am surrounded by people, many millions, who are worshipers at the shrine of Bill Gates."

Quince is not only familiar with the names of the main players, he is sharp enough to realize that sticking his head in the sand will get him nowhere. He knows that he must become familiar with the nature of the beast and has read up on it to better equip himself in his battle against it, although the books he specifically names, Talbott's and Clifford Stoll's *Silicon Snake Oil*, would only harden his prejudice. But in *The Future Does Not Compute*, Talbott argues that computers and technology in general can be beneficial as long as we keep our excitement in check, the promises in perspective, and make the preservation of our own humanity top priority.

Quince, on the other hand, begs to differ with his pen pal. No, don't give computers even an inch—they will take a mile out of you. "Am I becoming a little hysterical? I sometimes wonder. But deep down, in heart and soul, I know that I am right to question the very existence of these machines... The screens are closing in... Yet I feel immensely sane in a mad, fragmenting world." Still, "[o]ne begins to feel marginalised, isolated, characterised as some kind of 'Luddite'."

Some kind of what? You may already be familiar with the term "Luddite," but bear with me a moment, there is a wild history behind it. As with most histories, a romantic legend at its center is surrounded by stray facts that only seem to confuse the issue. The legend has a fellow by the name of Ned Lud, whose sanity was evidently questionable in the first place, freak out entirely one day in 1779. He breaks into a house and smashes up two machines. Some say they were knitting machines, some say they were weaving machines or stocking frames, doesn't matter. The point is, no matter what you call them, they had to do with the textile industry—the bread and butter of Leicestershire (where Ned did his dastardly deed) and much of England at the time.

Exactly why Lud went nuts on that particular day is one of the great unknowns of history, but speculation as to why he chose these particular machines as his target is somewhat founded on the belief that the machines were destroying a centuries-old tradition of hand-weaving some of the finest stockings around anywhere. The problem with this assumption, however, is that the machines, too, had been around since 1589, when the Reverend William Lee invented them. Complicating matters somewhat is the unfortunate fact that machine smashing had been going on since at least 1710, so Lud was hardly the founder of a movement.

But the movement took his name nonetheless, gathering steam in around 1811, peaking in 1812, and finally tapering off in 1816. The Luddites got their name by storming factories, messing up the place, and then claiming it was all in the name of either Captain Lud, General Lud, or even King Lud. Some suggest they had used Ned's name sarcastically; others believe they meant to make a hero of the loon.

These might be the same folks who have recast Nottingham as the location of the original legend, either because Nottingham was also a Midlands sort of weaving town not too far from Leicestershire or for a grandiose sort of resonance, as in this passage from a page on the "Internet Town Hall's" web site: "Their army was a secret army. They controlled the night, they knew the back trails between villages. If threatened by government troops they would simply disappear into the same hills and forests that fostered the legend of Robin Hood. Most of all, they enjoyed almost universal support of the local people."

But not of the government. A notable exception, however, was Lord Byron, who was not known to show up all that often at sessions of parliament, much less speak. But he did show and speak up passionately in defense of the Luddites. Not even the poet's words, however, would keep any Luddites who were caught from being hanged.

How much were the machines actually responsible for the pinch felt by the English people of the early nineteenth century? Robert M. Adams suggests several more likely candidates for their misery in *The Land and*

Literature of England. 1815 would see the end of a quarter of a century of non-stop warfare, for example, what with Napoleon on the loose throughout Europe cutting off markets left and right and the Americans to deal with again in 1812. That war, in fact, cut off the main supply of raw cotton. Throw a series of bad harvests into the mix, and that misery index just goes through the roof.

The Luddites and their supporters may very well have been misdirecting their anger, therefore, but the irony is only multiplied when technophiles accuse the Luddite crowd of standing in the way of progress manifest in revolutions digital or industrial. First of all, as the novelist Thomas Pynchon notes in his 1984 essay, "Is It O.K. to Be a Luddite?," the industrial revolution was hardly "a violent struggle with a beginning, middle and end. It was smoother, less conclusive, more like an accelerated passage in a long evolution."

It wasn't even called a revolution until way after the fact. In this it differs significantly from the digital version, which has been called a revolution way before the fact. "Nevertheless," Pynchon continues, "the idea of a technosocial 'revolution,' in which the same people came out on top as in France and America, has proven of use to many over the years, not least to those who...have thought that in 'Luddite' they have discovered a way to call those with whom they disagree both politically reactionary and anti-capitalist at the same time."

The moniker is unfortunate, because at the height of the industrial whatever, anyone opposed to the way progress was being run would be cast by it in the same lot with the machine smashers. Sort of like the way we use the word "terrorist" today. It doesn't take much to be painted as an anathema to society. But there was a lot to be against in nineteenth century England, and you would think that you need not have been labeled an extremist to think so.

Adams again, briefly: "Because machinery was expensive, owners tried to keep it running; that meant thirteen working hours a day, six days a week, for children as young as seven. Children were cheap; weekly wages averaged three shillings six pence for boys, two shillings threepence for girls... A few humanitarians were heard to murmur that the schedule was a bit heavy, but the manufacturers, reinforced by the laissez-faire economists, stood firm: interfering with the free marketplace and the child's right to dispose of his labor would produce nothing but misery— bankruptcy for the employer, starvation for the child." Adams then goes on to describe living conditions in the industrial towns, but I will spare you the gory details.

Peter Quince, the English high school teacher, may very well have had such historical precedents in mind when he referred to the machines of progress today as "dehumanizing." Certainly there is a long tradition of distrust in technology, just as there is a long tradition behind its counter-argument. Back when the "noble savage" was all the rage, critics reminded romantics that life before civilization as we know and love it was, in the words of Hobbes, "nasty, brutish and short."

It is not all that easy to know where to place the blame when technological innovations come along that are meant to shorten the work week, take over hard or tedious jobs, and generally make life go a lot smoother, but instead result in the loss of jobs, a frantic, forever-catching-up sort of lifestyle, or the general feeling that we have become a slave to our tools. Glance around the room right now (if you are not so fortunate as to be reading this outside) and let your eyes light on a couple of the high- or low-tech gadgets you have in there. If they are yours, you most likely spent the time to go out and trade a portion of your hard-earned wages for them. You wanted them, and chances are you would rather not give them up—until it comes time to exchange them for better, newer ones.

Dishwasher, stereo, manual pencil sharpener. One by one, you can see the benefits of holding on to the thing. The machines themselves seem innocent enough. So where does all this (what else to call it?) *exploitation* come from? Well—and you can probably see this coming from a mile away—as Adams noted, machinery is expensive. Innocent as each single dumb object may be in and of itself, it comes with a price. Those most able to afford it are often the ones promoting its use, declaring it indispensable, and generally holding all sorts of economic and political theories that may not be in the best interests of everybody all around. Further, they often have the power to see them through.

A lot of so-called Luddite resistance to the so-called digital revolution has been incited not so much by the computers humming in every office and many homes as by the insistent rhetoric of the self-proclaimed revolutionaries. A wave of Internet backlash books swept through bookstores throughout 1995, from Stoll's *Silicon Snake Oil* and Talbott's *The Future Does Not Compute* to the collection of essays in *Resisting the Virtual Life: The Culture and Politics of Information* edited by James Brook and Iain A. Boal and Mark Slouka's *War of the Worlds*, among the more notable of many titles.

To the true digital revolutionary, all these titles are "Luddite." In fact, however, they represent a wide range of not-jumping-into-the-cybersphere-with-all-four-feet. Stoll's book is full of all the rabid disdain a former smoker has for other smokers. Stoll was once a computer nut who made a name for himself with the bestselling book on a hacker's outing that he made famous in *The Cuckoo's Egg*. Having just discovered real life so late on his own, I suppose it is only natural that he turn on what he perceives to be the thief of all those lost years. Just as natural would be a not unintelligent man's developing a sense of balance in a few years between the obsession with and the total denial of computers.

Talbott, as noted, and Slouka approach their questioning of the thrill of it all with reason and pleas for the same in their readers. All in all, there is a place for dissent in the current ongoing transformation, whether in hindsight we will indeed call it a revolution or "an accelerated passage in a long evolution."

And of course, we can be thankful the dissidents are not following their namesake's example in the most explicit sense. As Kirkpatrick Sale, leader of the Neo-Luddites (and proud of it), told *Wired* magazine's Kevin Kelly, "[W]e modern-day Luddites are not, or at least not yet, taking up the sledgehammer and the torch and gun to resist the new machinery, but rather taking up the book and the lecture and organizing people to raise these issues. Most of the people who would today call themselves Luddites confine their resistance, so far at any rate, to a kind of intellectual and political resistance."

"Online technology is like any other: made by human hands, blessed with our best intentions, and tainted with our worst vices."

David Hudson

Chapter Seventeen

What Ever Happened to the Future?

1926 saw the realization of one the greatest sci-fi flicks ever, Fritz Lang's *Metropolis*. As Lang's ship approached New York City by night and he saw for the first time that jagged cityscape glowing faintly with electric heat from horizon to horizon, some muse tapped his shoulder and whispered, "Imagine what it'll look like in 100 years..."

The story and its politics were assigned to his wife, Thea von Harbou. Lang threw all his creative powers into The Look. And it's The Look that has lasted—spectacular, exhilarating, frightening. A massive architecture that simultaneously dehumanizes and hails the achievements, the sheer gall of humankind. The seemingly perpetual night. The ghost-faced, two-dimensional characters jerking from pose to pose in Expressionist ecstasy. And the lights!

In 1926, Modernism was still going strong, a period in love and hate with its new machines. Just four years before, Eliot had written of the *Unreal City*, and not too terribly long before that, Picasso, Braque, and Gris were seeing everything in cubes and cubes in everything. Traffic beeped and honked its way into the symphony halls. Sleek blocks rose skyward, bigger, faster—more—than anyone Lang's age could have imagined in his or her childhood.

The radical change in the physical reality around them was certainly partly responsible for populations' susceptibility to the rhetoric of the two prongs of totalitarianism that wreaked havoc on the rest of the century as well as that of the equally grand schemes of cigar-chomping capitalists drawing up plans for other populations. But no rhetoric could match the vertical expansion and horizontal speed anyone could see with his or her own eyes. The sights and sounds of a present that would not stand still were evidence enough. The future would be like this. Project the outward unfolding of bridges and factories, highways and skyscrapers to its logical, linear conclusion: Metropolis. By 2026.

A terrible beauty, to echo another Modernist, Yeats. But somehow, we got the terrible without the beauty. When U.N. delegates huddled in Istanbul seventy years after the premiere of *Metropolis* to fret over the utter disaster that has become of most inner cities, no one really expected any doable, concrete solutions. And if there are answers, they will surely be stumbled over at the local level.

By the 50s and 60s, it had become clear what was happening to a future built from the ground up, so we moved it off the planet altogether. If imaginations were to be captured, the trap would have to lie in wait far, far away from urban rot and the conquered countryside. We were all going to space, maybe to start all over on a fresh planet. Our on again, off again love affair with the future was on again.

The idea of a manned mission to Jupiter scheduled for just around the corner from right now in another all-time great sci-fi flick, *2001: A Space Odyssey*, threw no one for a loop a mere three decades ago. People who supposedly knew exactly what they were talking about spoke with absolute certainty about space colonies within the lifetimes of everyone within earshot. Perhaps the discovery of ancient microbe life on Mars will rejuvenate a wound-down space program. Without a doubt, however, we will approach any new way-out-there projects with new caution and a wiser sense of realism.

After a serious bout of nostalgia throughout the 70s and most of the 80s (with the freaky exception of Reagan's plan to launch nuclear weapons into orbit over our heads), the future has come home again. To burrow its way into all the little boxes we nestle in our boxed homes, our PCs and TVs, and maybe even into our own bodies. If the real Last Frontier was unconquerable, we will reconstruct it in virtual space, plant electrodes in our brains, and go surfing through it on alpha waves.

In *Metropolis*, the identity of the savior figure, Maria, is stolen by the archetypical mad scientist, Rotwang, in much the same way. It is one of those ooh and ahh scenes—electrodes, flashing lights, a robot that rises and walks. Because *Metropolis* is a movie, the transformation must be communicated visually. But even if we don't go as far as actually invading our physical bodies, we need not succumb to a less visually blatant seduction. Much of our identities is already encoded and our movements within the rudimentary prototype of virtual space are fairly easily tracked. Banners call out Put Your Bank Account Online. Register, It Only Takes A Moment. Tell Us About Yourself.

No need to go overboard with this, of course. We are still free to say no, thank you. The invisible pull, the imagination trap of our own post-a-lot time, is the promise held out like candy that when anything and everything we do in the course of a day is done online, it will all be so much easier. This, despite our failure to figure out why we keep picking up and abandoning utopias like the ones described in this chapter. We haven't even nailed basic questions like, For all the gadgets designed to lighten our workloads, why does it seem we have less free time than ever before?

Part of the answer to that one may be that we are spoiled. Life in the developed world is a piece of cake set next to life a couple of centuries ago or life in the undeveloped world right now. So what makes us such brats? Why do we feel shortchanged? Maybe because the bill of goods we were sold is not delivering what was promised as part of the package deal. Sure, there is a lot of fun stuff in the box with a wire to the world, but it is not taking us where we want to be—out of the here, out of the now.

One of the only certainties we can probably all agree on about online technology is that it brought a refreshing element to the uncertainty of the collective consciousness. All our thinking about the future again presents a marvelous distraction from the day-to-day anxieties of job insecurity, a collapsing health care system, ethnic clashes in declared and undeclared war zones, all that heavy late twentieth-century baggage.

The funny thing about the future as escapism is that the diversion does not have to be a rosy picture. In the summer of 1996, people lined up around the block hoping to get into a theater near you to watch aliens blow up the White House. But of course, it all turns out hunky-dory in the end. That's the movies, and Hollywood knows one of the most profitable aspects of its business is to purge our fears for us.

Not so in the sixty-second commercial, evidently. That same summer, I saw CNN run one for NEC Multimedia. A suit with a microphone takes us on a tour of a happy family home, all earth tones and warm sunlit oranges and yellows. Imagine a virtual house call, says the guy with the microphone, and behind the bed of the ill but cheerful Grandpa, a different sort of alien materializes out of a shaft of unearthly light. Why, it's the family doctor!

The house is rife with angelic aliens ushered in online. A smart-looking fellow in a cap and gown steps from the heavenly light and hands Mom a diploma. Meanwhile, Dad is conducting an international business meeting. At home! An Asian-looking fellow (just to show you how very international this business meeting is) flickers holographically in front of him like Obi-Wan, and the two shake hands. Deal sealed. All thanks to the wonders on their way via your modem.

Dark or bright, the future is big business. You can make a career out being a futurist. The irony behind the NEC commercial is that it was paying for a report on CNN about IBM's fears of a hacker break-in at its Olympics site. As it turned out, of course, hackers were the least of that site's problems—that's another story. As I watched the spokesman talk about raising firewalls and an "ethical hacker" task force conducting a day and night vigil around them, I couldn't help but notice all the man-the-battleships terminology being tossed around.

Now, I am not for a moment going to even pretend to know the first thing about hacking, cracking, the whole scene. It is, therefore, no surprise to me that I'm not the first to associate computer break-ins with plain old-fashioned warfare. Throughout 1996, Edupage, an excellent e-mail news list that sends you pertinent clippings three times a week on information technologies, clipped and sent paragraphs the editors (John Gehl and Suzanne Douglas) headlined with alarming words such as "Information Warfare."

Beneath those screamers, you learned, for example, that the U.S. General Accounting Office reported that 120 countries have computer attack capabilities. Or that Deputy U.S. Attorney General Jamie Gorelick testified before a Senate subcommittee that the country is vulnerable to "an electronic Pearl Harbor." Good heavens. Our dependency (so soon!) on computer networks opens up the entire information infrastructure to attacks that "can disable or disrupt the provision of services just as readily as—if not more than—a well-placed bomb." The same subcommittee was also told that each year, a quarter of a million attempts are made to crack the Defense Department's computer systems. And guess what? About 65 percent of them succeed. Sleep tight tonight.

Maybe it will help to know that Defense is working on its defense. It has financed a Computer Emergency Response Team to stand guard over "the Internet, the telephone system, electronic banking systems, and the computerized systems that operate the country's oil pipelines and electrical power grids." There's a hint right there of just how far that term "information infrastructure" actually reaches—not to mention airport control towers, security codes all over the place, and hey, your money.

1996 was also the summer the Bank of London admitted to being blackmailed out of $619 million by hackers. No wonder CIA director John Deutch has said that "information attacks" are "very, very close to the top" of the Agency's list of worries.

Meanwhile, the FBI's special agent heading the division in San Francisco released a survey of private companies, 42 percent of which admitted to having their computer systems broken into, 47 percent of whom "felt it could have been a foreign competitor or foreign government." You wonder how many have been broken into but are too embarrassed to admit it. Note that besides Edupage, it seems that even the FBI lumps competition between businesses and nations together as the potential causes of warfare. The implications would clarify many a historical puzzle, but that is yet another story.

These are just the intentional snares. We don't even have to delve into the unintentional ones, far more common if usually less consequential. Even those who had never laid a finger on a keyboard learned all about crashes in the summer of 1996 when America Online went down for nineteen hours, making old media headlines and infuriating 6.2 million customers. Rare indeed is the computer system that does not occasionally misread 0 or 1 and go tumbling through all nine circles of Hell. So the flames swallow a few files. Hey, it is only information. Except of course, when it is a rocket. The software screw-up that brought down Ariane 5 that summer of screw-ups certainly makes you glad Reagan never got the chance to launch his little wars up to the stars.

Wow. Crashes, blackmail, and information warfare. And to think that some had even predicted that digital technology would change human nature itself. Is this what has become of the euphoric visions of cyberspace as a pastoral idyll in which old enemies, like the proverbial lion and lamb, would settle down together, maybe set up house in the 'burbs of the new global village? Sure enough.

Online technology is like any other: made by human hands, blessed with our best intentions, and tainted with our worst vices. Nothing is wrong with the hopes for a virtual world to run to when the real one gets too real, but don't be surprised by what happens when your fellow humans follow you there.

References

Adams, Robert M. *The Land and Literature of England*, W.W. Norton & Company, 1983, pp. 361–362.

Alderman, John. "Brian Eno," June 5, 1996.
http://www.hotwired.com/popfeatures/96/24/eno.transcript.html

Ars Electronica Festival '96.
http://web.aec.at/

Ars Electronica Festival '96 Symposium.
http://web.aec.at/meme/symp/

Barbrook, Richard. "Ars Electronica '96: Memesis Critique."
http://web.aec.at/meme/symp/contrib/barbro.html

Barbrook, Richard. "Never Mind the Cyberbollocks..."
http://web.aec.at/meme/symp/panel/msg00076.html

Bennahum, David S. MEME 2.09.
http://www.reach.com/matrix/

Borsook, Paulina.
http://www.transaction.net/people/paulina.html

Brain Tennis.
http://www.hotwired.com/braintennis/96/33/index3a.html

Burke, James.
http://homepage.interaccess.com/athand/burke_news.html

Dery, Mark. "Culture Jamming: Hacking, Slashing and Sniping in the Empire of Signs," The Open Magazine Pamphlet Series, 1993.

Dery, Mark. *Escape Velocity: Cyberculture at the End of the Century*, Grove Press, 1996, pp. 3, 45–48.

Dery, Mark. On Club Wired, February 21, 1996.
http://www.hotwired.com/club/special/transcripts/96-02-21.dery.html

Dawkins, Richard. As quoted by Mark A. Ottenberg, "What is a Meme?" December 28, 1995.
http://www.clark.net/pub/nhp/nge/lib/what_mem.html

Edupage.
http://www.educom.edu/web/edupage.html

European Space Agency, "Ariane 501—Presentation of Inquiry Board report."
http://www.esrin.esa.it/htdocs/tidc/Press/Press96/press33.html

Extroprians.
http://www.c2.net/arkuat/extr/

The Extroprian Principles, V. 2.6, Max More, Ph.D., 1995.
http://www.primenet.com/maxmore/extprn26.htm

Frequently Answered Questions About Extropians.
http://www.c2.org/arkuat/extr/exifaq.txt

Habitat II, United Nations Conference on Human Settlements, Istanbul, June 3–14, 1996.
http://www.undp.org/un/habitat/

Heylighen, Francis. "In defense of 'Memesis.'"
http://web.aec.at/meme/symp/contrib/heyligh.html

Hobsbawm, Eric. *Age of Extremes: The Short Twentieth Century, 1914–1991*, Abacus, 1994.

Hypermedia Research Centre, School of Design & Media, University of Westminster.
http://www.hrc.wmin.ac.uk/

Internet Multicasting Service, Internet Town Hall, "What's a Luddite?"
http://town.hall.org/places/ludd_land/whatsa.html

Jargon File Definition, "meme."
http://nmsmn.com/cservin/jargon/m/meme.html

Johnson, Paul. *Modern Times: The World from the Twenties to the Eighties*, Harper Colophon Books, 1983, p. 1.

Kelly, Kevin. "Interview with the Luddite," *Wired* 3.06.
http://www.hotwired.com/wired/3.06/features/saleskelly.html

Krantz, Michael. "Cashing in on Tomorrow," *Time*, July 15, 1996 Volume 148, No. 4.
http://pathfinder.com/time/magazine/domestic/1996/960715/technology.html

Lebkowsky, Jon. "The R.U. Sirius Interview: It's Better to be Inspired than Wired," *CTheory*, 30 Cyber-Days in San Francisco 1.6.
http://www.ctheory.com/cd1.6-inspired.html

Leonardo.

http://www-mitpress.mit.edu/Leonardo/leohome.html

Lynch, Aaron. *Thought Contagion: How Belief Spreads Through Society: The New Science of Memes*, Basic Books, New York, Release: September 27, 1996.

More, Max.

http://www.primenet.com/maxmore/

nettime.

http://www.desk.nl/nettime

"Peering into the global meta-mind," *The Boston Phoenix*, May 2–9, 1996.

http://www.bostonphoenix.com/alt1/archive/books/reviews/05-96/MARK_DERY.html

Penrose, Roger. *The Emperor's New Mind: Concerning Computers, Minds, and The Laws of Physics*, Oxford University Press, 1989, Vintage edition, p. 579.

Pynchon, Thomas. "Is It O.K. to Be a Luddite?" *The New York Times Book Review*, October 28, 1984, pp. 1, 40–41.

http://www.pomona.edu/pynchon/uncollected/luddite.html

Rhizome Internet.

http://www.rhizome.com

Schultz, Pit. "Tactical Toilette Training: Five questions to RU Sirius," nettime mailing list, May 31, 1996.

http://mediafilter.org/ZK/Conf/Conf_Email/June.13.1996.04.06.40

Stocker, Gerfried. "Memesis—the Future of Evolution."

http://web.aec.at/meme/symp/contrib/stocker.html

"Techwatch," *Time International*, July 29, 1996, Volume 148, No. 5.

http://pathfinder.com/time/international/1996/960729/techwatch.html

Talbott, Stephen L. Editor, and Peter Quince, "A nineteenth-century man confronts the computer: Conversation with Peter Quince," *NETFUTURE: Technology and Human Responsibility for the Future*, Issue #8, February 26, 1996.

http://www.ora.com/people/staff/stevet/netfuture/1996/Feb2696_8.html

Woolf, Virginia. "Mr. Bennett and Mrs. Brown," (1924), as quoted in *Modernism: 1890–1930*, Malcolm Bradbury and James McFarlane, eds., Penguin Books, 1976, p. 33.

Wright, Robert, "Can Machines Think?", *Time*, March 25, 1996 Volume 147, No. 13.

http://pathfinder.com/time/magazine/domestic/1996/960325/cover.think.html

Part IV

The New Terms of the Old Debates

"The final complication is that the whole show is not being run in a test tube or on some SimSociety computer game, but rather, by very human personalities in a very volatile world."

David Hudson

Chapter Eighteen

Abstracts

uto·pia \yōō tō´pē ə\ *n* [Utopia, imaginary and ideal country in *Utopia* (1516) by Sir Thomas More], fr. Gk ou not, no+ topos place 1: an imaginary and indefinitely remote place often capitalized 2: a place of ideal perfection esp. in laws, government, and social conditions 3: an impractical scheme for social improvement—

INT. SALON, NIGHT

Oda lifts her right hand.

ODA (in a changed voice): "And I'm the right!"

Mild laughter. Oda stands in the salon in front of her charmed family. Another reading night. All are gathered. Oda performs a little pantomime with her hands, commenting along the way.

ODA (her normal voice): "And this right one is a little drop of water. Just a single drop of water. But the left one..."

She bends over and grabs the black cloth chicken with her left hand that Griselda holds in her arms.

ODA: "The left one is a black chicken. The black chicken is walking along through the cabbage patch."

Oda performs this.

ODA: "And then the chicken sees the water drop hanging from a leaf and is about to pick it off. But in this drop of water..."

Now the other hand portraying the drop of water is brought to life.

ODA: "There are little intelligent beings, and what do we call little intelligent beings that live in drops of water?"

No one can answer her.

ODA: "Microbes."

General amusement.

ODA: "The microbes have had time to evolve and live their lives, to make discoveries, to buy and sell, and to be bought and sold. They've had their ancient period, their dark ages, they've had their disarmament talks! The microbes have had their Moses and Caesar and Bismark! But the black chicken doesn't see any of that. Silent and greedy, he circles the water drop."

Oda plays the silent and greedy black chicken circling the water drop. She contorts her face into silly expressions to go along with the act.

Everybody laughs.

ODA: "In the water drop, of course, all hell has broken loose! 'The end of the world!' cry out the pessimistic microbes. 'Indeed!' cry out the optimistic microbes. The religious microbes cry out for Jesus Christ. And the black beak comes closer and closer."

The family is enchanted with Oda's charm and talent.

ODA: "Then the socialist microbes say: 'Let's work together! Let's try to make the drop of water fall from the leaf! Let's all go over in this direction!'"

The audience is suddenly uneasy.

ODA: "'No!' say the liberal microbes. 'Everybody should do whatever they want! 'No!' cries out the capitalist microbe, 'you'll empty out my factories! No no no no!' And the dumbest and most reactionary of the microbes just call out: 'Long live our Czar Nicholas!'"

An icy silence falls over the room. Only Apa Kügelgen wakes up again, stands and pathetically calls out.

APA KÜGELGEN: "Long live our Czar Nicholas!"

He sits back down and falls asleep again. Utter silence in the salon. Clearly, each and every one of them is in shock. Oda, caught up in her acting, hasn't noticed and looks up in surprise.

ODA: "What is it? Am I boring you?"

Two items, both a bit unusual, kick off our overview of the political landscape of the Net. The first reminds us that for all the jabbering about techno-utopias, the collective phasing out of our present human form into some sci-fi fantasyland, the word itself was originally meant to be applied politically. What Thomas More dreamed up was to be the end result of social, not biological, engineering. To an extent, all political theories are utopian. No matter how intricately mapped out they are, no matter how many raw statistics are called on to back them up, no matter how much cold hard experience of the real world informs them, the resulting theory is an ideal, a model for a way to run things.

The second item, a scene in which a thirteen-year-old girl from Berlin visiting her Russian family in Latvia attempts to provide the evening's entertainment with an impromptu puppet show, reminds us that in practice, theories often get readjusted on the fly. Instead of being designed as methods for society to move toward an ideal goal, theories are often called on for quick answers to immediate emergencies, for ways with which to steer society away from impending disaster (even ultimate dystopia).

Political theories, in other words, are often called on as corrective measures in terms of how they suddenly spring to prominence in the public arena. But it gets complicated. We just can't get around the well-founded suspicion that some theories have been dreamed up in the first place as counter-maneuvers to perceived imbalances or threats to personal or collective interests. Often, they actually work for a while as long as the original problem is still around to even out the forces of the zealously applied solution. After the problem is overcome, however, the scales are sometimes thrown out of whack all over again, and the whole process whiplashes and rolls on, but backward, like a movie being projected in reverse. This is the kind of thing that has made the word "reactionary" an effective insult to toss at your political opponents.

And then it gets even more complicated. Political theories can rack up points in the great debate by directing our attention to a current crisis and forecasting its dire consequences with eloquence and accuracy. The problem is that a terrific diagnostician does not always make for the best doctor when it comes time to prescribe the cure. I remember well my shock when my second semester history prof, a free market capitalist at a Baptist university, ranked Karl Marx as one of the top three historians of all time. Of course, he did think that Marx's cure led to one of the great catastrophes of the twentieth century. When it came to the old German's views on just why nineteenth-century Europe was such a mess and how it got that way, however, my professor (author of a more than a few history books himself) was the first to puff his pipe and tip his hat.

The final complication is that the whole show is not being run in a test tube or on some SimSociety computer game, but rather, by very human personalities in a very volatile world. A rotten idea can make a lot of headway when it is being pushed by a telegenic face, someone well-placed in the corridors of power, or that old standby...a lot of money. Likewise, a great idea may get lost in the fray when its spokesperson mumbles incoherently, hasn't got the ear of anyone who counts, or just cannot afford to advertise.

Over the next few chapters, we won't be diving into the nitty-gritty of many of the specific political issues that have been raging since the Net went wide, the flammables such as censorship and privacy. Instead, we touch on them briefly, and then dwell longer on open questions that comprise the overall framework for the sizzlers. We will start with one so broad that for now we will just denote it with that ocean-wide resonator, "democracy."

Chapter Nineteen
Empowerment, Entertainment, or Enslavement?

Who asked for the Christmas wedding? That was the first question that came to my mind when I came upon this sentence toward the end of "Winner Take All," Time magazine's cover story of September 16, 1996, the one aimed at helping anyone stuck in line at the supermarket catch up on those thrilling browser wars: "Explorer 4.0, when it ships, will complete the unification of the computer and the Web."

Surely, the question in big bold blocky lettering on the cover of the newsweekly is rhetorical: "Whose Web Will It Be?" The answers danced around in the article, which describes an "epic battle...taking place between Microsoft and Netscape. Each company wants to be your guide to the Internet, the key to personal computing in the future. The victor could earn untold billions; the loser could die." But on the cover, with its little symbols for Netscape, Apple, and so on, tangled up in a web, front and center, is the disembodied head of Bill Gates, "not just a great hacker but also a world-class CEO," glowing with money, smiling for darn good reason and topped with that 'do that makes him look more like an aged Beatle than a spider.

As soon as it hit the stands, the article got quite a bit of coverage all over the Net. When the mainstream offline media cover the Net or anything vaguely related to it, onliners get very excited. It is like getting your own picture in the paper—just one gauge of how much emotional attachment and identification goes on between the technology and its heavy users. The *Netizen's* Jon Katz, certainly one of the most fun, provocative, and engaging columnists on the web, devoted a day to it. And although I often find myself nodding in agreement as I read him, this time I just didn't get his reading of *Time's* take on the browser wars.

I was right there with him, all the way, regarding his comments on Microsoft itself (in sum, Bill wants the world), but I couldn't see what he saw in that article. According to Katz, *Time* did us a favor by sounding the alarm (Net threatened by monopolization!) throughout offline America and offline elsewhere, but that is hardly the tone or the message of the piece, not even between the lines. An "epic battle" between Microsoft and Netscape? When I hear "epic," I think Homer—ten years of tooth and nail, and then ten years limping home. No, entertaining as the competition on the browser front has been, both companies have since been distracted. Just months later, we were not even hearing the word "browser" all that often any more. Netscape was sending scouts into new territories, intranets and extranets, while Microsoft was busily keeping all the balls it had picked up juggling in the air.

But the article was a hoot and did present a few tidbits to chew on.

Time's robotic slice-of-life formula ticking away, we open with a dollop of classic Timese: "On a cloudy morning last December, as the white light of winter picked its way across the face of Mount Rainier..." Ahem. Turns out, we're actually in Bill's bedroom as he rolls out of bed, no time for breakfast, just a shower, and so forth. Yes, America needs its heroes, and the Hacker CEO certainly fits the bill in 1996. But must we watch him shower? Those eight cheeseburgers (yes, we get to read what he ate the night before, too) still working their way through his digestive tract?

Finally (after a twenty-minute drive), we get to that Internet strategy presentation wherein we hear how the Great Helmsman all but single-handedly steers his ship toward the Net. Oh, really. Other versions have other visionaries banging their heads against the wall because it took so long for Mr. Bill to even notice the Net before it rammed the company head on.

But that is hardly epic or heroic. But clearly, *Time* does want us feeling good about this guy hijacking the information age.

Back to my own rhetorical question. Who wanted the web and the computer unified anyway? Who, precisely, was asked?

I pose the question rhetorically because the specific answer does not matter all that much. What matters is that this little nugget of technical information tucked at the end of a popular newsweekly article is presented as if this rather significant move on the part of a single company is the most natural development that could transpire in the competitive arena. And of course, there is nothing legally or even morally wrong with a single company jazzing up its product with what may turn out to be a pretty nifty feature.

Microsoft certainly is not alone in its pursuit of a seamless integration between everything you used to do offline and everything you can or will be able to do online. Besides, any company great or small can release any gadget on to the marketplace it darn well pleases. After all, it is a free country! No one has to buy anything. If you want to compute on a Commodore 64, go right ahead. On the other hand, if you want, or even feel you need, the latest and greatest, go for it.

If you can afford it, that is. Myself, I have had a helluva time keeping up lately, and you know what? I'm hardly alone. I know a lot of folks who consider me pretty lucky for the computing power I do have, and I'm sure as hell not foolish enough to disagree. Of course, if I had the extra cash lying around, I would love to upgrade and see what the fuss is about, but I don't, so I won't.

And neither do most people. How much of the information of the information age will gradually be upgraded out of reach of the majority? The curve inherent in the question is not necessarily what is going to continue to happen, but it isn't necessarily what won't happen, either. At any rate, at present, as the competition heats up, it is what's happening now. Which is ironic. Because the Net and all its related technologies were supposed to be a great boon for pure democracy, at least according to the prophets of the "digital revolution."

Online technology enhances democracy in a couple of different ways. Jeff Johnson, a software designer and former Chair of Computer Professionals for Social Responsibility, notes two of the lesser ones in a speech delivered to the Association for Computing Machinery's 1995 conference on Computer-Human Interaction, "The Information Hypeway: A Worst-Case Scenario," and blows them away. "The popular term 'electronic democracy' suggests that the Information Highway will enhance democracy by allowing citizens to communicate with elected representatives and participate more effectively in government policymaking. In some fantasy world, perhaps, but not in this one."

The first problem with this fantasy is that online technology won't have any effect on real-world demographics. In other words, in terms of strict availability alone, representatives can already be reached via snail mail and the phone. You can write or call the office, voice your concern, and have an aide chalk up a mark on your side of the issue, or you can e-mail the same office (provided the representative has an e-mail address, of course, and slowly but surely, the ones in the U.S. at least are coming online) and score the same chalk mark. Your opinion and your vote carry exactly as much or as little weight as they always have, no matter how you deliver them.

Speaking of your vote. "Most of the hype about 'electronic democracy' is really just about rapid electronic polling," Johnson continues, picking up the second assumption about online technology creating an ideal democratic society. "But polling is just 'acclamatory democracy,' a degenerate case of democracy. True democracy involves discussion and deliberation and is slow by definition. It requires debate, not just clicking on For or Against buttons. Furthermore, it requires opportunities for citizens to influence important issues. Instead, the Information Highway will give us more opportunities to vote on issues such as whether or not the First Spouse should dye his or her hair. Instead of democracy, we'll get Oprahcracy."

That may be overstating the case, but even if instant elections are conducted on the Net on more serious issues, on referendums, candidates for office, and so on, as we can tell by the polls already being conducted daily, instantaneousness does not serve the democratic process. This is Johnson's main point and it is certainly well-taken. The utopian version of "electronic democracy" again, as so many utopian visions flaring up around new technologies do, overlooks the sad circumstance that no matter how beautiful the system you dream up is, after you plug real human beings into it, you have got yourself yet another mirror-image version of human society on your hands, with all its warmth, quirks, and deficiencies.

At the same time, one pair of aspects of this new technology is good news for democracy, for the engagement of citizens, and even for activism. First, quick and easy access to information—specifically, government documents, transcripts of congressional hearings, and the like—as can be found on several databases, public and private. One of the more obvious examples is THOMAS. As the "About" page phrases it, "Acting under the directive of the leadership of the 104th Congress to make Federal legislative information freely available to the Internet public, a Library of Congress team brought the THOMAS World-Wide-Web-based system online in January 1995, at the inception of the 104th Congress." In other words, it is a Newt Gingrich thing, and credit must be given where credit is due; it is a terrific idea, right up there with Al Gore's High-Performance Computing Act of 1991.

The second positive aspect of all this is the access to other citizens that online technology makes possible, and in some interesting ways. Although, as Johnson points out, debate is a slow process, it does actually occur in spades online. A lot of it is mere flaming for flaming's sake, but the same can be said for offline debates as well. Further, although it is next to impossible to measure just how people get informed and how their opinions get shaped by their online communications, we can pretty much safely assume it happens, over time—and over great spaces, too. Discussion and debate can, and literally does, occur worldwide.

But—there's always a but—in the early days of the Net, some fairly similar characters were the ones doing the discussing and debating. The online population was hardly representative of the offline one, not that the Net was designed to accommodate such representation. Remember, after the initial structure was up, the Net can hardly be said to have been designed at all. Then, as more and more people opened accounts and as the population did gradually morph into something a bit closer to the broader demographic picture you might see on a bustling city street, another phenomenon began to take effect. People found and tended to gravitate toward others who shared similar tastes, opinions, interests, and lifestyles. Precisely because the Net population had become so huge, getting to know everybody was, of course, an absurd proposition altogether. Soon, however, so was wading through, say, even all the descriptions denoted by the titles of all the thousands of newsgroups that had sprung up overnight.

"Newbies" faced with what seemed to indeed be a whole new world would naturally hit some overall hierarchical guide to resources and subsets of populations within populations, choose a broad interest (maybe arts), and click their way toward a manageable evening's worth of browsing, chat, and message exchanging. By that time, many had arrived at a slice of online life so thin in terms of the range of its interests that the idea of the free exchange of ideas with any sort of real relation to "democracy" as the word is applied to the way a whole country gets run had become rather silly. Even sillier is the whole notion of a single Net community. In the old days, yes; now, no.

Nevertheless, some things do get done. The bright and shining example is the mass lobbying organized and, for the most part, carried out online against the Communications Decency Act, part of the monolithic Telecommunications Bill of 1996. The lobbying didn't keep the U.S. Congress from passing the bill nor President Clinton from signing it, but it did keep the debate over this one particular portion of it, the CDA, alive and kicking and can probably be said to be largely responsible for its getting declared unconstitutional by a Philadelphia court.

What is worth pointing out within the framework of the idea of online technology making democracy work in some new and unique fashion is that, by any definition, the CDA was an extraordinary case. If passed, upheld, and actually enforced (as much as that would have been possible), almost no one online would not have been affected in some way. Being on the Net (or a BBS or any other online service) was the single most motivating criteria for joining up with others in what was, essentially, a special interest group—although offliners concerned about the CDA's threat to the First Amendment were naturally welcome to pitch in, and many did. There were, it must be told, notable vocal groups online that supported the CDA.

Still, the movement to repeal the Act was largely supported by those who had a direct stake in the outcome of the decision and those familiar with what the online experience was actually like. Accordingly, online petitions, an endless stream of information, and shows of solidarity such as the blue ribbon for free speech tagged on to web pages (which went black for a while to protest the CDA's passage) were prevalent. Meanwhile, those in favor of the Act seemed for the most part to have been persuaded by sensational offline media coverage (such as *Time*'s infamous "Cyberporn" cover story) that suggested (quite profitably) that the Net was one great global orgy of pornography.

Because support and opposition pretty much fell along these lines and because of the unique nature of the issue, the CDA became a thrilling example of the possibilities of "electronic democracy," but also a deceptive one. Such activist solidarity when it comes to an issue such as abortion, for example, is highly unlikely. And yet the hype surrounding just what connectivity can do for a society as a whole, while wearing thin as more and more people do get connected and things continue more and more sort of the way they always have, rolls on.

Quotes such as this one from John Perry Barlow, that lyricist and co-founder of the Electronic Frontier Foundation, abound: "All the current power relationships on the planet are currently being disassembled, it's going to be up in the air. Ultimately, centralized anything is going to be greatly de-emphasized and redistributed." These things are a dime a dozen. If you happen to collect them, pick up any copy from the first couple of years' worth of *Wired*'s issues, close your eyes, and let your forefinger fall where it will. Chances are it will have landed on some eloquent and exhilarating claim for the next wave (the Third one, actually, as numbered by Alvin Toffler). And among the many claims, you will read that the digital age will be one in which the old hierarchies are leveled. Democracy unleashed at last!

Yet if you set the rhetoric next to an item such as the *Time* cover story we opened with, the one announcing a redirection of the total online experience, it seems that in truth, matters have been cleanly swiped from most of our hands and the hierarchies are more pronounced than ever. We are on the sidelines now, hoping we will be able to afford the show.

Richard E. Sclove, executive director of the Loka Institute, in an interview with Steve Talbott, grants that "the Internet can undoubtedly give small groups or dispersed populations some opportunities to organize and coordinate in new ways, or to access some useful sources of information, thereby empowering themselves to challenge inequitable concentrations of power." Turning to the application of this microcosmic model to Barlow's macrocosmic one, however, "The question is whether that empowerment of the 'small and weak' can outpace the continuing empowerment of the 'large and potent.' E.g., multinational corporations, government bureaucracies, affluent professionals and the super-rich will retain vastly greater capabilities to adopt powerful technology more quickly, to amass and analyze information, and, in many cases, to act on it."

Sclove has written a book called *Democracy and Technology*, and although it deals with technology in general, he has applied the gist of the book to the Net noting, "as a wider range of people choose to join in (or find they have to, as a condition of employment or to be able to access social and commercial services that will increasingly be available only online) it's important that their concerns and perspectives also play a role in influencing the evolution of information systems (and the dynamic transformations between cyberspace and life off-screen)."

Is this still a feasible option? Decisions are being made right now— radical ones—redirecting the course of the digital r/evolution (that's what I like to call it); its infrastructure; the ways it will work; the ways it won't; how often we will be bumping into it; and how often and how effectively it will chase us down, throw its arms around our knees, and bring us face down to the artificial turf. And neither you (assuming you are not one of Adam Smith's Invisible Handful) nor I, nor even the scampering cheerleaders we used to cringe at and refer to as the digerati have even as much as one of those wadded up little flags to toss out onto the supposedly level playing field.

There is no conspiracy at work here. No one consciously decided it would turn out like this, which is part of the problem. But we could not possibly have expected a call some time back, asking, "Text that, like, blinks on and off... what d'ya think?" But we got blinking text and it was the butt of many an online joke throughout 1994. Or a year or so later, another call, "We know that window's kinda small already, but what if we frame it off into lots of even smaller ones? You can still sorta read 9 pt. Times, can't you?" But frames stuck.

But the real players, the big software companies, content providers, and webmasters, are all too often too busy scrambling over the ball, pushing for that extra yard, to call a time out and consult the rabble. Instead, runners trot back our way with whatever they have overheard at the huddle. "Ditch your PC, we're going back to the time sharing, mainframe model." Rats. And I'd just gotten used to running my own programs without any over-the-shoulder coaching.

If you think it is semi-tough resisting the shove back up to the stands now, just wait until the playoffs. So a couple of questions arise. Is there more than blinking text and other stupid aesthetic tricks at stake, and if so, can we afford not to shove back? And if we can't, is there a doable shove in the game plan that will get us back out on the field? Answers: Yes, no, and probably not. But what the hell.

"Unfortunately," says Richard Sclove, "if we wait to involve everyone in decisions about [information] systems until most people are already online and have begun to experience economic and social consequences they don't like, it will be largely too late. By then many important decisions will already have been made by corporate conglomerates and glamorized netreprenures, and embodied in multi-billion dollar systems. Hence the challenge (about which I am politically pretty pessimistic) of how to develop new institutions now—not later—for involving everyday people, including affected non-users (i.e., everyone) in system design."

At this stage in the game, the pessimism is surely healthy, but nevertheless surprising from a guy who has put forward several comprehensive ideas about engaging the general public in the process of making the decisions on the development and applications of the technologies that affect their lives. Decisions the public is not in the habit of being in on. The ones businesses, the military, and universities perceive as their own turf, the ones on which sort of energy resources we ought to exploit, what to do with our map of the human gene after it is drawn up, which sort of weapon we would prefer to blow our enemies away with, and yes, who gets wired and how, among other questions— the ones we are hardly ever asked to worry our pretty little heads with. After the congressional hearings, advisory panels, and policy studies are neatly wrapped up, the papers and CNN are usually the ones to let us know in due course how it has all turned out.

In his article for the July issue of *Technology Review*, "Town Meetings on Technology," Sclove outlines a set of ideas for turning this self-regenerating flow of power around, for realizing the radical notion of actually reaching these decisions democratically. And he backs them up with the concrete and thorough illustration of the consensus conference as applied primarily in Denmark, but in the Netherlands and the United Kingdom as well. At present, the European Union, Canada, New Zealand, and Australia are giving serious thought to trying out the consensus conference. Because it works. Briefly, here's how:

Let's say, to summarize the article's main example, the issue of whether it is a good idea to allow biotech companies to patent genetically engineered animals is about to come up in the Danish parliament (as it did in 1992). The Danish Board of Technology actually places ads in the papers:

Who wants to be in on this? A couple hundred people write in, saying, yep, I'm there. Around fifteen are selected; they keep it as demographically diverse as possible.

These lay folk get to know each other first, and then they meet up with the experts, also a panel comprised of members from a broad range of related fields. Questions are raised, readings recommended—in general, everybody familiarizes himself and herself and each other with the details of the question at hand and the concerns each representative has brought to the conference.

After a few days of this, the media, members of Parliament, and the public gather for a howzit-going open session. Views are aired. There is some give, there is some take. Eventually, the experts and the lay folk split, and the lay folk compiles its report. The experts are given a chance to look it over, correct any factual errors, but not comment. And the report is delivered to the public at a national press conference.

Here's the important part. The report is not binding in any way, legally or otherwise. Parliament could ignore it and pretend the whole conference never happened if it liked. But being the smart politicians they are, they pay darn close attention to that report as it gets passed around to local debates throughout the country sponsored by the Board of Technology and generally bathed in national attention.

Moreover, as a result of the care taken in the process, the panel's reports are exceedingly fair. In this particular case, the precedent of treating living beings as products was deplored, and several environmental concerns were raised. At the same time, however, the use of genetic engineering toward finding cures for disease was encouraged.

Rewired

And get this. As a result of the 1992 panel, Novo Nordisk, a large biotech company, actually shifted its focus away from creating bigger, meatier farm animals to just that: medical research. Novo Nordisk thus raised its standing in the eye of the Danish public. Everybody wins.

So, great. Could or should such a process be applied to the development of information technologies? As Sclove has said, "the real story about cyberspace is not about life or culture within cyberspace itself, but how cyberspace—especially as it commercializes—is going to dramatically alter the economy and, via the economic transformations, society and politics...everywhere, for everyone, all the time (i.e., offline)."

But his very next sentence begins, "Much of this change will be involuntary and coercive...," and sort of goes downhill from there. After all, he did say that he is pessimistic about the prospects for a truly democratic policy regarding the development of information technologies.

It is late out on the field and up here in the stands. The teams down there are not for a moment going to stop and suggest we all have a nice long chat about where we are headed. How long, one wonders, has democracy been a spectator sport?

Chapter Twenty

Hot Buttons and Slow Burners

Many of the debates that have blazed across newspaper headlines, magazine covers, and the evening news in the last few years over the impact of online technology and what to do about it have been cast in a hyped-up terminology that makes the questions at hand look as exotic and new as the Net itself. But scratch any of them and you will find an issue that most likely goes back for centuries. Granted, we can't afford to deceive ourselves. There are new twists to old unsettled matters of business, and they must be taken into consideration.

But at the same time, there is little need for irresponsible hysteria. The most famous example of unfounded scare-mongering in all Net history would have to be *Time* magazine's "Cyberporn" cover story with the illustration of the wide-eyed child on its cover, aghast, staring out at us, horrified by an image so deranged that the illustrator has left its reality to our imaginations. No, contrary to the fraudulent Martin Rimm "study" on which the story was based, merely establishing a connection to the Internet would not load your screen with pornographic imagery. If you want to see naked people, you will have to do some clicking. You will have to go find them—because you want to.

Is it important to discuss the questions raised by a new sort of availability of pornography in the light of our kids? Absolutely. All the old issues are just as vital as ever, and therefore, require level-headed, informed deliberation. Sensationalism just muddies waters we need kept as clear as ever.

Now about that porn. There was a lot of back-patting on the Net when the Communications Decency Act was overruled by a Philadelphia court. To hear some people tell it, the web pages that went black in protest to its signing and the blue ribbons they sported in support of the fight against censorship went a long way toward influencing the decision. There is little reason to mock this viewpoint and little gain in doing so other than to point out that there is a danger in overconfidence based on an unrealistic idea of how the law actually works. The decision was based on the nature of the Net, and not on any activities taking place there.

But what I would like to avoid in this chapter is a journey down well-trodden lines of argument. Instead, for each of the hot button issues and slow burning questions this chapter briefly touches on, let's take a less formal approach. In the case of censorship, for example, we could recall the great cases of the past and then point out how the Net makes this issue a whole new ball game.

It is also worth keeping in mind that when CompuServe struck some two hundred newsgroups because of some backwoods Bavarian court ruling, instructions for how to reroute and read them anyway were rampant. Or that when France tried shutting down two ISPs and UseNet access, alarms went off all over the Net. Paul Garrin's New York-based Media Filter shot out, "[T]his is idiotic...to cut off all newsgroups...and unnecessary," and then proceeded to list several public access news servers. "Forget about the stupid local laws!" the message concluded, "They would have to filter all outgoing international packets to stop the access to these feeds from France."

Sure, outright censorship of the Net is utterly futile. Any network built to withstand nuclear attack is not going to buckle under mere political pressure. Of course we should keep on our toes. Fight the good fight and all that. But the CDA was hardly the only game in town. Even as the post-CDA euphoria was just beginning to cool off, several crises far more threatening to individual freedom and privacy are brewing on a variety of fronts, and few were thrown into the new media spotlight like the CDA was.

In Germany, for example, a new telecommunications law, or Telekommunikationsgesetz (or even better, the TKG), was passed right on the heels of the CDA decision in the U.S. However you pronounce it, it explicitly spells out an absolute disaster for the most basic of individual rights in any country calling itself a democracy. Further, it sets a dangerous precedent; usually, that is journalism talk for "something not to be taken quite so seriously yet, but listen up." Similar legislation is bound to make its way into the parliaments and congresses of other governments. Instead of being laughed off the floor as anyone in his or her right mind would expect, the idea will parade in wearing the cloak of legitimacy.

Here's the deal. Paragraphs 85 and 87 of the new law require all— all!—online and telecommunication service providers to make their users' data available to a new government watchdog office, which will pass on whatever it perceives to be valuable information on anyone jacked into a phone line to security officials, the Sicherheitsbehrden. Chilling, isn't it? But that's not all. This new office is to have complete access to all user data at any time. And the service providers are to set up the technical apparatus to make this access possible (and pay for it). At an estimated cost of around 50,000 German marks per provider, that totals over $30,000.

I am not making this up. And get this. Although the providers are to foot the bill for the government's snooping into its users' affairs, they are to do it in such a way that not even they themselves are to be aware that the snooping is going on.

I won't even get into all the ramifications except to say this: Imagine being told by the police to knock out a wall and build a back door to your living quarters, pay for it yourself, and arrange your house in such a way that they can stroll in any time and go through your and your family's stuff without your being aware of it.

As noted, the law passed, but the story is far from over. It will be fought over, challenged, and bounced around. As Nico Reichelt, who has been maintaining a web site with news resources on this story at the Institute for New Media in Frankfurt, asks, "When will the first providers be required to set up the access over which they have no control? When will the first provider no longer be able to handle the financial costs? When will the first trials be held?" As of this writing, these questions remain unanswered.

Now, I consider myself a fairly Net savvy sort of guy, but this story all but blew past me until Armin Medosch of the excellent German web publication *Telepolis* tipped me off. After we had hashed through the details, he commented, "Isn't it strange: Many people in Germany seemed to be concerned with the CDA but with something much worse in their own country nobody (or better: not many people so far) is doing anything about it."

Strange and not so strange. For all the heady talk of the unique, global community the advent of online technology is supposed to bring us, for all the off-the-wall declarations of independence for cyberspace, the Stamp Acts of digital nations intoxicating even normally leveler heads, the U.S. and its concerns dominate the Net.

As Medosch's comment reveals, this is not solely the "fault" of the Americans. Yes, the U.S. had a head start in the race to cyberspace. The Net's backbone was built by the U.S. Defense Department, true. But speed aside, there is nothing in the architecture itself that inherently requires American domination any longer. Claims of American cultural imperialism or comments such as those of Anatoly Voronov, the director of Glasnet, an Internet service provider in Russia, quoted by the *New York Times* don't cut it with me. Throwing around nineteenth-century buzzwords as he does when he calls the web "the ultimate act of intellectual colonialism" just flies in the face of the reality of how information gets out there. Want more of it to be Russian, Indonesian, or Angolan? Put it up.

Of course, I'm stepping out onto thin ice here. Although the Net's structure is open in theory, the practical reality of economics shuts out much of the world. Still, and again theoretically, the Net ought to be a step in the right direction. Costly as it is, there is less of a "breaking into the industry" phase involved than there is in other media. The point is that online technology itself does not represent any one nation's hegemony. Furthermore, I sincerely doubt that the Net, which was all but an accident in the first place, was ever intended as such. With all that in mind, the unfortunate conclusion we would have to draw if we were to try to define a "digital nation" would be that its shape would look very much like a map of the lower 48. The open question on this issue is, How do we color in the missing pieces?

The word "access" is often coupled with "universal," making the matter seem rather abstract. It isn't. It can be a complex problem to sort through, no doubt. Real people, however, are struggling with those complexities on a very specific level: "So I have $20 to produce this piece of work—how am I going to make this $20 go far enough to reach my goal?"

What performance artist and writer Rebecca Levi is talking about is the nitty-gritty, not-so-fun side of her work. "$20 is not really enough to produce a zine unless you can steal paper and xeroxing services. I could do a street performance. I could put it up in a show where I didn't have to put any money up front, and spend the $20 on 4-up xeroxed handouts that I can pass out and leave in prime locations."

I met Rebecca Levi just after she moved back to New York, wrapping up a couple of years in San Francisco. A weird and lucky chain of events brought her to Berlin even before she'd had a chance to settle into her new life in her favorite city in the world. Both of us tromped through the rain under an oppressively grey sky to meet face to face for the first time in a bookstore on Oranienstrasse in Kreuzberg.

It's weird. Most of us have gone through something like it. For months, we had been exchanging e-mail almost daily, and then suddenly, there you are. She tries her German out on me, "Ich habe Hunger," and that breaks the ice. Back out into the rain in search of that ever elusive decent yet affordable bite.

The place on the corner calling itself a Taqueria might be a hoot. On our way, we talk zines. She publishes a terrific one, *Your Head on a Platter*, and I had been hounding her for months, trying to get her to let me help her put a few of her works online. Rebecca writes what I would call prose poems; the first one I saw utterly floored me. It had evidently lodged itself somewhere under my skin, because I couldn't shake it for days and I went back and read it more than a few times again. It took me somewhere I knew I had never been before, but at the same time, it seemed both terrifyingly and reassuringly familiar.

Nachos for DM 7.50? That's around $5. Enchiladas, $15. Back out into the rain.

I know a cheap but good place. I point to it with the little pocket memo recorder she knows she will be speaking into. Because the other hand, as usual, sports a smoldering cigarette, so very Berlin, yet I know she hates them, so very San Francisco, so I don't want to wave it around.

"When I talk about being concerned about issues of distribution, I am rarely thinking primarily of the electronic domain. In fact, it's usually my last concern. For the most part, what I'm thinking is, I want to get a piece of work—performance, fiction, whatever—out there in the world. Who is my target audience? What is the medium I want to present it in? For me, the first answer is usually my immediate community, and so, the second is performance."

I've translated the menu, and she has decided to go for local flavor: Speckknoedel mit Sauerkraut. Okay. Now, what if you want to go beyond your local community? "A zine is a good idea, though distribution is extremely time consuming and you have to work hard to even make back your costs in most cases. But it can be done for the low or no budget zine publisher; look at *Cometbus*, for instance. But for getting beyond the local community, sure, I think electronic publishing is invaluable. Or let me qualify that: potentially invaluable."

Let's back up. She did a longish stint for Luna Sea Women's Performance Project, a two-year-old professional theater space in the Mission, "dedicated to producing the work of women without censure. And that includes economic censure. Economic censure is a tricky thing."

Luna Sea is devoted to producing the work of women who wouldn't otherwise have access to a professional theater space, "partially because of the content of their work, partially because almost every other environment requires an initial outlaying of money."

Back to the concept of economic censure. Some examples? "An underground performance space requires a professionally produced video tape from a performer to get booked in that space. A funding board that funds new programs has a grant application that takes 72 hours to complete—for a volunteer organization like Luna Sea that means 72 volunteer hours—of not doing the books, not finding new performers or producers, and perhaps most significantly for an artist-run organization—not producing our art."

I nod a bit too vigorously and light another. "Most other organizations have a paid fundraiser who's writing the grant during her eight-hour day at work, not after it. One of the most ubiquitous examples of economic censure I've seen—and this is totally unacknowledged—is the 'reading fee' or 'contest fee' attached to almost every call for entries listed in those pages. What's nice about electronic publishing is that the do-it-yourself aspect can enable you to bypass the admissions process. That is, if you have the funds to get up there at all."

Which reminds Rebecca of her participation in a group of Bay Area literary organizations responding to a Field Report written by the NEA about literature. "It was a horribly written, grossly inadequate project, not surprisingly, written by a research company, I believe, and not by someone actually in the field. I co-wrote a response to the section on writers, which was largely a critique of the happy-go-lucky, optimistic view of this section."

In what way? "Oh, 'there are more people writing, more places to get published, more writing programs than ever,' etc. But our question was, Who is writing? Who is getting published? Are emerging writers getting published? Are people of color getting published and going to MFA programs? Are people outside of New York City getting funded? Do you have to go to school to get published? What about the issue of access... Who has access to what?

"And that's my concern about electronic publishing. When someone says, 'almost anyone can afford a computer and put up a web page,' who is that 'almost anyone?' Look, I think that electronic publishing has enormous potential, but for now, for me, it would mean trading in one community for another."

Beaming over my Pils and smoke, I'm congratulating myself for bringing my recorder. "Right now, for instance, of the approximately 50 people I automatically send my zine to, I believe about ten percent have e-mail, and maybe a third of those have access to the web. Obviously, replacing my zine with an electronic format would mean losing my primary readership."

Just to play devil's advocate... "Sure, on the other hand, there are thousands of people who could have access to the zine on an electronic format, who I would never otherwise have access to. Now, that is very exciting. And it doesn't cost me anything more to expose 50, 500, or 5,000 new people to my ideas. Fantastic!"

Well, actually... But it's too late. Rebecca's on a roll. "You know, if Luna Sea could send out all our announcements electronically, we would radically reduce our number two expense of mailing calendars. For show updates, this would be equally invaluable, because the shows later in the two-month calendar tend to get lower audience turn out, and it wouldn't cost a thing, practically, to send e-mail updates."

We? But we live in New York now, don't we? "Well, still, it's something that could very practically be put into place. Keep doing the bi-monthly calendars, then compile a list of e-mail addresses for weekly updates—a supplement, not a replacement." What have I done?

But Rebecca's fork stabs the air. "The problem. That we're denying access to this information to the vast majority of our audience and our community. We could not afford to mail to those who don't have Net access. Yet we're committed to not excluding women from our activities on any level." I watch the fork playing in the sauerkraut. "A tricky one, no?"

There you have it, Rebecca.

"I don't know, maybe we should try it anyway. Someone—not from Luna Sea but someone who had seen a flyer—posted one of our audition announcements for a gender identity festival we were doing to a cyberdykes subscription list, and we got about five new performers that way. That was great! Because looking at it another way, the flyers were posted somewhere where they weren't—they didn't have access to the physical flyers, and this was the only way they would have found out about it."

A tricky one indeed. Just to make things more complicated, we talk about her preference for the BBS we met on over the web. "I find a lot more discussions on many more topics, a lot more voices coming from different places." Which is interesting, because the BBS is local and the web's big asset is supposed to be the worldwide angle.

But it's time to go. It is late afternoon, the Americans are waking, checking their e-mail, and I've got to get back. We say our goodbyes, and as much as I hate to end my brief foray into the 3D world with its sense-o-round amazements, I have to get back to the all too terrifyingly and reassuringly familiar. The computer, with its eerily claustrophobic window out on to the world.

Sometimes you have got to ask yourself, What "virtual class?" Just sometimes. Because you know they're around, these netrepreneurs shoving one technofetish after another out on to the market (though they're the only ones with the money and the know-how, if not the time, to fondle them), overseeing web ventures in the confidence that, despite *Business Week*'s diagnosis that "the number of losers still exceeds the number of moneymakers by more than two to one," they can always jump ship and still land on top.

We know they are there because many of us have actually seen them, watched them, dreamed our lives were like their lives, so much so, in fact, that we actually pretend—at least in public—to number among them. Tapping the PowerBook keys with one hand while steering two tons of metal with the other? But of course. Gotta work, work, work to keep up that virtual lifestyle.

Truth is, for the most of us, the genuinely virtual aspect of the charade is the affluence. What with the economy the way it was throughout 1996, the Clinton administration having created ten million new jobs in the U.S., raised the minimum wage (yes, that actually means something to a lot more people closer to our real lives than many of us would care to admit), and overall wages increasing (okay, it is a drop in the bucket toward replenishing the disastrous Reagan/Bush drainage, but getting wages to rise up and over the rate of inflation while keeping unemployment down was quite a trick), you'd think the denizens of the industry of tomorrow would be bathing in opulence.

But just how are the foot soldiers of the digital revolution faring? Well, David Kline points to some numbers in a study by the Working Partnerships USA, a non-profit policy institute, and draws a couple of right-on-the-money conclusions summed up pretty well in his phrase: the "Silicon Valley Squeeze." Turns out the Microserfs are even worse off than they were when that silly "novel" was released in their name.

Forty percent of them are temps. While those at the head of the virtual class are chasing down their next flight, the would-be's are chasing down their next job. Less than ten percent have any sort of health insurance. And of course, since the Clinton health plan was shot down, that over 90 percent remainder will just have to go on doing without, hoping for the best and pretending they will never grow old. Temp or not, insured or not, since 1989, their wages on average have fallen 15 percent despite the national rise. Over the same period of time, the highly skilled are even worse off. They're down 28 percent.

As Kline notes, "The dark side of 'disintermediation' revealed by the declining status and eroding opportunities of high-tech workers is much more than just a bleeding heart moral issue. It poses serious risks to the health of our economy, to our nation's competitiveness in world markets and to the hope that the Information Revolution can help create a reinvigorated American dream for the 21st century."

If he could turn up the volume on any one facet of *Road Warriors*, the book he co-authored with Daniel Burstein, this would be it: "If I felt I had no part of the 21st century," he commented during a phone chat, "I'd run out and start burning houses down. It's in no one's best interest to have that much cleavage between the two classes. Things are getting better for a minority, but worse for the majority."

How can such a revolution in convenience, convergence, or sheer hip (and hence marketable) newness have such a detrimental effect on the very people with their hands right on the making of it? Or for that matter, the rest of us? Consider Gerry McGovern's observation that he "can't help but feel that [he's] become a Digital Age farmer." What he means is...well, let's back up.

McGovern, an Irishman, grew up on a farm. And as we all know, a farmer's work is never done. "You milked the cows in the morning, delivered the milk to the creamery, cleaned the byre out, washed the milk buckets and cans, fed the calves, sowed, tended or harvested some crop, repaired a gate, cleared out a ditch, began draining a field, worried about too much or too little rain, watched over the cow who was about to calve, and when you were about to do something else, you realised that it was time to go up for the cows again."

Sounds terribly picturesque, but also just plain terrible. But there was a post-war blip in there somewhere, a point at which we had achieved a measured realization of the idea of leisure.

Leisure. What a foreign-sounding word it is. We don't even sip our iced coffees any more without feeling the impulse to choose a cybercafe to do our sipping in, click on, and keep up. McGovern means that he is "tied to my information like my parents were tied to the land. I am farming information, an agricultural boy who must sow, tend, and reap, with the ever present knowledge that this year's work is for this year's crop, and that next year the whole process must start again."

Would that the cycle were as slow as the years. But as the Critical Art Ensemble noted as it turned its acerbic eye to the often dissected AT&T "You Will" campaign, "The corporate intention for deploying this technology (in addition to profit) is so transparent, it's painful. The only possible rejoinder is: 'Have you ever been at a work station...24 hours a day, 365 days a year? You will.' Now the sweat shop can go anywhere you do!"

And not just your job is following you around either. The persistence of technology, online or not, was driven home to me on a visit to my parents' place in Texas. Now Texas is one of the more amazing of the U.S.' 50 states. It has all the makings of a culturally, geologically, atmospherically, linguistically varied country, which in fact it was briefly over a century ago. Many, in fact, would justifiably claim it still hasn't got over its brief shining moment of independence.

Wrapped up in the Texas myth and genuine Texas pride is that strain of individualism that is so often preceded by the adjective "rugged." So when my father handed me an article in *The Dallas Morning News* that began, "Tom Thumb wants to know more about your shopping habits," I knew that, however subtly, this story will play here differently than it would in a lot of other spots on the globe. As columnist Molly Ivins has put it, "Texas is a reality check for the rest of the nation. People can see right through the bull people in other parts of the country might buy."

Tom Thumb is a supermarket chain run by Randalls Food Markets Inc., based in Houston. Randalls sank $13 million into what it is calling a frequent-shopper card program. The company isn't the first to set up a computerized system to keep track of what its customers are buying. Vons Cons Inc., with 325 supermarkets in Southern California and Las Vegas, for example, has been at it since 1991. Around 14 percent of all U.S. supermarkets run similar programs.

On the consumer end, it looks like this. You bring your driver's license into the store, fill out an application, grab your Reward card, shop, and save, save, save! The day after that *Dallas Morning News* story, Tom Thumb slipped a four-color, eight-page advertising supplement into the same paper, and hey, these savings were substantial, ranging from 30 percent on Diet Coke® to 50 percent on cookies to around 70 percent on a ten-pound bag of potatoes.

You can also look forward to receiving coupons for all your favorite products in the mail—and also samples of products Tom Thumb thinks you're gonna like. And just so you can sleep at night after basking in all this reward, Tom Thumb will donate a percentage of your annual grocery bill to your favorite charity.

On Tom Thumb's end, it looks like this. For starters, based on the data gathered from similar programs, the chain expects to increase its sales by ten percent. Further, they will be able to get up close and personal with their customers. Oh look, those newlyweds are having a baby. That didn't take long. Well, send them the Pampers coupons and the Gerber samples. Jones has been drinking again. Thirty percent off his next bottle of Jack Daniels. Let's see if he can find his way to the store.

Sinister? Probably not. Spooky? Definitely. I couldn't help but note that the president of the chain, Mark Prestige (seriously), goes out of his way to point out to the *News* that all this electronically stored and highly valuable information will be kept confidential and that Tom Thumb wouldn't think of selling it to anybody. Maybe not Tom, but one of his disgruntled Thumbsters perhaps?

My father showed me this article because he knew I'm up to my ears in all this Internet stuff, and the thought that came to my mind is that he recognized the connection probably more quickly than most people up to their ears in all this Internet stuff would. Many of us who all but live online may be all torn up by the most hotly debated and widely publicized privacy issues that the Net seems to have almost exclusively given rise to, but we stumble on through the pesky real world, leaving clumsy tracks and losing not a thought over anyone who might be interested in them.

Yes, we might go to the trouble of stripping our identities before browsing by stopping off first at http://www.anonymizer.com/, picking up a bit of encryption, or e-mailing Lexis-Nexis to tell them to get our names and numbers out of that P-TRAK database. But we tend to forget that information comes in all sorts of unexpected forms and can be extracted in ways we don't usually deem worthy of our conscious attention. Sometimes I wonder whether the most Net savvy of us overlook the proverbial forest while quibbling over the trees.

Which morsel of info on you has more value? That spicy PGP-mangled love note you sent to that special someone, or your pack-a-day smoking habit? Obviously, your insurance company couldn't care less about the note, but they might sit up and take notice of your purchasing habits. Which is more potentially incriminating—clicking a link to the leftist pub "Radikal" or dropping some cold hard cash at your local weapons retailer?

Where you drive or fly to, where and with whom you stay after you get there, the books you check out of the library, the magazines you subscribe to, the TV programs you watch—all of it is potentially storable information, and all of it is potentially valuable to someone somewhere. Little of it, I believe, is actually gathered in the interest of any sort of

Rewired

conspiratorial force, but rather, innocently made possible, step by step, by entities as innocuous as Tom Thumb who claim only to want to serve you better. Of course, though, they have their eyes on their own bottom line. Who could blame them for that?

Privacy is a frustrating quagmire, no matter what your political stripe. The right to know slams head on into the right to be left alone. But closing our eyes to wherever the issue may arise will have us sinking into that mire all the more quickly. My parents like Tom Thumb and they like to save money. But they haven't exactly leapt at that Reward card. As of this writing, they still haven't yet decided whether they will go for it or not. What price rugged individualism?

References Chapter Eighteen
Abstracts
Chapter Nineteen
Empowerment, Entertainment, or Enslavement?
Chapter Twenty
Hot Buttons and Slow Burners

"A.Word.A.Day—utopia," A.Word.A.Day Archives.
http://www.wordsmith.org/awad/

Barlow, John Perry. Quoted in Karrie Jacobs, "Utopia Redux," *Word*.
http://www.word.com/textword/machine/jacobs/index.html

Cover image.
http://pathfinder.com/time/magazine/domestic/covers/960916.covbus.jpg

Critical Art Ensemble, "Utopian Promises—Net Realities."
http://www.well.com/user/hlr/texts/utopiancrit.html

Ivins, Molly. Quote taken from Lynton C. and Joan Wiener, *The Best of Texas*, Peter
Pauper Press, Inc., 1993.

Johnson, Jeff. "The Information Hypeway: A Worst-Case Scenario."
http://www.1010.org/Dynamo1010.cgi/LiveFrom1010/team1/johnson.html

Katz, Jon. "Time Tells," Media Rant, *The Netizen*, September 11, 1996.
http://www.netizen.com/netizen/96/37/katz3a.html

Kline, David. "Silicon Valley's Dirty Little Secret," *Upside*, September 3, 1996.
http://www.upside.com/online/columns/netprofit/9609.html

Kroker, Arthur and Michael A. Weinstein. "The Theory of the Virtual Class," *Data Trash:
The Theory of the Virtual Class*, New York: St. Martin's Press, 1994.
http://www.ctheory.com/ga1.4-theory_virtual.html

McGovern, Gerry. "Digital Farming," *New Thinking*.
http://www.nua.ie/NewThinking/Archives/newthinking013/index.html

Radikal.
http://ourworld.compuserve.com/homepages/angela1/radilink.htm

Ramo, Joshua Cooper. "Winner Take All," *Time*, September 16, 1996 Volume 148, No. 13.
http://pathfinder.com/time/magazine/domestic/1996/960916/cover.html

Rebello, Kathy with Larry Armstrong, Amy Cortese, "Making Money on the Net,"
Business Week, September 23, 1996.
http://www.businessweek.com/1996/39/b34941.htm

Reichelt, Nico. Web page on the Telekommunikationsgesetz, Institute for New Media, Frankfurt.
http://www.inm.de/people/nico/tkg.html

Scene 63 from Poll. A screenplay by Chris Kraus, 1996. Translated from the original German by David Hudson. Reprinted with the author's permission.

Sclove, Richard E. and Steve Talbot. "A Quick Guide to the Politics of Cyberspace," *Netfuture*, Issues 6, 7, and 8, 1996.
http://www.ora.com/people/staff/stevet/netfuture/

Sclove, Richard E. *Democracy and Technology*, New York: Guilford Press, 1995.
http://www.amherst.edu/loka/sclove/toc.htm

Sclove, Richard E. "Town Meetings on Technology," *Technology Review*, MIT Press, July 1996.
http://web.mit.edu/afs/athena/org/t/techreview/www/articles/july96/sclove.html

Telepolis.
http://www.heise.de/tp

THOMAS.
http://thomas.loc.gov

Part V:

One Dark Future

"Look, the question is no longer what sort of statists we should be supporting: Republicans or Democrats, communists or fascists. The question really is what sort of libertarians we should be supporting. There is no alternative to a world that's out of control. Central power not only doesn't work, it is not even possible anymore."

Louis Rossetto

Chapter Twenty-One
"The Voice of the Digital Revolution"

"Look, the question is no longer what sort of statists we should be supporting: Republicans or Democrats, communists or fascists. The question really is what sort of libertarians we should be supporting. There is no alternative to a world that's out of control. Central power not only doesn't work, it is not even possible any more." That, in a nutshell, is the political philosophy and professed modus operandi of Louis Rossetto, co-founder and editor-in-chief of Wired magazine, chief spokesman for a strain of libertarianism that has sprung from a hybrid culture. This strain of libertarianism is a mutant cross between San Franciscan psychedelia—the ferocious entrepreneurial spirit (and its accompanying greed) of the 80s—and the massive wave of disenchantment with all things governmental that has swept through the 90s.

It is impossible to talk about the phenomenon of "techno" or "cyber" libertarianism without dragging Wired into the discussion. Hardly news to anyone with the even scantest familiarity with online culture. But even if you are pretty convinced that you couldn't care less, don't have a computer or any plans to get one, have never read Wired, or you're just plain sick to death of all that techno mumbo jumbo about some "digital revolution" going on, it is high time to sit up and pay attention.

As the global economy begins to quake, shift, and go online, the stakes are rising at lightning speed. "Who stands to gain and who will lose? How will power be distributed in the new order of things? Will existing sources of injustice be reduced or amplified? Will the promised democratization benefit the whole populace or just those who own the latest equipment? And who gets to decide?"

Langdon Winner posed these pertinent questions in "Peter Pan in Cyberspace: Wired Magazine's Political Vision," published in a 1995 *Educom Review* special edition about *Wired*. Winner, who teaches science and technology studies at Renssalear Polytechnic Institute in New York, concludes, "About these questions, *Wired* shows little awareness or concern."

Writer Paulina Borsook quite aptly articulated: Even if these questions don't matter to *Wired*, they matter to "what Apple Computer once disingenuously called 'the rest of us'." In a big way. Like it, love it, or hate it, online technology is about to become a very big deal in your life. The ongoing mating dance between the web and television has already spawned WebTV, with more media convergence to come. Your address, phone number, and maybe a lot more personal information than you may realize is already on the Internet. Even your bank is now zipping your financial stats (and soon, your money as well) along its private lines, little intranets sitting like so many packages under a Christmas tree—just waiting for some clever hacker to come along and unwrap them. It will be tough to get away from it all if you're the type to try. Just about every electronic appliance you touch throughout the course of the day is about to get wired. For everyone from Bill Gates to the CEO of a tiny start-up company running out of a garage to the guy just now trying to figure out where to stick that free America Online disk into his spanking-new computer—for everyone driven by the need or mere curiosity to keep track of how all this is coming along—*Wired* is indispensable. Period.

Wired's vision of the supposedly very near future and the readers it finds there, outlined in the interview with Rossetto that follows, is at times beautiful, at times strange, and so forward-looking as to be entirely out of touch with the realities of the present. In that future, parents must shop for whatever education they can afford for their kids, the minimum wage is banished along with every other labor protection law so sorely fought for, the environment is up for grabs to the highest bidder, and the top percentile prospers while the "losers" just flat out lose.

Wired has its critics, but even the harshest (for the most part) do not want to see this magazine fade away. Why? Because after nearly four years of publication, *Wired* is still the only periodical with the guts and the savvy to tackle the issues central to these rapid fire changes. MacThis and PCThat are selling computers. *Net.Guide*, *Internet World*, and that bunch are chock full of how-to hints and technology updates aimed at the casual user. *Upside* and *Red Herring* are business magazines. Of the online cultural magazines, *bOING bOING* is all but gone, and who knows what exactly happened to *Mondo 2000*. *Wired* covers the entire span of what it proclaims to be the "digital revolution,"—but digs deep—hiring some of the sharpest writers around and letting them run on for three, five, eight thousand words at a time, whatever it takes to get at the roots of a fully developed idea and get it across to its readers. Hacker culture, new media art, netrepreneur profiles, e-money, encryption, censorship, all of it!

When one nun whispers news of some techno-gadget to another in an IBM commercial and adds, "I read about it in *Wired*," the joke works. For one thing, it is the only geek magazine everyone in television has heard of; for another thing, *Wired* invokes just the right tinge of sin.

Educom Review editor John Gehl introduced the special edition of his magazine devoted almost exclusively to another one in an almost apologetic tone, informing readers that he has invited six prominent writers to expound on the pros and cons of *Wired*. He then signs off with, "Our next issue: back to normal." Lew Perelman was one of the invited, and in his "Weird, Feared, Revered?," he writes a few nice things, then a few not so nice things, and finally concludes, "But that's okay. Don't worry about it.

"IT'S ONLY A MAGAZINE."

Certainly a healthy dose of perspective.

When writer David Bennahum zapped over a point-by-point breakdown of the themes governing *Wired* via e-mail, he wrapped up: "And now a step back—who cares really? What on Earth are they, or me, yapping about."

But even stepping back for a good hard check with reality, we have to be careful not to step too far lest reality be left behind as well. Hitchcock may be famous for the remark, "It's only a movie," but he lived to make them (and not for much else). Books are only books, paintings only paintings, TV only TV. But books get banned, Congress gets worked up over the NEA, and the impact of television certainly needs no explication here. Culture, pop or otherwise, matters. "In 1985, we had 2,500 consumer magazines," notes Samir Husni, acting chairman of the University of Mississippi journalism department, in an interview with Bob Andelman (a.k.a. the web's "Mr. Media"). "Now we have 4,100."

What's the appeal? Any marketing director of any magazine could tick off a dozen reasons for the proliferation of and fondness for magazines. Identity would certainly rank way up there.

Magazines wrap up a world view and update it regularly. After finding one to subscribe to, you have got something to replace your face with on a crowded subway. A handful of titles have even become cultural artifacts. Like presidential campaigns or blockbuster movies, you can't escape them, and you sure don't have to subscribe to them to find yourself enmeshed over dinner in a lively discussion of such-and-such an article or the wandering editorial direction of one or another of the older institutions. "One tribute to the mark *Wired*'s made," Gehl points out, "is that it has received far more than a magazine's fair share of rants and raves."

Quite an accomplishment in a crowded market.

People love to complain about what Tina Brown has done to *The New Yorker*, but no one was talking about *The New Yorker* at all any more until she came along. Getting talked about is the first step toward getting a foothold on your corner of the cultural landscape. At the same time, there is a thin line to walk between getting talked about for the hell of it (à la Howard Stern) and getting talked about because you have something new, something eye-and-ear-catching to say—even better if it catches on and sticks.

Without a doubt, *Wired* fits into that second category. Sure, it *is* splashy and noisy, but there is definitely something behind the pizzazz to bite into and chew on. One of the ranters in the *Educom Review* special issue was author Mark Dery who, in "Unplugged," observes that some *Wired* critics slam it for being all fluff and no substance. "On the contrary, I would argue that *Wired*, far from being depthless, is dense with ideas. Indeed, it has become a bully pulpit for corporate futurists, laissez-faire evangelists, and prophets of privatization."

Chapter Twenty-Two
The Other L-Word

Although just about everyone has heard of *Wired*, seen it in the supermarket, or ever-so-casually tossed on the well-dressed coffee table, or found a copy lying dog-eared and abused on the floor of the college dorm lounge, far from everyone is aware that a ferocious struggle is going on. That struggle is all about how to get from the present to the future. And *Wired*, with all its ubiquity and influence, is sitting squarely on one side of the argument—the libertarian side. "Libertarian" is the other L-word. Frankly, it should be taken at this juncture a helluva lot more seriously than Republicans' pathetic revival of "liberal" as a stone to toss at Democrats.

"Libertarian" harks back to the seventeenth and eighteenth centuries, when the hottest debates were over religion. God is God, one side insisted. Humans have no control. All is predestined. The libertarians were the ones who argued, No, humans are blessed with free will to do as they please and to accept responsibility for their own actions. How far we've come in a couple of centuries. How did we get from that past to this present in which probably the most strategically placed libertarian of our time is the one arguing that we have no control? First, it should be noted that although Louis Rossetto is hardly a lone voice in cyberculture in his promotion of libertarianism, the term itself cuts a variety of ways. In his FAQ (Frequently Asked Questions) critiquing the movement, Mike Huben notes that the "two major flavors are anarcho-capitalists (who want to eliminate political governments) and minarchists (who want to minimize government).

"There are many more subtle flavorings, such as Austrian and Chicago economic schools, gold-bug, space cadets, Old-Right, paleo-libertarians, classical liberals, hard money, the Libertarian Party, influences from Ayn Rand, and others."

Kooky as many of these labels may be, the point is, plenty of them are out there—most of them well-versed in the ways of the Internet. Indeed, they saturate the Net, picking fights, propagandizing, and recruiting. As Mike Godwin, staff counsel for the Electronic Frontier Foundation, has written in *Wired*, "Libertarianism (pro, con, and internal faction fights) is the primordial net.news discussion topic. Anytime the debate shifts somewhere else, it must eventually return to this fuel source."

These UseNet tangos are not for the squeamish. Things can get really ugly really fast. To be fair, the same can be said of many online discussions on just about any topic (political or otherwise), but the hit-and-run nature of online discourse attracts these lone individualists disproportionately. A *Wall Street Journal/NBC News* poll reports that "Internet users are more Libertarian in thinking than non-users, not just on free speech online issues but also on topics unrelated to the Internet, like abortion." To anyone who has been out and about on the Net, the findings are hardly surprising. The poll found Net users to be more anti-minimum wage, pro-free global trade, and so on, and so forth.

Further, libertarians' Net know-how makes them keenly tuned in to the date, time, and "place" of the next clash. When the Markle Foundation and Crossover Technologies sponsored "Reinventing America," an online simulation game that had Net users collectively "rewrite" the federal budget, Crossover's president reported "a strong libertarian streak early on," before everybody else caught up and kicked some balance back into the make-believe budget. And when *Mother Jones* announced that Paulina Borsook, the author of the controversial essay "Cyberselfish," published in its July/August 96 issue, would appear in *MoJo Wire*, its online public forum, the "pro-individual rights" mailing list "Freematt's Alerts" got word out quickly. Borsook had been critical of libertarian leanings of Silicon Valley culture, and the word in short was: Go get her. They did. Bryan Griffin turned in a critique, "Comments from a Libertarian, Mistakes and Misleading Statements," that actually surpassed the length of the essay itself.

For fun evidently, *Mother Jones* conducted a series of online polls—one each week—during the 1996 election season. The mood, as you may remember, throughout that campaign could probably be summed up in a single word: Blah. For those who love to kick back and enjoy or even actively dive into the USA's quadrennial circus—those who look forward to it years ahead of time—it was hard in '96 not to think, "What a gyp!"

If the Republicans hadn't bumbled into their own version of the race the Democrats ran in 1984, we all could have had quite a blast. Although it is true that even in the tightest races the candidates rarely butt heads over real issues, when the ideological stakes are high (as they were in, say, 1980), pundits and spin-masters, husbands and wives, bartenders and hairdressers do lock horns. And it's great, great fun. Not this time.

So how do you liven up a political poll during one of the dullest races of the century? Humor helps. *Mother Jones* asked its polled to come up with a new slogan for Bob Dole, one he could remember, and then chose its top ten from the bunch. My favorite by far was number 3, submitted by John Gerardi: "You kids knock it off back there or I'll stop this country and you can all walk to the 21st century!!"

But at the same time, the numbers that turned up in answer to the more straightforward questions were not as amusing. No need to make a big deal out of this, but without a doubt, something was going on. First, to state the obvious, the results were a far cry from any sort of scientific slicing of the voting public. They didn't even reflect the online population. What they reflected were the leanings of around 480 people who stopped by *Mother Jones*'s *MoJo Wire* and had the free time and just the right what-the-hell attitude to click around a bit.

Looking back, it really doesn't mean much. But see whether these results don't raise an eyebrow or two on your face. The question, "If the elections were held today, and all these candidates had an equal chance of winning, who would you vote for?" drew these percentages: 32 percent for Harry Browne (Libertarian), 31 percent for Ralph Nader (Green Party), 25 percent for Bill Clinton (Democrat), 5 percent for Bob Dole (Republican), 3 percent for Ross Perot (Reform Party), 2 percent for (No Preference), 1.3 percent for Howard Phillips (U.S. Taxpayers Party), 1.3 percent for John Hagelin (Natural Law Party), and 0.4 percent for Lyndon Larouche (Democrat).

Browne and Nader: A landslide for radical change. Although Clinton, the candidate of change last time around, maintained the twenty point spread he was enjoying over Dole at the time, two out of three of the respondents wanted nothing to do with either of them.

More alarming is the choice of alternatives. Of the Nader supporters I had listened to (another highly unscientific sampling), most were liberals disenchanted with Clinton's recent lurch to the right, probably most blatantly signified by his signing on to welfare "reform." They turned to Nader and the Greens out of frustration, but didn't have much of an idea what Nader would actually do if he were elected. No one in their right mind saw that happening anyway, so it was a protest vote.

This is not meant to denigrate, by any means, those who know precisely what Nader's about and genuinely want him in there seeing to things or those who hoped to use their vote to plant the seeds for a vibrant Green Party in the future. But for the most part, it was a "none of the above" sort of sentiment that I was sensing among them.

Browne's supporters, on the other hand, knew very well what they were after. It comes as no surprise that they would race over to the nearest online poll and chalk up another one for the libertarian dream of voting the government right on outta here. The Net is top heavy with these dreamers. Times are good for the libertarians. All signs are pointing their way. While the Net continues to fill up with new users of blander political leanings, it's the independently minded, smart libertarian who already knows the way around and how to use that savvy to his or her advantage—and therefore, is most likely to get heard first.

Further, although Clinton occasionally put on progressive airs as the campaign itself progressed, he appeared more and more to be the embodiment of old school politics. He backed up his 21st century rhetoric with a reference or two to the Net during the televised debates without outlining how or why he sees it as a part of the future, much less the present. Granted, by the time his State of the Union speech rolled around in January '97, he was advocating Net literacy for all U.S. schoolkids, but the numbers and the specifics were conspicuously missing.

In mid-October of '96, though, the Net did show up on his agenda when he pledged $500 million to install what some call Internet II—a high-speed network linking a hundred universities and research institutions, the core of the original Net that has been frustrated by what high traffic has done to its privileged communications. In other words, Clinton came off looking as if he were throwing money at the Net. Not good. The money was good for the Net's infrastructure, of course, but everyone knew it wasn't his to throw. Worse, his pandering to the clearly descendent conservative ideology with his signing of the Communications Decency Act and his insistence on holding the key to everyone's encrypted lock only infuriated liberals and libertarians alike. In short, while the ascendant libertarians pointed to this sad excuse of an election as the last dying embers of electoral politics, Clinton was inadvertently fanning the flames.

The Libertarian Party claims to be the third largest political party in the U.S., and when Ross Perot takes the day off, that may well be true. But Rossetto and his fellow "technolibertarians" or "Cyber-Libertarians"—

the labels vary (we'll stick with "techno")—most likely don't give a flip. To this new breed of libertarian, electoral politics is already dead. The future is here. We are living in the 21st century.

Louis Rossetto has some very exciting things to say in the interview, and the "electoral politics is dead" schtick is certainly right in there among them. Just watching Bob Dole and Bill Clinton propped up like two stiffs behind their podiums to trudge through the charade of the televised "debates" in 1996 was more than enough inspiration to entertain the idea of what at times seems to be a long overdue funeral.

But Rossetto's usurper for the role electoral politics has played in democracies is network communications and, frankly, the Net didn't perform quite as expected in the election of 1996. As Tom Watson wrote on the "@NY" site, way-new media was supposed to usher in the age of way-new politics. Starting now. "The Net would help level the playing field, it was said, giving the voting public better access to candidates, and leading to an open and informed election the likes of which the Great Republic had never witnessed. The Presidential election would be a watershed event in the history of the new medium, proving its power and its worth as television had four decades before. Well, it didn't happen."

You would think that if it was going to, the 1996 election would have been a terrific time to start. After all, if there was ever a vacuum to be filled—an opportunity to jump-start radical democracy—this was it. As Rossetto explains, "[The] equation of democracy with electoral politics is entirely inappropriate now... People believe electoral politics is democracy because they have been brainwashed, period."

So, we won't have to go through charades like the one played out every four years for over two centuries ever again. On the one hand, that prospect is awfully tempting. It would certainly save us all bunches of money, money we now spend to be repeatedly insulted in 30- or 60-second jolts that interrupt our regularly scheduled daily dosage of televised sedation. Doing away with these pesky elections, chucking it all, and starting from scratch packs quite an emotionally appealing wallop.

But it is not entirely unproblematic, is it? For starters, we would have to scrap the U.S. Constitution. Not that that bothers anyone who would take way new democracy to its logical extreme. In fact, a rough cut of "The Netizen," *Wired*'s venture into way-old media, the final cut of which aired just days before the last election of the century (last ever?), treats the Constitution as a disposable beta version of something far better to come: namely, Constitution 2.0.

"This segment inspired my only strong content criticism regarding the first show," the EFF's Mike Godwin commented in his role as consultant for the program. "Specifically, it's built on the premise that the Constitution (and, by extension, laws in general) are inherently static and rigid and therefore eventually and necessarily obsolescent. In my experience, deep study of the Constitution reveals the opposite to be true. I believe I can demonstrate to just about anyone willing to read a few cases that in fact the Constitution is dynamic, constantly evolving, responsive in countless ways to social problems of the moment or of the decade."

In other (admittedly lesser) words, this sturdy little program is capable of updating itself, thanks. Before succumbing to the urge to tweak it out of existence, we had better have something pretty wonderful with which to replace it. So far, despite the ample opportunity, networked communications are not quite up to speed.

Before we do away with representative democracy and the U.S. Constitution, therefore, we had better have something really marvelous and really solid to put in place of it all. That something is very hard to pinpoint in all of Rossetto's exhilarating verbiage. It is tough to extract a clear picture of the future according to Louis Rossetto—what life is actually to be like on the streets, in the houses, condos, and apartment complexes where real people really live.

Chapter Twenty-Three
The Techno Elite

Louis Rossetto wrote in the very first issue of *Wired* that the magazine would be covering "social changes so profound their only parallel is probably the discovery of fire." As for the hyperbole, to sell his magazine, he has got to sell his revolution. "I do believe that being digital is positive. It can flatten organizations, globalize society, decentralize control, and help harmonize people..." Perhaps you recognize that voice from the first chapter. Nicholas Negroponte is not only the author of *Being Digital*, his back-page column is a standard feature of *Wired*.

When his column "Market Forces" was discontinued by "HotWired" shortly after his dissection of some of Negroponte's positions, Kline insisted over and again that the decision was not political—despite Negroponte's crucial role in the founding of *Wired*; when Rossetto and Metcalfe washed up in New York City, out of money and out of work, it was Negroponte who provided the funds to get them to San Francisco, hire a staff, and realize their vision.

One *Wired* insider claims that the column was cut because it wasn't performing, and no "meritocracy" will stand for low hit counts (that is, the number of times a web page is viewed). But Kline's got the numbers to prove he was coming in just a nose behind Ned Brainard's popular gossip column, "Flux." So, what happened? Kline suggests he was traded in for a bigger name, Michael Schrage, who has written for the likes of *The Wall Street Journal* and the *L.A. Times* and has worked, coincidentally enough, at the MIT Media Lab. But with a couple of *Wired* cover stories under his belt, an impressive résumé with other publications, and an excellent book co-written with Daniel Burstein, *Road Warriors: Dreams and Nightmares along the Information Highway*, Kline isn't exactly a lightweight. When Kline submitted an 8,000-word opus critiquing the right-wing elitism of such libertarian digerati as George Gilder (a buddy of Rossetto's), the piece was fine by Kevin Kelly. Rossetto tells his side of the story in the interview, yet rumors persist that he ditched Kline's piece, "Is Government Obsolete?" and then only grudgingly resurrected and eventually printed it in the January 1996 issue after editorial staffers complained about the silencing of divergent views in a magazine that purports to be the "voice of the digital generation."

If anything, mainstreamers Kline and Burstein's treatment of Gilder— who has definitely had his say in *Wired*'s pages—is fair. This is the author of *Wealth and Poverty*, after all, the supply-side wetdream of a book Reagan handed out to any White House visitor who would take it. Gilder is presented as "articulate," full of "unique insights," and possessed of "a gift for distilling complex technical issues into popular language." That "Gilder's powerful critique of outmoded, big-government, industrial-age thinking has thrust him into the spotlight as a leading voice in Newt Gingrich's inner sanctum of high-tech gurus" is just the facts, ma'am.

So why not go ahead and add, "To advocate replacing government today with some sort of marketocracy of the technologically enabled would, for starters, disenfranchise the 70 percent of Americans who don't own computers. It is precisely in such proposals that one can see the fundamental elitism of today's ultralibertarians."

It doesn't take a raving liberal to be alarmed at the widening gap between rich and poor in this country, no matter what sort of age we're entering. Just as Kline has written on how to make the Net a better place for business, so too, has he warned in *Upside*, for example, of the deteriorating state of affairs facing the footsoldiers of the digital revolution—the real workers of Silicon Valley.

"If I felt I had no part of the 21st century, I'd run out and start burning houses down," Kline says. "It's in no one's best interest to have that much cleavage between the two classes. Things are getting better for a minority, but worse for the majority." Maybe wiring the world can help. It all depends on how we go about it.

Chapter Twenty-Four
"The Californian Ideology"

As with political decision-making, when it comes to education, corporate monopolies, any specific law or institution, the role of government in general (of course), and even the Netscape/Microsoft browser wars, Rossetto's answer is, "Hands off!" There's an underlying, almost Zen-like passivity inherent in the idea that not only must we let the universe decide matters for us, we have no choice.

At the same time, *Wired*'s heroes, its road warriors, renegade hackers, sleepless entrepreneurs, and even Rossetto himself are hardly kicking back and going with the flow. The individual cells are hopping around, dividing like mad, driving lesser cells out of the petri dish, while the creature that comes of all this...well, who knows? The only guarantee is, it will be lovelier than any made by design.

With the "Utopia" chapter already read, you must have already realized that the biological metaphor is not accidental. Many of these ideas come from fellow *Wired* editor Kevin Kelly's book *Out of Control: The Rise of Neo-Biological Civilization*. As a quick refresher, writer David Bennahum sums up the implications of the argument this way: "We are ushering in a golden age, a 'digital nirvana' where the collapse of mind-body separation through the unification of binary 0-1 and biological A-G-C-T (DNA) will essentially bring us closer to God or its equivalent." And there's not a darn thing you can do about it.

It is an interesting formula, this cosmic Darwinism. Richard Barbrook, a founder of the Hypermedia Research Centre of the University of

Westminster in London, thinks it could only have come from California—specifically, the Bay Area. "This new faith has emerged from a bizarre fusion of the cultural bohemianism of San Francisco with the hi-tech industries of Silicon Valley...the Californian Ideology promiscuously combines the free-wheeling spirit of the hippies and the entrepreneurial zeal of the yuppies. This amalgamation of opposites has been achieved through a profound faith in the emancipatory potential of the new information technologies. In the digital utopia, everybody will be both hip and rich."

That excerpt comes from the provocatively named essay, "The Californian Ideology," which has been circulating in one form or another around the Net since 1995. Europeans in particular have picked up on the alert inherent in the piece, and the title has been tossed around in online arguments as an epithet standing for a lot more than Barbrook and his co-author Andy Cameron originally intended—from the use of the Net as a force for American cultural imperialism to a blunt insult akin to some dumb blonde joke.

In the spring of 1996, I was sitting at a cafe in Berlin, chatting with Pit Schultz, moderator of the excellent nettime mailing list. We covered a lot of ground, but my ear kept catching one phrase in particular time and again. Pit, who is as sharp and Net savvy as they come, perceived California—specifically San Francisco—pretty much as a colony of *Wired* and all it represents. I should say "perceived," because I set him straight (insert blinking emoticon here). He was quick to admit that (yes, the moment he gave it a second thought) it only makes sense that there would be a large number of detractors from the hard line and from what he constantly referred to as "The Californian Ideology." A lot of that detraction would naturally be based on sheer economics, the rest of it on common sense.

Thing is, wherever he is invited to speak on Net issues—Budapest or London, Trieste or Madrid—and whenever Pit and his fellow Euro Net Critics toss around the term, "The Californian Ideology," everyone knows exactly what is meant. The feeling of some sort of cultural clash between the U.S. and Europe on just what the Net is and what it is for, even among the two groups of Net enthusiasts, has always been around. In Europe, however, a name for "the other side" only jelled after Richard Barbrook and Andy Cameron gave it one.

Barbrook is terrific at detecting and dissecting cyberblather, and although I certainly had no bone to pick with his pinpointing and tearing into what he calls "The Californian Ideology" in terms of its politically offensive stance, I quibbled with him on the "Rewired" web site about the name. Barbrook summed up the gist of "The Californian Ideology" in a piece called "Hypermedia Freedom" for *CTHEORY*, an open-ended online publication edited by leftist cultural critics Arthur and Marilouise Kroker.

"The ideological bankruptcy of the West Coast libertarians derives from their historically inaccurate belief that cyberspace has been developed by the 'left-right fusion of free minds with free markets' (Louis Rossetto, editor-in-chief of *Wired* magazine)... [N]eo-liberalism has been embraced by the West Coast version of Kroker and Weinstein's 'virtual class' as a way of reconciling the anarchism of the New Left with the entrepreneurial zeal of the New Right."

The targets Barbrook is aiming at are right on; what needed to be cleared up in my mind is the "who" that is said to represent them. The "virtual class" may be a lot smaller and less influential in its hometown than it is generally thought to be elsewhere. This is not mere nit-picking. Barbrook is right to point to California (and specifically, Bay Area political history) and outline why this ideology couldn't have come about anywhere else. Indeed, a brief glance at the unique role San Francisco played in the Net's salad days turns up several interesting implications related to the real geography behind the curtain of virtual space.

The jamming of Silicon Valley, a thriving art scene, and a tradition of embracing The Next Big Thing turned it into the cultural HQ of the Net. HQ has since set up offices all over the place, but some oh-so-Northern-Californian ideas did feed into a sort of foundational, unwritten constitution of Net behavior while setting the tone for what the Net was supposed to represent—spoken of in the early days (and still is in some corners) in nothing less than cosmic terms.

Had "The Well," *Wired*, much of the Electronic Frontier Foundation, and so forth all been happening in New York or Los Angeles or Washington back then, the Net as a whole would have had a very different flavor indeed. You can argue that all that is over. With the rampant commercialization or even the very globalization of the Net this set of ideas called for, all innocence has been lost. But we are all marked by our births, even abstract entities such as nations and networks.

The bone I do have to pick with the title has to do with the construction of a legitimate argument that in turn is put to use in the second half of the essay to put forward Barbrook's agenda for a European policy designed to counter what ultimately boils down to more American cultural imperialism—which is another subject altogether. For now, however, let this suffice: Europe could kick ass on the Net (you want culture? we got culture!), but instead, it is sitting on its own.

It should be stated as a minor footnote that besides the several active and activist networks engaged in direct online combat with "the entrepreneurial zeal of the New Right," AlterNet (to name just one), besides the lively and vibrant virtual communities thriving on BBS's that are anything but "The Well" and bustling with a population derived from anywhere but the "virtual class," the San Francisco Bay Guardian Online (to name just one again), the Bay Area is chock full of organizations, groups, and colorful individuals, online and off, struggling to make ends meet and to make it easier for others to as well. And charged with very other Californian ideologies.

"Okay, it was a bit slack of us to lump all Californians together," Barbrook admits in a post to the "Rewired" site in response to my critique. But Barbrook and Cameron had heard enough loose talk from their friends and associates who "as usual" had not "been slow in copying the latest fad from America." They hadn't thought things through.

"As normally sane Europeans, they wouldn't believe that, for example, deregulation and privatisation were the best way to run our health service. Yet, because they were regularly reading *Wired*, they accepted that [laissez-faire] policies would inevitably triumph in the process of digital convergence." What Barbrook and Cameron were after was to show that "a contradictory mix of technological determinism and libertarian individualism" was rapidly and unquestioningly becoming "the hybrid orthodoxy of the information age." Voilá! An ideology—à la California.

The essay is not without its problematic moments. Barbrook has admitted that proposing the French Minitel system as an example of positive state action in the field of telecommunications was unfortunate. Louis Rossetto was quick to spot the loophole in the argument and fired off a response which, in what Barbrook notes, is a "rather hysterical tone." Rossetto slams the author not only on this, but on many other points as well, expanding into a continent-wide rant on the way Europeans run their affairs in general.

How much personal history informs this rant is impossible to say, but it is interesting to note that Rossetto and his partner Jane Metcalfe did work on getting a publication called *Electric Word* going in Amsterdam. It never really took off, went bankrupt. When they moved the redesigned project to San Francisco, however, boom.

Nevertheless, objections to the Californian tag on this ideology persist. Mark Stahlman, a former Wall Street analyst and current president of the New York New Media Association, wrote something of a reply to Barbrook and Cameron in an essay entitled, "The English Ideology and Wired Magazine," which ran on the "Rewired" web site and the nettime mailing list in November 1996. Stahlman traces not only libertarianism but the specific brand of cyberlibertarianism back to Barbrook's home turf.

"*Wired* magazine is not an American institution, nor is it even distinctly Californian (although its association with San Francisco is certainly undeniable). And its ideology is also not nearly as novel as Barbrook/Cameron and some other European commentators seem to suggest—although, arguably, it is appearing in a new and, therefore, potentially confusing form. Each of the magazine's elements, including free-market economics, hedonic lifestyle, techno-utopianism and, crucially, complete disdain for the uniqueness of human consciousness are all specifically and historically English."

Needless to say, the essay raised several eyebrows and more than a few guffaws across the cybercultural landscape. In short, it was ripped to shreds and strewn across online forums ranging from "The Well" to the "Rewired" conference board, from nettime to Electric Minds. Stahlman himself is an intriguing figure who can be soft-spoken and generous one moment, and then seemingly rash and cruel the next, especially when criticized. Although many are quick to dismiss him altogether, others spot flashes of insight here and there in his entangled prose and are intrigued enough to investigate further. After all, Mark Stahlman has hobnobbed with many of the figures mentioned in this book as well as several others who have made significant marks for themselves in a wide variety of fields—as he is often quick to point out.

In "The English Ideology," Stahlman traces the history of *Wired*, assigning an even more significant role to "Anglophile" Negroponte than other *Wired* histories have. Many suspect that Stahlman's near-obsession with England and its influence is rooted in his earlier flirtation (and again, personal confrontation) with Lyndon LaRouche, to whom many attribute off-the-wall conspiracy theories that would put Oliver Stone to shame. So when he examines the financial relationship between *Wired* and the Global Business Network, the philosophical relationship between this whole crowd and the tenets of the major thinkers of the British Enlightenment-era thinkers is a natural next step.

Indeed, the Information Age would be more appropriately named the New Dark Age, Stahlman says. It is *Wired*'s ties to this imminent future (and its English origins) that Stahlman aims to outline. *Wired*, he says, is designed to propagate the "optimism meme," that is, to make us feel good about the "digital revolution," even if the social upheaval this revolution would bring about would throw most of us into anxiety-ridden chaos and poverty.

Richard Barbrook agrees that the U.S. form of libertarianism is derived from classical liberalism, and that (sure) many of those classical liberals were English. But he pretty much stops right there, claiming Stahlman utterly miscasts the roles of H. G. Wells and Frederick Hayek, for example, in the grand scheme of things.

More immediate objections to "The Californian Ideology" have been raised by writer and occasional *Village Voice* contributor Mitchell Halberstadt. "When you refer to the Californian Ideology as a 'bizarre hybrid'," Halberstadt writes to Barbrook, "I still must question whether this is a deliberate libel, or the result of a genuine misunderstanding of the American counterculture. Much has been written on both the local and more general relationship (as well as disparity) between the New Left and counterculture."

To which Barbrook replies, "Within the Bay Area, the differences might have seemed to be very great, but, from the outside, they both seem very distinct from Social Democratic or Leninist forms of leftism." Halberstadt: "Within America! Here, the differences between New and Old Left (which narrowed as time went by) seemed relatively parochial leftist concerns, while the counterculture itself seemed to be 'quintessentially American,' in the tradition of Walt Whitman."

And when one reader of the *San Francisco Bay Guardian*'s cover story of November 6, 1996, "Digital Dark Ages," saw Barbrook and Cameron's remarks, he just about flipped his lid. Writing on the *Guardian*'s online service, he asks, "Yuppies and hippies are the same people. That's what's wrong with them—they're insular, spoiled brats that can only see what's in front of them. Last year it was getting stoned, this year it's making money. Why do you think that the two most monstrous and self-destructive initiatives on the state ballot this year—[Prop.] 209 [banning affirmative action in public education, employment, and contracting] and [Prop.] 215 [legalizing the medicinal use of marijuana]—passed with significant majorities? Because the majority of California voters are white baby boomers—self-centered, money-grubbing NIMBYS. They're your parents, and they're real assholes."

His personal opinion on Proposition 215 aside, he has got a point. The freewheeling hippiocity and freewheeling "entrepreneurial zeal," as Barbrook and Cameron put it, are very closely related. They are not opposites, not any more. But what Barbrook and Cameron mostly likely had in mind is that they once were (at least culturally, if not politically). Todd Gitlin's excellent book, *The Sixties: Years of Hope Days of Rage*, has a sort of sad chapter toward the end about that decade melding into the Me Decade, the 70s. Here's where a bit of historical probing would be in order to try to figure out how "let's get stoned" turned into "let's get rich."

This angry reader asserts that this generation was selfish from the get go. But it is hard to generalize. Possibly, the activists of the New Left for the most part have remained liberal while the hippies and yuppies, who were always butting heads with their political partners in revolution, are either now as destitute as Mannie the Hippie or running sleek businesses and preparing for a very comfy retirement.

The linkage of the two California propositions, however, is right on target. On Thursday, November 14, 1996, John Heilemann wrote in his "Impolitic" column for *HotWired*, in an article entitled "Westerly Winds," the following:

"...although the CCRI [Prop. 209] was backed most ardently by 'conservatives' and Prop. 215 was backed most ardently by 'liberals,' the two initiatives actually didn't fall neatly into either category. In truth, both were basically (if unwittingly) rooted in a common world view: libertarianism. Indeed, the statistic I'd most like to know coming out of this election is how many people voted in favor of both; I suspect the figure is surprisingly large."

Agreed. This opinion was expressed in one form or another all over the Net during the run-up to the election: Out with quotas, in with pot. Libertarians are not conservatives, despite the appeal of renegade critic Bob Black's assessment of them as "Republicans on drugs." More powerfully, libertarians are in a position to capitalize on the disgruntlement of the public and open the door to what seems to be a very enticing set of politics—that is, no politics at all, or as *Wired* likes to put it, "post-politics." The '92 election was supposed to have been about "Change" and the '94 election about "Revolution."

Hardly. Both were all about throwing the bums out, regardless of their political stripe. The only reason the voting public went for more of the same in '96 is that the economy was supposedly running along relatively well, Dole offered nothing to catch the interest of anyone, and Gingrich had been making a fool of himself for two years.

The well-taken central point of Heilemann's column is that in 1996 the action was in the state and local elections. And what happened in California is eye-opening. As he concludes, "California, of course, has always nurtured a strong strain of libertarianism—and so maybe the results aren't so contradictory after all. The question is whether, if both these initiatives are replicated in other states, it's a sign that libertarianism is on the march as well."

And we all know the old adage, "As goes California, so goes the nation." This is the nerve that Barbrook and Cameron struck with their essay, or more to the point, with their title alone. Further, they saw that it is next to impossible to talk about *Wired* without bringing both California and the 60s into the conversation. This was reiterated by Paul Keegan in a cover story for *Upside* magazine profiling Louis Rossetto. Keegan notes, "If *Wired* is about youth culture at all, it's about '60s youth culture...

"To be sure, this 'digerati' class emerged from a narrow slice of '60s counterculture: libertarian technophiles whose idea of expanding consciousness and doing their own thing meant starting a computer company.

"By making itself the mouthpiece of the digital revolution," Keegan continues, "Wired Ventures has tapped into a virulent strain of libertarian capitalism pervasive among the computer industry's movers and shakers, many of whom believe this new technology can be a tool for transforming society (to say nothing of their investment portfolios). As a child of the '60s, Rossetto seems to share those convictions, but with one caveat— libertarians are not extreme enough."

Plain vanilla libertarianism, that is. The kind that goes to the trouble of laying out a program addressing contemporary issues and running candidates for office in the hope of seeing that program implemented. Whatever the origins of this new set of beliefs regarding this sort of old-fashioned electoral politics "not extreme enough," and whatever we end up calling it, "cyberlibertarianism" has a foothold on what has often been the first stepping stone toward a genuine national movement, California.

Whether it succeeds is an open question, of course. But the most dangerous choice we could make at this juncture would be to ignore it.

Chapter Twenty-Five
Isn't It Ironic?

Barbrook's proposed alternatives may not be everybody's cup of tea. Although Barbrook remains a steadfast Euro Social Democrat, many critics of libertarianism wouldn't go that far. There is a delicate balance to be achieved, and *Wired* is pushing on the wrong end of it. Even as the government in the U.S. has been turned into "a sycophantic lap dog by corporate power," the "Tofflerist-Gingrichist alliance" (*Wired* has not only celebrated Alvin Toffler, author of *The Third Wave*, and Gingrich in its pages, but has also contributed to the Progress and Freedom Foundation—Newt's unofficial think tank) is revving up the rhetoric machine, calling for a more individualist streak in an already polarized society.

For Dery, all this "is really a very transparent thread-bare blind for, on the one hand, utterly unraveling the social safety net...and simultaneously...dismantling the rickety framework of the nation state that even now only just constrains corporate power to clear the way for transnational media monoliths whose power is utterly unconstrained and answerable to no one."

Louis Rossetto just might like a part of that diagnosis—the unconstrained part. Constraint is what the nineteenth century was all about. Notice how often it pops up as the ultimate barb throughout his comments, almost always contrasted to the twenty-first century, which is to be all about out-of-control freedom from constraint. Notice, too, the missing link, the dog that didn't bark in the night.

Except for a few moments plucked from it to prove a point, the twentieth century (and it has been a big one) is all but ignored—maybe for perfectly legitimate reasons. Looking at the big picture, we could be seen to be moving from the industrial era as defined by the nineteenth century directly into the twenty-first, a post-industrial information age. That is certainly the way Toffler sees it: from the Second to the Third Wave. Thinking in vast, bold strokes is more or less part of a magazine editor's job. But it is also hard to fight the suspicion that Rossetto would like to conveniently forget a lot about the twentieth century. Take this remark from the interview, "The Net was never in anyone's control." Astounding.

It was, after all, the U.S. Defense Department (specifically, ARPA), that built the Internet, eventually turning it over to the National Science Foundation, which ran it for years, pouring oodles of money into it, setting standards and what not. What's more, when the government no longer saw a need to stay involved, it pulled out. To this day, entities still oversee the little that needs attention, but someone has to do it. At the end of September 1996, representatives of the Internet Society, the International Telecommunication Union, and the World Intellectual Property Organization got together in Washington to try to figure out how to go on handling the registration process for assigning Internet domain names.

Technolibertarians love to envision the Net as the perfect model of anarchy that works. Technically, they have a lot of points in their favor, and if no humans ever plugged into it, it would be a very sleek beast indeed. But they do, and the Net is becoming less and less anarchic with each passing day and resembling much more the not-so-pretty picture of the real, 3D world most people hang out in.

Barbrook notes an eerie irony to all this. "One of the weirdest things about the Californian Ideology is that the West Coast itself is a creation of massive state intervention. Government dollars were used to build the irrigation systems, highways, schools, universities, and other infrastructural projects which make the good life possible. On top of these public subsidies, the West Coast hi-tech industrial complex has been feasting off the fattest pork barrel in history for decades."

This is the very irony central to Paulina Borsook's "Cyberselfish," the essay that had libertarians jettisoning alerts to each other. Borsook grew up in California in a culture that appreciated what government had done for it, "from the GI Bill to interest deductions for home mortgages to the vast expansion of government funding for R&D—they felt society in general, as manifested in the actions of the government, had an obligation to help everyone in it."

But then she took up work in Silicon Valley in the 80s—a different culture altogether. On social issues, the people of the culture there bore all the good liberal credentials she had expected, but when it came to the role of government, no dice. Worse, she discovered it was not just a Valley thing. She found herself butting heads with libertarians on "The Well," "smack in the middle of tree-hugging, bleeding-heart-liberal, secular-humanist Northern California."

What makes Borsook's essay click on a level different from, say, Barbrook's, are the hardcore examples, the details that concretize the issues at stake in this debate. Example: She describes a week at the Lake Tahoe getaway of a successful "Silicon Valley guy." They argue politely, and when she scores a point, she allows it to reverberate in real time and space.

"I was also thinking about the fine system of interstate highways that made his trip from Silicon Valley to the Sierra a breeze; the sewage and water-treatment facilities that allowed his toddlers to drink safely out of the tap in his kitchen; the fabric contents-and-care labels on the sheets and towels freshly laundered for each new house guest; and the environmental regulations that keep Tahoe the uniquely blue, gorgeous, and safe refuge it is—precisely the lateral, invisible, benign effects of the government he constantly railed against."

Borsook is just as precise when she ticks off examples of her accusation that technolibertarians are "violently lacking in compassion," pointing out friends and relatives who, despite their considerable talents and education, despite their persistent get-up-and-go, are not finding steady work in this downsized society—real people, in other words, who are already getting left out of the digital revolution.

In August 1996, I interviewed Borsook for "Rewired." Almost from the moment it went up on the site, a bizarre chain of events was set in motion. Yet a full picture of what we will be talking about once we get there is nearly impossible without a look at what exactly was said and posted. Herewith, Paulina Borsook, unplugged.

"Just as 19th-century timber and cattle and mining robber barons made their fortunes from public resources, so are technolibertarians creaming the profits from public resources— from the orderly society that has resulted from the wise use of regulation and public spending. And they have neither the wisdom nor the manners nor the mindset to give anything that's not electronic back."

Paulina Borsook

Chapter Twenty-Six

The "Rewired" Interview with Paulina Borsook

(Part I)

Suddenly This Summer

July. A cryptic e-mail from a friend: "Check out this essay." An URL. And that was it. Doesn't get much more urgent than that. I clicked and found myself at...*Mother Jones*? Goodness, I hadn't even thought about them in years. As it turns out, I have been missing out on a much better magazine than the one I gave up on some time ago, but that's another story.

The real story was the essay in front of my face. It is not a grab-you-by-the-lapels piece. The first couple of paragraphs establish a set of well-informed liberal credentials, sort of warming up to the audience, and then spices the résumé with dates and encapsulated job descriptions from over a decade of time served in "the culture of Silicon Valley." And then the punch is thrown:

"Although the technologists I encountered there were the liberals on social issues I would have expected (pro-choice, as far as abortion; pro-diversity, as far as domestic partner benefits; inclined to sanction the occasional use of recreational drugs), they were violently lacking in compassion, ravingly anti-government, and tremendously opposed to regulation."

Whoa! Look where we're going. It wasn't the last time I would blurt out Whoa! before I hit the double-whammy of the last two sentences:

"Just as 19th-century timber and cattle and mining robber barons made their fortunes from public resources, so are technolibertarians creaming the profits from public resources—from the orderly society that has resulted from the wise use of regulation and public spending. And they have neither the wisdom nor the manners nor the mindset to give anything that's not electronic back."

The essay, of course, is "Cyberselfish" and the writer is Paulina Borsook. I zapped a reply to my friend immediately. It is not just that she has taken on the libertarians, nor that she does such a fine job of it by focusing on the essential irony of their position. It is that she's doing it in a forum that not only is not as hopeless as UseNet, for example—where liberals and libertarians have been bashing each other for years—it isn't *Wired* or *Boardwatch* or *Red Herring* or some such either.

She has barged straight into the heart of a complacent moderate-to-left establishment—not to preach to the converted, but to trip their wires. *Mother Jones* may have a web site, and old school card-carrying Democrats may rest assured that Net-savvy Al Gore will take care of whatever comes up, but few, sadly few, are aware that the ghost in the machines that they are trusting to bring about a new age in democracy has been spouting off views that would be an anathema to the most centrist among them.

August. A transatlantic call to Paulina Borsook. No, it turns out, *Mother Jones* didn't really have any idea what she was getting at. And this after shopping it around for nearly a year as a book in New York. "I didn't used to believe in the liberal east coast media establishment, but now I do," she says in parentheses. Yes, you can hear the parentheses.

Paulina Borsook is not just a helluva writer, she is a helluva talker as well—not just in terms of the range of ideas, the sensibility steeped in issues as geeky as the IETF, as arcane as intellectual property rights, as pop as TV. That didn't surprise me. What surprised me was the sheer word-happy speed of the aural deluge.

And I had half-expected to have to coax a few usable quotes out of a lone warrior, exhausted after a week of fending off sniper fire from libertarians at the *MoJo* site followed by another at "Brain Tennis." After all, via e-mail she had referred to the call as "...a break from being screamed at by extroprians and libertarians. i do -not- take well to being misconstrued, being attacked for what i didnt say nor for positions i dont hold — nor ad hominem attacks in general. sigh..."

But no, Paulina is juiced. I don't mind admitting she pretty much left me eating her dust. She is so damn fun to listen to, I would keep forgetting it was actually my job to propel the conversation. I had already ditched my list of questions and could just as well have scratched out each one and scribbled in its place, "Go on, please...don't mind me..."

At any rate, for the longest time, no one was interested in doing the book that eventually became "Cyberselfish." But someone on the *MoJo* staff clued in the others. Instead of doing an excerpt from the proposed book, how about an essay. Finally, an outlet. "So I'm not doing this to capitalize on a trend, it's something I have been pursuing for a long time. It takes a while for whoever sanctions these things to catch up. I wasn't thinking, 'Oh, gee, libertarians are fashionable, I should write about them.' It's just that it's something I have been observing for a very long time—and it matters."

It does. Just about every mailing list or BBS I pay any attention to got word out. I saw libertarians put out the call to go dis Paulina Borsook at "MoJo Wire," liberals actually relieved that finally someone had given a voice to a creepy feeling they'd had while wandering the online landscape. A friend dumped a 50 K file of argumentation the essay had sparked in my mailbox. Europeans, baffled and put off by the ruthless meanness of the industry, alerted each other to the new insight into the sick creature inhabiting at least one nook of the American mind.

I saw more "Check out this essay" e-mail fly than I had since John Perry Barlow declared cyberspace an independent...whatever. Suddenly, Paulina Borsook, who has been working at it for years, is hot. When I got to her, she had just wrapped up a session with *The Wall Street Journal*. Hell, there's even a fan club. And now the book will be done after all. *The Deadly Embrace* is the tentative title and HardWired Books is doing it. Isn't that, you know, as the song goes, a little ironic? After all, what entity online or off could have done more for the cause of libertarianism?

"What do you mean, how much *Wired*'s shaped the terms of the debate?" There we go. "I think *Wired* is reflecting what's out there. In other words, if they are celebrating the Gilders—the worst of them—they're doing their job. They've got a good gut instinct about who the creature is. I don't know why *Wired* chooses these people, but I think it just externalizes what they feel about it." Indeed.

"And you know, I've heard horror stories..." And she goes through a few: The scene after Jon Katz's review was killed by Kevin Kelly, the ones she touches on in wired_women. "So there is this thing about how they have their worldview, or actually religion. 'Don't contradict with facts, please.' But you know, they have their point of view, as does *National Review* or *Details* or anybody else, and that's what people are buying."

Of course, another thing they have—and keep—is Paulina Borsook. Plus, they have tolerated Katz's rants, Heilemann's near-endorsement of the Techno-Communitarians (a hilarious name—I keep expecting to hear a Westbam remix of the Internationale)... What gives?

"Good question. You know, it's really funny, because Louis [Rossetto] wants me to keep writing for them which is kind of strange." Her agent, who has been given pretty much whatever he wanted, made the remark, "'What, did Louis have a spiritual awakening? What's going on over there?' 'Cause it's certainly never been like that in the past, so maybe they are changing somewhat." Hey, it could happen. "I don't know why I have a place in this organization, I don't quite understand it, and there are other people that Louis has been far meaner to, or far more vindictive to, or pronounced an anathema on or has said, 'Traitor! I never want to see you again' or... It's a mystery to me. You tell me why."

Well, the word "token" comes to mind, as in "Wired's token feminist/humanist/luddite/skeptic." She's chosen it herself as the one-line intro to nearly every online appearance she makes. The words between the slashes change occasionally, but "token" is always there.

"Well, the 'token' thing is interesting. There are more women who write for the magazine now than there were when I was there the first year. That's really just a gender thing, and that's better now. The 'token' thing is kind of sarcastic. The sensibility that I have is not one that is very representative of the magazine. I think, though, that it's sort of the sensibility that a lot of the people who work for the magazine have. Which is that, you know, we think that technology is a good thing but it has its downside. In other words, I think I represent a lot of people who, say, work in South Park or a bunch of other places who just don't get heard."

No, they don't. "When I first started writing for them, they really didn't understand who I was, I didn't really understand who they were, and then about a year into it, to our horror, we both realized who each other was. What were we going to do?" [Laughter all around.]

"And when I really got fed up with them, you know, when I wrote my feminist rant about Wired, actually things were far worse than what I put into that essay. And there were things going on there that were making me so angry, that were so humiliating to me that I didn't want to write for them any more. It's been interesting. They have apologized and done everything they can to bring me back, you know, 'We want to keep you here,' and it's weird—I cannot get away from Wired. There's "Suck," there's HardWired with the book contract, there's this "Brain Tennis" thing... It's not false modesty. I don't completely understand how it happened."

Maybe it helps them bring their own views into greater relief? "Maybe." The only one-word answer of the whole chat, the only awkward silence, the only time I scrambled for the list of questions I had scratched. Because in the long run, in the grand scheme of things, who cares? Magazines come and go, and those who run them are all but expected to act according to stereotype. Far more to the point would be the political movement she has set out to dissect, the one that stands a genuine chance of shaping both the near and distant future. This would be the meat of the talk, the part that had me listening most keenly and Paulina talking faster than ought to be humanly possible. And a note to libertarians: Paulina Borsook takes you a lot more seriously and is a lot more willing to listen—as long as you don't scream— than you may imagine.

(Part II)

Because It Really, Really, Really, Really Matters

"Did you see that movie called *I Shot Andy Warhol*?"

Nope. Hasn't made it to Berlin yet. This is the second movie Paulina Borsook has brought up in our phone call. Not insignificant, I think, and not just because I'm nuts myself about movies and Andy Warhol. Fluent as she is in techspeak, Paulina Borsook doesn't approach the Net within the vacuum of its own culture. Although the cyberlibertarians will often— not always, but often—come at you brandishing "logic," which is of course vital, they sometimes come off sounding as if they were speaking from inside the very machines they are tinkering on. Paulina Borsook is able to step outside, where the logic of reality is a lot fuzzier, look back in, and make the sort of connections that make deep sense to the living, but which no system of binary switches could ever stumble over. Like this one.

"It's an excellent movie and it's one of the few movies I've ever seen that gets the 60s right as I remember them. I remember watching the movie and thinking that back then when I was a kid—and I was a hippie, you know, or whatever—being a little fascinated with the whole Warhol subculture, what little I knew of it. Because I had a sense that even though it was scary and hostile and inimical to my way of being and inhospitable to who I was as a creature, and a whole bunch of other things, that it was nonetheless fascinating."

Flying in the face of natural law, Paulina's words actually pick up in pace and vigor. "And I also had a sense that this really, really, really, really matters. This really, really matters. There's something new here that I haven't seen before. And a lot of the things that spun out of that scene, a certain kind of cynical commodification of self, the way certain kinds of elements in gay culture would come to matter more and more in the rest of our cultural life—a lot of things spun out of there which are in their way as important or more important than what the counterculture was about."

Kids, those of you so young as to lump Warhol's Factory and flower power in one great ash heap of 60s history may need to be reminded that a cultural war was going on between the two camps that would have made Pat Buchanan blush. To bring it way down to our own ho-hum decade, imagine Eddie Vedder and RuPaul in the same room; maybe that helps, maybe not. "Well, I hadn't realized this until I saw the *I Shot Andy Warhol* movie, but I'm having the same experience thirty years later with libertarians. They scare the hell out of me. They really do. Yet I know that they really matter and there's that kind of intellectual view here that I think will matter culturally all over the place. And I need to understand it and borrow what's good from it, or at least get a better system of antibodies prepared against it. I feel that very strongly."

Now, libertarians, listen up, because Paulina Borsook is fully aware that "there are some really smart people with some interesting ideas in that community, and it's not intellectually as—not bankrupt, but exhausted the way our leftist community is. And again, I think most of them are insane, but there's something interesting there that's worth listening to or looking at or thinking about. It makes you think, What are my values and what do I think matters?"

She knows the territory and has even plucked a few of its fruits. "I do believe in the law of unintended effects," that government sometimes, and maybe even often, screws up its own best intentions. And get this: "I tend to call myself a 'left libertarian.'" Hmm.

"So that's the foundation of my book," due in the Fall of '97. "You can't just go on and yell about them. It's not that simple. You have to ask, Why does it matter? What is it they're sort of an antidote to in our culture and why did they come about in the first place?"

I wonder out loud about the non-libertarian (or maybe unconsciously libertarian) anti-government wave so many congressional freshmen capitalized on in the '94 elections. If libertarians tap into these general, more emotional strains, could this set of ideas be corrupted by them?

"You know, that's interesting, because I think for a lot of people, CDA was a watershed. Because I think a lot of libertarians were horrified to see that a lot of these Republicans that they felt they could be for and held common cause with sold them out on CDA.

"And there's another interesting idea there. Someone suggested to me, and I don't think it's so far off, that it was a really interesting move getting all the civil libertarians much more in a lather about CDA as opposed to paying attention to how telecom deregulation—the same bill—are basically allowing a total deregulatory feeding frenzy for the big bad communications companies which may really screw up consumers and businesses because we don't have freedom of choice. Big business is taking everything over, so you're really screwed. So in a sense, it deflected a lot of political energy onto something that was guaranteed to get a lot of people riled up, but it's defeating the main issue which is the economic one."

Then again, "some libertarians will stay out of government, they'll say that they don't act or vote or do anything anyway. I don't know how much say they will have in American electoral politics." The mere mention of American electoral politics sets her off on another tangent.

Researching her book, preparing for a trip back east, "I was just calling around, mostly in New York and Washington, asking, you know, are there any policy wonks or analysts or interesting people I should talk to. And much to my surprise, no one in Washington gets it. Whereas I did find some people in Boston.

"But it's amazing. I have a cousin who's been active for a long time in the Democratic Party. He's a really smart guy, but he doesn't know anything about any of this, and when I asked him, 'Who can you, of all the people you know in Washington, and you've been there for 15 years, who do you know who would be useful to talk to, who understands libertarianism and American life, and in particular has some understanding of technology culture.' And he could think of nobody. Which is not a reflection on him; what it says is that people in Washington aren't thinking about this stuff."

Big difference between having a web site and an e-mail address and "getting it." Has she seen that article... oh, what was it... (later I checked my notes: Ronald Brownstein's "Rage Against the Machine")...that article pitting the "Cyber-Libertarians" against the "Techno-Communitarians?"

"Oh, that's *Fast Company*." Right. "Right. Everyone has been talking about that article. Yes, a bunch of *LA Times* reporters and they're hopping on this a little late. I thought it was okay, but as usual, I thought it was superficial, and again, I felt that the polarity set up isn't real in that tech and Net culture is so heavily weighted toward the libertarians, and there are so few lefties, or whatever communitarians are going to call themselves, and they generally tend to be so clueless about technology that it's not a fair fight."

Example: She was invited to the First Congress on Media and Democracy and what she saw there was a bit disturbing. "They asked me to be one of their online media activists, which is a joke, because you know I'm not an activist." I laughed, but I also knew she may be having more of an effect, positioned where she is, doing what she does best. "I was appalled that here were all these self-serious, well-meaning lefty people who thought of themselves as online media activists but they hadn't heard about 24 Hours of Democracy, and I'm thinking, Excuse me? Who are you talking to?" After realizing who *she* was talking to, she figured a little net.culture 101 was in order. She told them "the dominant issue and culture of the Net is libertarianism, but there are many issues that we on the whatever you want to call it, the lefty side, can find common cause with, and if we can link with these people on the areas that we do have commonality with, then we can engage their support on some of the other stuff, which is maybe more important to us.

"But if you cannot meet them on what is most important to them, which is crypto, privacy and freedom of speech, they're not going to listen to you.

"And they were sort of like, 'Who invited her here?! Get her out of the room!' Again, I was struck with the left talking to itself and how it doesn't understand many of these issues. Whereas, I'll give it to the libertarians. They understand that culture a lot better. So, it's not a fair fight, I think, between the 'Techno-Communitarians' and the 'Cyber-Libertarians' because there's so much more power and juice on the side of the libertarians." Instead of punctuating her sentences with full stops, Paulina jabs those in-between spaces with questions: "Does that answer your question?" "Is this what you're after?" "What are you looking for?"

I tell you what I'm really looking for—a real cool word for moderate. Not utopian, not luddite... "Well, see I don't like that word either. One of the reasons I'm using [luddite] myself is because we don't have a good word for someone who thinks that technology can be fine but who also sees its downside and is critical of it. We don't have a word for that. And it's too often called luddite, and if you come up with a word I'll grab it and steal it from you!"

I'm working on it. "Moderate" is clearly asking for trouble, too milquetoast. I would like to get "realism" in there some how, but we've had "Realism" and "neo-realism" and I sure as hell don't want "cyber-realism!" "Humanist?" Taken. Hmm. "net.realism." "I'm a net.realist" ...nah. I'm working on it. If I find it, Paulina, it's yours.

Chapter Twenty-Seven
The Fall Out

Date: Tue, 20 Aug 1996
From: Paulina Borsook
To: David Hudson
Subject: emergency news bulletin .RM50/just thought you
should know hardwired canceled my book contract today
because of the comments I made on "Rewired."

To anyone who doesn't devote an undue amount of attention to the
quibbles within San Francisco's cliquish new media scene, this emergency
news bulletin might not have warranted much more than a blip on their
cultural radar. But a shot had been fired in a war of ideas over how to
usher in the information age (or whichever buzzword you prefer), and
the immediate casualty was a work that would likely have gone a long
way toward raising pop consciousness of the conflict and its significance.

Fortunately, that wound was seen to in short order. Paulina Borsook's
Deadly Embrace will be published by Broadway Books. The irony is that
the shot ricocheted, spilling bad blood throughout the Net, visible in
spots such as web sites *c|net*, *Salon*, and *Rewired* itself, which covered
the ditching of the book. Rumors, accusations, and innuendo rippled
through various conferences on many a BBS where the literati of the
digerati hang, and via something of a private e-mail intranet linking all
who follow any buzz with the name *Wired* humming in it. In short, the
shot backfired on *Wired*.

Now the twist to the strange and clumsy unfolding of events that
followed is that as fellow *Rewired* publisher Andrew Sullivan and I were

working on an article on all this (which in turn eventually expanded into two, one for the *LA Weekly* and one for the *San Francisco Bay Guardian*), an early draft of the piece leapt out of the loop of editors and writers with relentless glee and persistence from one private desktop to the next. It can go pretty darn fast and really screw up your game plan.

Example: When asked to comment, Louis Rossetto had already seen the story in all its rough and tumble glory and gore and snapped, "Seems kind of arrogant to me to have made up your mind about a story, actually written it, actually circulated it, and then expect me to be an accomplice in my own trashing by supplying you with quotes which you can mangle to your heart's content to make the points you already decided should be made."

A damn good point. When I snapped back that the story wasn't actually written yet, that I sure wasn't the one who had actually circulated it, things cooled down. And he was an awfully good sport about the whole thing, patiently trading lengthy e-mail messages almost daily for well over a week, an exchange that rapidly developed into the interview that follows, knowing full well all along that *Rewired* is in part about calling that vision into question and proposing alternatives.

The funny thing is, the story that got away even as its editors were sharpening their red pencils and issuing instructions for round two was sort of unofficially published, or at least circulated—ever widening circles reverberating between the private and the public, little intranets. Remarkably, though, many are inhabited and run by approximately the same people. More or less.

Mark Stahlman of New Media Associates was actually the first to post a public mention of the book's demise. He did so in Threads, "HotWired's" open bulletin board. Strangely, there was little reaction out in the open, but the flames of private gossip were fanned all the higher. The proportion of whispers to the out-and-out spoken word was simultaneously staggering and hilarious. A bit sad as well, because those who knew what they would have to say about the mishap didn't feel free to say it. Indeed, Borsook's cut book stood out like a disembodied head on a pole as a warning to all *Wired* insiders as to just what can happen.

Until that Tuesday in August, Paulina Borsook had been having a pretty terrific summer. As she mentions in the interview, besides "Cyberselfish," she had placed a couple of pieces at the überhip web daily "Suck," a *Wired* outlet, lobbed a few high ones back and forth with Extropian Max More for a round of "Brain Tennis" ("HotWired"), and then that contract with HardWired, *Wired*'s venture into book publishing.

That's a lot of *Wired* for one summer, and if you toss in the generous handful of articles she had written for the magazine proper over the years, you are looking at what most would consider a fairly solid writer/publisher relationship—one with a history to it, one you could count on. Who would imagine that a few innocuous comments made to a fledgling webzine such as *Rewired* could send it all up in flames overnight?

After all, Borsook and *Wired* had already had their big spat. When the collection of essays "wired_women" was released and Borsook's opened, "I suppose it all came to a head one night past midnight... *Wired* magazine had brought me to that too-often described 'aha' state of women and ethnic minorities and gays and anyone else who feels marginalized and badly done by...," and then crescendo'd into what she called her "feminist rant about *Wired*," naturally, *Wired* was not pleased. But everybody got over it.

What made this run-in turn out so differently? The abrupt snub seems all the more unjust considering that the supposedly offensive comments were hardly central to the two-part *Rewired* interview itself, were even played down in the piece by the author (me), and to top it off, were not exactly news. What she said, in sum, was that although she and *Wired* had had their differences, they always had her back, and that, yes, she'd heard "horror stories" regarding the treatment of writers typical of probably any publishing institution run by a single strong personality, but that they were pretty much common knowledge. Oh, and the political thing: *Wired*'s right-wing cyberlibertarianism versus Paulina Borsook's stance—not too terribly far to the left of center—but hey, they got along.

Boris Groendahl, a media consultant who has had a hand in *Wired*'s negotiations with German publishers during the long struggle to get *Wired Germany* launched, put it this way. Borsook's comments were actually "great PR for *Wired*. The interview demonstrated that they're willing to give important voices of all points of view an opportunity to express themselves."

Which would be precisely the sort of PR *Wired* could have used, and not the sort this incident generated. Stunts such as this one get everyone speculating on the "why" of a seemingly pointless and self-defeating move. c|net's gossip columnist, for example, remarked, "[Wired Ventures] and its mercurial co-founder Louis Rossetto apparently don't take kindly to criticism from the magazine's writers. Fuming over trenchant comments..." ...and so on.

Notice the immediate assumption that it was Rossetto who raised the axe. At the web publication *Salon*, Scott Rosenberg traced a tentative line back to Rossetto as well. "It's tough to try to identify the sections [of the *Rewired* interview] that might be contract-breakers—except, maybe, for the section where Borsook, after bemusedly noting *Wired* publisher Louis Rossetto's apparent good will towards herself, mentions his being 'vindictive' to other people or drumming them out as 'traitors.'" And there's the very foundation of the assumption.

Add to the mix that Rossetto is no great fan of Paulina Borsook. "According to Paulina's argument, the very fact that people don't believe in using the government to correct social ills is QED a manifestation of their selfishness. It's like she read her Rand too closely."

Further, Borsook's comments to *Rewired* did tick off Rossetto, though he claimed to have read them only after I contacted him—above all, it was that phrase "horror stories." He didn't like seeing it in the *Rewired* interview, and he didn't like seeing it in the early draft of that article, either. "What I object to is repeating Paulina's allegations about 'horror stories' without documenting the stories. Paulina saying there are 'horror stories' isn't good enough... You need to dig out the 'horror stories' themselves. Otherwise, all you're doing is repeating unfounded allegations, spreading bad memes."

But what an interviewer does for the most part is pass on what the interviewee has said. And a story on the overblown consequences of that interview, whether it be Rosenberg's or the one I eventually wrote, is going to try to put its finger on just what it was that caused the whole thing to blow. At the outset of my e-mail exchange with Rossetto, he all but made discussion of the "horror stories" a condition of carrying on.

A dilemma. Name names? No. You need permission from all the protagonists, and that, as Rosenberg discovered as well, is a tricky business. Rosenberg describes the pattern of reactions you run into when you go after *Wired* insiders to source stories you have overheard again and again. "First, they will profess their deep admiration for what *Wired* is and what Rossetto and his partner Jane Metcalfe have achieved in growing it from a tiny start-up to the media icon it has become. Then they will express concern that an arbitrarily and erratically enforced party line of technolibertarianism has begun to make the magazine and its sister ventures less interesting, more predictable and less fun to work for... They describe a media company that is in 'empire-defending mode.'"

Then, fully aware of the consequences of revealing both sides of a story, they request that their comments be kept off the record. You will find plenty of current or former *Wired* employees who are perfectly willing to rake the company over the coals in private, but who freeze up when it comes time to go on record. For one thing, despite their experiences, in their heart of hearts, most don't want to see *Wired* tumble. For another, they have got their eye on that axe.

After all, merely mentioning that there are horror stories to tell can get you living one yourself within hours. But HardWired boss Peter Rutten officially took full responsibility for this one. "I'm the 'bad guy.' Each time your report (the early draft—yes, his desktop, too) assumes a *Wired* role in my decision to revise the delivery schedule of the Borsook contract, or in any of my decisions, it is factually 100 percent incorrect." Borsook's agent, Stuart Krichevsky, concurs. "I have neither reason to think nor evidence to suggest that the decision was made by anyone but Peter."

PR aside, was it a good one? Some within the *Wired* walls are well aware of the danger posed by the common perception that, politically at least, *Wired* has become a one-trick pony. "The number one problem," said one insider, another who'd rather not be identified, "is Louis's editorial slant." A book on that slant, its roots and ramifications, from another angle might not have been be a bad idea. Only if alternative views do eventually get aired in a manner that denotes more than sheer tokenism do either the magazine or its extended ventures have a ray of hope of reaching anyone outside one of the thinnest demographic slices of the reading public, namely, rich white guys. A mere twenty percent of *Wired*'s readers, for example, are women. It is as if the digital revolution according to *Wired* were preprogrammed to serve a single elitist batch and to shut out the rest of the world.

This is why Paulina Borsook has been so immensely popular. Her work addresses the concerns of those into Net culture, but "who feel marginalized and badly done by" each time they pick up their "voice of the digital revolution" and find it full of technofetishes, technotranscendentalists, and technosnobs. I'm not aware of any other *Wired* contributor that has actually had fans, much less fans so devoted that they have set up a home page on the web ("chez Justine," named after Borsook's "Suck" nom de plume), linking to all her online articles.

So it didn't make sense. Why shoot down one of your finest assets in her prime? When word got out that Paulina Borsook was the subject of an interview at *Rewired*, the site's hit count increased ten-fold. Borsook had made a tremendous impact with her frequent online appearances throughout the summer.

"Cyberselfish" in particular hit a raw nerve. Many unfamiliar with the essay's subject had appreciated Richard Barbrook's clarification of "The Californian Ideology," but Borsook cast the ideology in real terms, in snappy language laced with the occasional personal anecdote, making its import and implications concrete not only to a global online audience, but to the offline readership of *Mother Jones* as well. She spoke straight into the heart of a constituency that may have been least aware of the libertarian strain running throughout Net culture, but would be the most likely to want to do something about it.

Both were and are important, landmark essays, and in a sense, they could even be seen as a complementary pair. But when Borsook goes on to describe face-to-face encounters with the true believers who are in a position of tremendous power but utterly clueless as to what day-to-day living means for the majority, the abstract points are driven home.

Because "Cyberselfish" was more or less the essay version of the book Paulina Borsook was to write and HardWired was to publish, all the signs of keen interest in, and hence, a market for the book were there. The essay was hotly debated on BBSs and mailing lists, and *Mother Jones*'s own online forum drew quite a crowd from both sides of the issue.

When I originally phoned Peter Rutten, head honcho at HardWired, to ask him why he would cancel the contract for such a book, he insisted over and again that "canceled" is the wrong word. But he wouldn't disclose what actually happened that Tuesday. "I don't talk to the press about specific clauses and arrangements. That's between an author and a publisher." Fair enough, at the time.

After media attention heated up and the arguments on both sides with it, matters were revealed to be far more complex and depressingly weighted with legalese than anyone might have assumed at the outset. But in humanspeak, Rutten's side of the story goes like this. There was no contract. Borsook and her agent hadn't signed. And then he saw the *Rewired* interview. It upset him. It upset him because he and Borsook had talked a lot about her "sarcastic tone," he had been instructing her not to use it, and there she was, using it on a worldwide webzine. He took action. Immediately.

Now, when I heard this for the first time from Rutten, the tone thing was a difficult objection for me to fathom. He did what he did because in the interview, "she said some very sarcastic things about cyberculture and about people at *Wired*." Rutten, with his noteworthy history in publishing before HardWired, had taken on an author despite his distaste for Borsook's "tone," her "angry sarcasm?" It didn't add up. "Cyberselfish," for example, was "too sarcastic and poked fun at the political culture here on the West Coast."

But doesn't tone define a writer? "Well, Paulina's a fine writer and we felt she had a marvelous book in her, but we told her not to use that tone." But isn't Paulina's tone responsible for her tremendous popularity?

And hence, marketability? And wouldn't this be true in Paulina Borsook's case more than in probably any other writer's on the cyberbeat? "We knew she had a constructive critique in her, and that's the book we wanted." Sounds more like HardWired wanted the Borsook name stamped on the cover of a book written by someone else, someone a little less "sarcastic" when it came to covering *Wired*'s home turf.

The course of action Rutten decided to take was not, however, a straightforward "You're fired!" This is where it gets slippery. The way he sees it, he's 100 percent factually correct in saying he did not "cancel" the contract. Instead, "I proposed to change the number of installments from two to four for the first draft and to include two additional drafts. These new installments were to be based on delivery of 40 percent, 60 percent, 80 percent, and 100 percent of the manuscript. Not very unusual in book publishing."

Maybe not. Until you look at the payment schedule: 5 percent of the advance when she signed; 5 percent on delivery and acceptance of 40 percent of the first draft; and 5 percents all the way through, until she had written the whole book. Then a mere 11.5 percent when she had done the entire second draft, another 11.5 percent for the third draft, and finally, after Rutten had by his own admission "monitored" the progress throughout, 52 percent on delivery and acceptance of the final draft.

Unusual? Krichevsky: "I can only say that in over sixteen years in the agency business I never encountered a situation where a publisher wanted to change the payout schedule even after we shook hands on a deal, to say nothing of at this late stage, when we were waiting for countersigned contracts and a check."

Hold it right there. Legally, after the thing was signed, sealed, and dropped in the mailbox, that's that. You've got yourself a contract after all. And the check? Rutten's own e-mail to Krichevsky reads, "I have decided not to countersign the contract for Paulina's book, 'Deadly Embrace', and not to send you the fully processed check." Someone processed a check, approved it, for a full 50 percent of the original advance, but didn't consider this agreement an actual contract?

Cybersavvy lawyer Steve Arbuss took a look at the situation and could not get around the legal fact that in the first place, "a valid and enforceable contract was almost certainly formed when Paulina and HardWired made a verbal deal for the publication of her book. The people at *Wired* ought to have known better than this. A deal's a deal. Just ask Kim Basinger."

The final twist in this particular tango was Rutten's assertion that, gosh, he would like to have done that book but "they walked." Borsook and her agent terminated negotiations with an e-mail. "Yes, we terminated," says Krichevsky, but take a look at the conditions Rutten demanded and would not budge on despite Krichevsky's offer that they all get together to talk things over. If "they walked," they were all but forcibly escorted to the door.

This is HardWired's version of hardball. Insiders were whispering throughout the duration of the mess that another book announced for the company's Fall list by yet another woman writer—this one on the topic of women, social change, and technology—was summarily dropped at the same time as Borsook's. The tale sounds just as nasty, just as politically and personally motivated and legally out-of-whack. After the *LA Weekly* story on the mess, however, those rumors whiplashed and reversed: The book was back on the list.

The consequences of all this hiring and firing are not pretty for *Wired*'s hired and fired. Borsook, for example, "spent the summer winding down my freelance projects, turning down work and not taking on new assignments, setting up interviews and travel plans, and generally preparing to run a nine month book-writing marathon, as my contract said I would be running." Not only was the summer spent, but a lot of money as well.

A minor irony here is that Borsook has often written on topics as arcane as how the Net throws a whammy on intellectual property rights and so on, and in the process, has met a lot of lawyers. She knew full well that she "might possibly stand a pretty good chance in court. But I don't want to go to court. I don't even want to go on a Children's Crusade against *Wired*. All I want to do is write a book that's truthful by my own lights. Which has been my sole intent all the way along."

After two months of squabbling and poverty, she finally regained that chance.

Chapter Twenty-Eight
How Tired Is *Wired?*

Wired knew it goofed, knew that the decision—made hours after the *Rewired* interview went up on the web—was rash and irrational. But the "why" question still hasn't been tackled and done with.

David Bennahum, a writer who has contributed to the *New York Times* as well as to *Wired*, has an interesting observation on that one. The world according to *Wired* "is divided into two clans, the Tired and the Wired," a reference to the infamous *Wired* version of the standard "what's hot and what's not" list. But *Wired*'s either/or's represent two warring factions, a far less sane interpretation of fashion.

To Bennahum, what happened to Borsook and so many others was only to be expected. Consider the timing. In August 1996, *Wired* was gearing up to step back out on to Wall Street, go public. "When all you have is your name, and you are trying to do an IPO based on *Wired* = Wired, any credible implication that *Wired* = Tired is a deep no no. People who wrote for *Wired* are articulate critics. Second, the world at large is getting educated about the culture of high-tech, and as they do, they are sensing [*Wired*'s] editorial themes," that ruthless libertarianism championed by *Wired*'s heroes—figures who would most probably show up in Borsook's book and face serious critical analysis rather than day-glo fan mail. "Criticism accelerates the decline, and weakens the IPO. Ironically, a public company would probably wind up canning a good part of the editorial to boost circulation which has been stalled for ages."

The ultimate irony of many in this story is that Paulina Borsook's book was shot down over remarks that were hastily interpreted as "*Wired* = Tired" when in fact, what she actually says in the *Rewired* interview is that she kept coming back to the various manifestations of the *Wired* empire and had every intention of doing so in the future.

Rewired is not about spreading "bad memes" about *Wired*. Its writer, in fact, hopes *Wired* (even better, a more politically balanced *Wired*) is still around long after the twenty-first century breaks, hopes many of the nice things *Wired* has been saying about it come true, but at the same time, feels quite strongly they won't if the technolibertarian agenda wins out, and further, worries that the state of Wired Ventures, even its financial status aside, is in deep trouble meme-wise.

Off-the-record comments such as, "You can't preach technolibertarian radical democracy if you run your affairs and your company like a Stalinist," or the commonly whispered observation that there's "way too much Louis" throughout the *Wired* media empire are the memes that will eventually surface and nudge *Wired* either toward a more inclusive editorial stance or to extinction.

The first brush eLine and I had with the *Wired* meme was in a shot of e-mail from one of the literally hundreds of companies with the name "wired" nestled within its full name. It was a warning that *Wired*'s legal posse was on the prowl for anyone using the *Wired* name in vain. Imagine *Time* or *People* pulling such a stunt. As the e-mail noted, "The word 'Wired' is a very generic term on the Internet, used to imply 'connectivity to the Internet,' and used in such phrases as 'the community of Monticello is now wired...'". Suppose you see online technology being bent out of shape, and to speak out against that trend, you're silly enough to wander out on to the playing field level only in rhetoric with a site called *Rewired*? Another silly misfire during the summer of '96.

Some have even gone as far as to weave theories about the slew of bad news that hit so many *Wired* insiders during that August. At about the same time Borsook lost her book, paychecks were getting sliced. Too many real numbers attached to too many real names have been put forward to deny that something along this line went down, and interestingly, Rossetto doesn't address this issue at all in the interview.

One week before the *Rewired* interview that cost Borsook her book, at least temporarily, a very strange day transpired on the set of *Wired*'s foray into television, *The Netizen*. First, it should be noted that several people associated with *Wired* think this whole idea of Wired TV is ridiculous at best, and at worst, very damaging to all that *Wired* stands for in terms of celebrating new media over the old.

Jon Katz, a "HotWired" columnist who was asked to take part but declined, went on record with *New York* magazine to say so. This earned him an outrageous post in "HotWired's" discussion area, Threads, from Louis Rossetto. Rossetto says he did not attack Katz personally; Katz's reply suggests he sure took it that way, and besides, he had no idea that comments he had made in a private conversation with Rossetto would end up in a public forum.

Another who might have taken offense at the post was the show's first host, Lawrence O'Donnell, who is summarily referred to by Rossetto in the post as an "asshole." This surely didn't help *Wired* much in its litigation with O'Donnell over the contract they broke with him. Clearly, Rossetto had no idea who he was dealing with or how to deal with him.

As of this writing, O'Donnell was pretty confident as he prepared to go to court against *Wired*. "The basic problem here is that *Wired* does not understand contracts. According to Louis Rossetto's public comments, he fired me because he did not like me and did not like what he thinks I think. You cannot violate contracts with people because you do not like what you think they think. *Wired* doesn't know this."

Time to back up. MSNBC had committed to *Wired* for eighteen weeks of programming, but cut that back to fifteen when *Wired* didn't deliver the first show in the first week of August as *Wired* was originally obligated to do. When executive producer Grant Perry either left the show or, as the *Los Angeles Times* reported in October, was fired for trying to tone down Rossetto's hard line technolibertarianism, Louis Rossetto stepped in and took over. Now, not only was Rossetto editor-in-chief of the magazine and chief editorial officer of Wired Ventures, he was also the executive producer of a TV show.

He shook things up. "In one day," O'Donnell notes, "hiring someone of my background and experience went from being a good idea to a bad idea in his view." And Rossetto fired O'Donnell. At this point, the network, whose representatives had been refused entry to the set, reduced its commitment from fifteen weeks to zero. Quite a day's work for an executive producer.

"What *Wired* then tried to ignore was that it had signed an unbreakable contract with me the day before," O'Donnell adds. This was a contract for quite a sum of money, perhaps the largest sum *Wired* had committed to a single employee, and you can bet your own last dollar final approval of such a sum rested squarely with Rossetto.

O'Donnell readily admits he did not know much about the Net or *Wired* before he walked on to the set. "The one thing I was sure of was my position on encryption which was identical to *Wired*'s. The only thing that has ever given me the slightest doubts about encryption was listening to some of the *Wired* people talk about it with their frenzied political naivete."

Naive or visionary, surely *Wired*'s technolibertarianism was common knowledge to the former Moynihan aide? "It did not occur to me to mention to anyone there that I am not now and have never been a libertarian. There were two reasons for this oversight: I did not realize that any of them were libertarians, and I assumed that as the former chief of staff of the Senate Finance Committee who pushed through the biggest tax increase in history for Bill Clinton, my politics could not have been more obvious."

Now imagine the author of *Deadly Force*—an account of his own federal civil rights case brought against the Boston Police (no one before had ever won such a case, much less had it turned into a TV movie, as CBS did in 1986)—a Washington player, being required as host to ask verbatim a question as patently absurd as, "Mass production, mass communication, mass society, the rise of powerful central governments. Mass customization, networked communication, niche communities—isn't centralized, command-driven organization obsolete?"

"I have never been so heartsick as I was when I was at Netizen TV," former co-host Mike Godwin suddenly announced on the "Well" in mid-October. "I would say that I was lied to during the three days I was taping on the set more times than I was lied to during the six months or so that I devoted serious time to investigating the Marty Rimm fraud [the dubious study that led to *Time* magazine's infamously absurd "Cyberporn" cover story]." The deceit and backstabbing are not unique to *Wired*'s television division, Godwin adds, but instead "are more systemic at Wired Ventures, and I strongly believe that money concerns are the primary source of them."

Immediately following his remarks, Godwin posted transcripts of an earlier version of the show that aired on November 2 as well as a carefully worded point-by-point deconstruction he handed over to the top guns in his new role as consultant (after he, too, was replaced as host). Godwin's tightrope walk between a defense of the U.S. Constitution, for example, and the program's implicit proposal to scrap it and his desire to hold the ear of a staff known for its irrational jettisoning of dissenters is quite a piece of work. His overall critique of *Wired* is significant, not simply because of his position in cyberculture but because he truly believes that there is a need for *Wired* in the broader cultural landscape.

Wired went nuts during the summer of '96. Maybe, as Bennahum suggests, it was the IPO thing, the public humiliation of making such a show out of going public in June, taking a ride on that wave of outrageously overvalued Internet-related IPOs (Netscape, Yahoo!, and so on), and then being all but laughed off Wall Street. Although the *Washington Post* took note of the unique chutzpah of offering "branded content with attitude" to potential investors, it also couldn't help observing that the company has yet to turn a profit.

Just as *Wired* was on the verge of making the move again, a slew of really rotten press hit the company. At this point, it should be noted that not only is it not too smart to make writers mad because they will turn around, dis you, and do it well, but angering a media concern backed by Microsoft and NBC is not too clever, either. In early October, Christopher Byron wrote up a scathing report for MSNBC on the financial state of Wired Ventures.

In short, Byron posited that *Wired* and its underwriters, Goldman Sachs & Co. and Robertson Stephens and Co., were trying to pull a fast one on Wall Street. The company was originally presented to investors as worth $447 million. Just three months later, that figure had fallen 30 percent, to $294 million. Why? Because *Wired* was not only still not making a profit, its across the board financial status was swirling down the virtual toilet.

"Already this company is living on cash infusions from its backers," Byron pointed out, "which in May pumped in $12.5 million in return for a new tranche of preferred stock. Take that cash out of the picture, and *Wired*'s mid-year balance sheet is a catastrophe, with $14 million in assets propping up nearly $18 million in liabilities. On a balance sheet basis, this is a company with no value at all."

Worse, *Wired* owed a bank $5 million it didn't have. Without the IPO, few saw any chance of the company climbing out of the hole. The magazine, which accounts for 90 percent of all its revenues, lost $6 million in the first half of the fiscal year 1996, two-thirds of the loss posted by the company as a whole for the second quarter. *Wired* was in dire need of cash. Then and there. To attract investors, Wired Ventures and its underwriters cut opening prices again and again but still couldn't raise enough interest to support the offering. By Friday, October 25, it was all over.

We will return to the implications of the crashed IPO, but here is a fine place to stop and wonder, Can the company go on trying to embellish its main asset, attitude, by branding itself as a multimedia monolith? 1996 ended darkly for Wired Ventures, but the dawn of 1997 (the announcement was made on January 2) saw a shot of $21.5 million from a private investor for the company. More than the money, which is a nice start toward plugging the leakage, it was an important psychological boost, the first positive sign in a long, long while.

The questions now being asked are, Is it enough and will more private investment be forthcoming? How much will these unnamed investors have in the future decisions shaping the company, its direction, and its products? Did it try to skim the fat throughout the summer of '96 by eliminating pesky contractual agreements, or were these violations actually politically motivated? And whatever the explanation, are we likely to see the same sort of maneuvers in the future?

These are not pleasant questions on either end. The least pleasant of all may be, How long can a branded media presence go on propagandizing an extremist position and maintain its position as the "voice of the digital revolution?" Let's pick up David Bennahum's analysis of the magazine's monthly thesis and look at it strictly from a publishing angle.

First and foremost, according to Bennahum, *Wired*'s fire is lit by cyberdelia. "Technology, especially digital technology, is a continuation of the psychedelic 60s. Where once LSD would transform the world (and failed), computers are taking the mantle. All the puritan concerns about human-machine synthesis are essentially anti-pleasure, anti-enlightenment."

Louis Rossetto has said that he has aimed to make *Wired* the *Rolling Stone* of the 90s. It is a great idea, and he has succeeded in many ways. *Rolling Stone* became the quintessential late 60s, early 70s magazine, and certainly any future history of pop culture in the early to mid-90s that doesn't mention *Wired* would not just be incomplete, it would be way off.

To touch on that identity thing again, though, *Rolling Stone* then and *Rolling Stone* now are very different magazines indeed. Not just in terms of cultural importance, but editorially as well. A lot of the naivete about the power of drugs and rock to create a new and better planet dissipated from the magazine's pages when it dissipated in the real world.

Just as the naivete about computers and digital technology is rapidly dissipating now. Drugs and some form of rock are still around, and obviously, computers will be too for as far ahead as anyone can see. But attitudes shift with reality. Will *Wired* continue to follow *Rolling Stone*'s example and adjust accordingly, maybe even better than *Rolling Stone* has been able to?

Bennahum's second diagnosis: "Technology is an organism. It is alive. Human beings are mere pollinators of some nascent machine-consciousness. This is very important to *Wired*, because if that's true then everything today is fated and not designed by human beings. Therefore we have no control," hence Kevin Kelly's book. Harping on these themes and their implications won't hurt *Wired*'s circulation in the least. Science fiction continues to be a booming market.

Now this one I hadn't thought of until David Bennahum brought it up. "History is evil because history contradicts the idea that cyberspace is an evolving organism. History shows that c-space was designed, not destined, by conscious visionaries with an agenda. That is why the history of technology is never, ever covered in *Wired* with one exception—business stories about huge flops or successes. Business matches the Darwinian destiny evolutionary model of c-space; the out of control bit is nicely mapped to the world of laissez faire economics. So it is okay to talk about Atari or Apple."

It is an eye-opener, to be sure, but in the strict terms of *Wired*'s place in the culture of the near future, it is hard to say whether the exclusion of any particular topic (as opposed to the relentless pounding away at one) would have much effect. As *Rolling Stone*'s readers aged, we started seeing more retrospective look backs, best-of lists, and so on. Those issues, some pushed as collector's items, have sold well. So we'll see.

The next running theme is the most offensive: The division of the populace into, as Bennahum puts it, "two clans, the Tired and the Wired." As Bennahum reminded me at some other point, this sort of tribal thinking is thriving in the 90s in a variety of arenas. "Stories should emphasize the excellent adventures of the *Wired* clan, and denigrate the Tired clan.

This ranges from the stupid (Manhattan = Tired, San Francisco = Wired) to the intelligently sly—why high-tech executives (the princes among the *Wired* clan) have the vision, the fiery power, and the super-ability to build a righteous *Wired* future. Everything in their path—you name it—is Tired, and destined for extinction by the laws of evolution, therefore any reference to their needs is pointless, and a waste of column-inches."

That identity thing again. To a degree, it makes sense. You would expect readers of *The Nation* and *The National Review* to frown at each other from across their respective sides of the magazine rack. The danger for *Wired* lies in either angering too many people or angering the very people who ought to be its hardcore readership.

That hardcore readership should *include* persons such as web diarist and instructor Justin Hall, for example, who has certainly been right in there from the beginning as digital culture has become central to what the 90s have been about. "I am not supposed to feel left out of 'the digital revolution'," he writes on one of his countless web pages. "I saw an ad for wired, in Details magazine: it read, this is the digital revolution, you are either part of the steamroller, or part of the road.//give me a break. that ain't inclusive! that ain't encouraging! that's capitalist megalomaniacal pave-the-earth puffery."

And finally, Bennahum's "who cares really?" question. "This preposterous multi-millennial quest for earthly transcendence is a total yawn. As an atheist child of the Enlightenment, I find it hard to believe we still even talk about this. Oh well, but we do, and c-space is just the latest vessel for silliness, and *Wired* a leading flag-waver."

So, once again. For how long? And another question. How wide? I pose this one because, for one thing, *Wired* was planning that same summer of '96 to launch three new domestic titles. John Battelle, the executive director of editorial development, told the web news source Media Daily that the first would be "a combination of the *Economist*, *Wired*, and the new *Fortune*," and the second would focus on the cyberlifestyle, "a cross between *Martha Stewart Living* and *I.D.*" Both might get you scratching your head. Doesn't *Wired* pretty much already cover those areas? In fact, isn't that range one of *Wired*'s greatest strengths, especially when it's set next to all the other titles in the field?

It reeks of expansion for expansion's sake. That third project, by the way, was "top secret." A secret that may well never be revealed. The *LA Times* reported on the demise of that batch of projects as well. Also on life support as of this writing is *Wired Germany*, not exactly hot on the heels of *Wired Japan* and *Wired UK*.

"No one in Germany would say about any technology, 'This is cool.'" Just one of the hurdles to overcome, according to Boris Groendahl, that Berlin-based media consultant who was in on the negotiations between *Wired* and its potential German partners, Spiegel-Verlag and Gruner + Jahr. But negotiations have soured and its most well-known partner, *Der Spiegel*, even threatened to sue if *Wired* forged ahead without it.

But how much sense does this make in the first place? Germans link technology with authority, Groendahl surmises, and the Germans have this infamous thing about authority—a complicated mix of respect and suspicion informed by what Chancellor Kohl calls "Germany's special history." Respect and suspicion, neither suggest a proclivity to see anything particularly "fun" in technology. Perhaps this explains German computer manufacturer Digital's cutting back production in 1996 while one of the largest technology retail outlets, EsCom, on the verge of default, rushed to the courts for legal ammo with which to fight off its angry creditors. Digital revolution gear has stocked the shelves in Germany for almost as long as it has in the U.S., but even the Germans, the wealthiest of Europeans, aren't exactly snapping it up.

In an article for the online German publication *InSight*, Groendahl objectively outlined why a *Wired Deutschland* might work, and why it might not. About the best he could offer for *Wired*'s prospects is that there is nothing like it yet on the market.

Of course, there was nothing like it in Great Britain either before *Wired* joined forces with the Guardian Media Group to fill that niche. As Groendahl noted, "the differences between the Californian fast-lane company and the British publishing house, rich in tradition...were unbridgeable." Besides, the digital revolution may be global in theory, but in practice, it is way local. In other words, *Wired* didn't get the British, the British didn't get *Wired*, and the joint venture flopped. There was a relaunch, but just as the UK staff was getting a feel for its own way of doing things, *Wired* HQ in San Francisco let it go. The March 1997 issue was the last issue of *Wired UK*.

In Germany, *Wired* would face a skeptical crowd—of advertisers even warier of risk-taking than those in the markets *Wired* has aimed at before and of readers who don't like being advertised to at all, much less by Americans. When I suggested to Groendahl that *Wired* is, in fact, one great big advertisement for a certain flavor of revolution unpalatable to anyone earning less than an executive's salary, he took up the defense, and we haggled until we both gave in on some points and met on middle ground.

He admitted, that yes, as a package, the design co-opts a "subculture" the way MTV co-opts "alternative rock" to promote an agenda that is anything but "sub." I in turn admitted that in terms of content, *Wired* had recently hired on writers who have been permitted to dissent now and then from the party line, albeit all things considered, I still did not see that as anything more than tokenism. When the issue of the fetish page came up, however, we were bickering all over again, much to our own amusement. When I commented that it is a cruel teaser like the American TV program "Lifestyles of the Rich and Famous" or a Neiman-Marcus catalog, Groendahl countered, "I'm interested in all that stuff. I want to know what's out there." Fair enough.

What struck Groendahl as he sat down with Louis Rossetto, Jane Metcalfe, and Kevin Kelly in San Francisco was that although he felt the magazine itself was at least beginning to present varying points of view on the goals of the revolution, this trio running the show was charged with an almost naive zeal he found alarming. "Usually, it's the other way around," he noted, the magazine doing all the propagandizing while the editors retain a more human complexity.

"What makes Rossetto so zealous," I asked straight out, surprised that Groendahl had a theory at the ready: "Something in his past," he shot back, maybe a flirtation with the Left that turned sour, maybe something else, but at some point, he got burned. By an Electric Word?

A magazine that covers what essentially remains an intriguingly mysterious phenomenon in Germany, online technology and its cultural implications, could actually take off. But it won't be the one Germans already perceive as McNet. In other words, *Wired* already has a tremendous image problem to overcome even before it launches. The only way it could save its spin-off is to disassociate it from the Mother Ship.

That would have to mean, without exception, no translated reprints of any articles featured in the U.S. version. Anyone under forty who subscribes to the elitist politics of the U.S. *Wired* is fluent enough in English to take comfort in the *Ur-Wired* already available at "international newsstands," of which there's at least one in any town over here larger than Salt Lick, TX. Further, the Berlin staff would have to be brought to the fore. The impression would have to be made that they just bought the name to justify their own, uniquely German franchise.

And if you're Louis Rossetto, be prepared to swallow some antithetical positions with regard to issues such as universal access, government support and interference, and so forth. Germany is a country with a rich, deeply ingrained social democratic tradition, meaning the set of priorities for the Berlin staff is going to differ radically from that of the South Park, San Francisco staff in terms of just how the words "digital revolution" resonate.

Wired's uniquely American view of how the digital revolution ought to be run, or even why it is taking place amount to precisely the version of the revolution Europeans are beginning to perceive and reject. There is something about the European political landscape, brought out in even sharper relief in Amsterdam, that rubs Rossetto the wrong way (again, take a look at that response to Barbrook's "Californian Ideology").

Granted, it is just a theory. But why would such a brashly American reading of the meaning and potential of online technology be introduced as a viable venture in Europe? That's the perplexing question the theory is aimed at. In a sense, it reads Michael Corleone's famous line in *The Godfather* backward. "It's not business, it's personal."

Just before the IPO fell apart, the German news wires carried reports on the demise of *Wired Germany*. The complete text of the joint press release read, "Gruner + Jahr und Spiegel-Verlag geben bekannt, daß die Gespraeche mit Wired Ventures ueber die Herausgabe eines deutschen

Wired-Magazins ergebnislos zu Ende gegangen sind." Got that? Translation: "Gruner + Jahr and Spiegel Press announce that negotiations with Wired Ventures related to the publication of a German *Wired* magazine have ended without results." That was it.

But *Wired* was quick on the rebound. Two days later, the *Suddeutsche Zeitung* reported that Wired Ventures had announced that it will be going it alone. At some point in 1997, a German *Wired* will appear. As the single publisher, *Wired* will have absolute control over its product.

So what went wrong with Plan A? Horizont-Newsline added to the curt press release that the parties could never agree on the essential concept or personnel. The Kress news service went a bit further. They claimed to have had a hunch for quite a while. Despite haggling for months, the potential partners "couldn't even agree on the top-level editorial staff." According to Kress, "the Americans" were demanding too much control over a project for which the Germans were putting up the cash.

The very same week all this transpired, as Godwin was telling his Netizen story on the "Well" and sharply critical stories about *Wired* were sprouting up on the pages of *Business Week*, the *Los Angeles Times*, and *U.S. News and World Report*, Louis Rossetto, whose spirits were certainly showing no sign of wear, e-mailed a pep talk message to his over three hundred employees. Addressing them as his "Wired Ones," Rossetto had nothing but good news and cheers for his team. *Wired* was doing great, the IPO couldn't be better, thanks. Not one of these clueless reporters at any of these shoddy institutions knew how to read a prospectus. Ads were selling like hotcakes, page views at "HotWired" were soaring, two out of six HardWired books were moving nicely, and *Netizen TV* was to air, after all, on November 2, which in fact, it did.

Rossetto wrapped up the note with a quip from F. Scott Fitzgerald: Success is the best revenge. Of course, Calvin Tomkins, the insightful art critic who has lived longer and probably happier than Fitzgerald may have come up with the worthier observation: Living well is the best revenge. And by "well," he didn't mean "well-to-do."

Well, the memo leaked. When the IPO collapsed a second time, few of the articles in the resulting wave of media coverage neglected to mention the leak, even as most of those same articles admitted that the leak probably didn't break any SEC "quiet period" rules and certainly wasn't solely responsible for the demise of the IPO.

Meanwhile, back in Germany, the web site "Wildpark" sent journalist Jörg Koch across the Atlantic to roam the States, and naturally, *Wired* HQ was a stopover. There, he lounged on a sofa and chatted with editor Russ Mitchell. Mitchell has since claimed that what Koch reported back to "Wildpark" did not transpire, that Koch took no notes, but proceeded to misquote him out of hand in his article.

Whatever was actually said, there can be little doubt that the *Wired* editor and the European reporter clashed. That Mitchell talked up the virtues of the free market, whichever words he chose to do so with, is also more than likely. In his article, Koch claims to have remarked that the free market can't be doing all that hot in America—on his way to *Wired* HQ, he found himself zigging and zagging every few steps just to get around the homeless lying on the sidewalk.

Words were evidently traded and Koch got angry. "Even the laughably cut American social support is still too much for the digital elite. The free market will take care of it. The free market will ensure free communication. Free communication will make everyone happy." Then, in English and highlighted: "Bullshit." Koch comes away from *Wired* HQ piping mad, swerving around the homeless, muttering statistics to himself. 1 percent of the U.S. population holds sway over 40 percent of the wealth, the top 20 percent over 80 percent of the wealth, while the bottom 20 make do with 5.7 percent. I would just add to that the recent findings of the charity organization Bread for the World that place the U.S. at the top of the list of industrialized nations in a category no one could be proud of, child poverty. One out of five kids in America lives below the poverty line, 13.6 million often go to bed hungry at night, and the welfare bill passed by Congress and signed by President Clinton in 1996 will toss in another 1.1 million.

And to that, a personal observation. From 1985 to 1994, I lived in Munich. That's nine years away from "the old country." When I came back to what is still my favorite city in the world, San Francisco, I was appalled. I understand the shock Koch and so many other foreign observers go through when they set foot in America and see the stats translated into 3D, tangible human suffering. The administrations friendliest to laissez faire economics wreaked havoc on the U.S. and its people, tearing them apart into two classes, and rewarding the minority while punishing the majority.

After another paragraph or two of furious ranting about who mans the top at Microsoft, Sun, Netscape, and so on, how they got there while no one else would stand a chance, Koch concludes, "the so-called digital revolution, paired with an ascendant neo-liberalism, won't change this situation, it'll make it even worse."

That's his last sentence, but it follows a considerable swath of textual speculation on what in the world *Wired* would publish in a German or any European version of itself. How could it possibly fly? This from a guy who readily admits to subscribing to *Wired* and eagerly leafing through each new issue the moment it arrives. But as curiosity about the Net and its culture wears off and all those wow colors wear thin, only the ugly part is left.

Maybe it was the idealist in me that didn't want to see *Wired* get its comeuppance in terms as petty as money. Maybe that is why, when I first heard of the collapse of the IPO, I instinctively muttered, "Oh, shit." The magazine so many of us love to hate and hate to love was in deeper trouble than those at its helm either realized or would admit—hence what I perceived at any rate to be a dark pall over both supporters and critics when news of the collapse broke.

Even though *Wired* has sat squarely on one side of the fence, it has been a catalyst for some of the most important arguments to be played out over the last few years, many of them just now getting truly fired up. This may be a leap, but I felt like I did when Nixon resigned. I thought, You cannot rob us of this showdown. Let's do the impeachment, hash it out until the final curtain falls, complete the constitutional cleansing. But when the man slipped out the back door, he left us more corrupt than he found us, caught in some perpetual, labyrinthine Second Act.

Now the critics are worried that we won't have *Wired* to kick around any more. Supporters may not understand this need. They looked at us with those big black velvet painting eyes, their empty sad clown pockets turned inside out as if to say, Well, I hope you're satisfied. No, we're not. Wired Ones, we were hoping to get the chance to be there when, like some Deadhead whose acid has finally lost its punch, you realize, Hey, this music really sucks—maybe even to have been instrumental in the realization.

But the critics have taken up a very funny, paradoxical, and probably ultimately naive position as well. A lot of what really ruffles our feathers about *Wired* is precisely what makes *Wired Wired* (though not necessarily 'wired'). It is the old cake and eat it too thing. Would we, for example, like to see a writer as sharp and thorough as David Kline go after that story he has been dying to do for so long about the state of the digital revolution in Middle America, to answer the question, Has the Third Wave washed over the heartland? Of course we would. And it would have to be in *Wired*. Why? Because that is where that story would matter most. Why? Isn't it obvious? Because *Wired* is still the most important single media entity exploring, speaking to, even embodying what some call digital culture.

And yet *Wired* would never have achieved this position by withholding any of its arrogant brashness. Some Mr. Nice Guy at the helm would never have steered it to the forefront. The Middle America idea is evidently too middle for all-or-nothing *Wired*. At the same time, there is that old adage that the best campaigner doesn't always make for the best office-holder. Slogans are fine for slashing your way to the top, but after you're there, it is tough translating them into policy. Not that either a magazine or a multimedia high-tech company would have to. But mere sloganeering wears thin, grows boring, and "boring" is deadly for any brand name.

We could reach back even further to older adages about fat, stagnant kings and king slayers, cycles and seasons, but this would be getting far too cosmic for the topic at hand. This failed IPO—which garnered a remarkable amount of media coverage considering its actual import on the economic big picture (a sign that either *Wired* really is seen as symbolic of the net worth of the Net or that what goes around in media circles comes around)—is simply a signal that investors are no longer in the market for hype.

Indeed, as David Kline wrote in "Upside," "*Wired*'s IPO died for one reason and one reason only: it was a mangy dog of a stock offering that deserved, if only for mercy's sake, to be taken out and shot." Why? It boils down to one simple business formula. You invest in a company that shows signs of profitability. Not only had *Wired* never turned a profit in all its nearly four years of being open for business, prospects that it ever would looked very dim indeed. Naturally, Kline's article, which appeared on the "Upside" web site, earned him and the magazine a furious post from Louis Rossetto.

Although it would have been a lot more worthwhile (and fun) to put *Wired*'s slogans to the test ideologically rather than financially the first time around, we may well have *Wired* to kick around for some time to come.

Chapter Twenty-Nine
What to Do

Whether *Wired* pulls through or not, the technolibertarianism it has done so much to promote is on the rise. What to do?

The first step is awareness. If you are a "lefty," chances are the libertarians know a lot more about you than you know about them. Time to bone up. As Borsook, a good "lefty" herself, notes in the *Rewired* interview, at this stage in the game, "it's not a fair fight." In Net years, the libertarians are eons ahead. But if you recognize that "the dominant issue and culture of the Net is libertarianism," and then that "there are many issues that we on the whatever you want to call it, the lefty side, can find common cause with," maybe we can meet on that common ground and start from there.

This is not a compromise of essential principles Borsook is talking about, though a bit of open-mindedness on either side of the unfair fight won't hurt. Even if you are one of those liberals who agrees with Bob Black that, "A libertarian is just a Republican who takes drugs." Maybe you have even gone so far as to trace the fairly simple yet intricately laid-out arguments in Black's "The Libertarian as Conservative" and found yourself nodding in agreement when you weren't twitching in wonder or anxiety.

Because although you may be among those who refuse to loosen a grip on the cogs and wheels of reality to such an extent that you will go along with Black so far as to believe that the abolition of work is attainable (however worthy a goal in one's personal life), Black's second argument, that the state is the very least of anyone's problems in the daily swim upstream, rings a bell. Especially that uncharacteristically straightforward bit, "the source of the greatest direct duress experienced by the ordinary adult is not the state but rather the business that employs him. Your foreman or supervisor gives you more or-else orders in a week than the police do in a decade."

Perhaps you also can't help but crack a smile watching Black map out all the places in the libertarian argument that concede that the sheer existence of the state depends on consent rather than coercion. Even as objections pop off in your own liberal mind like so many randomly fired synapses (the truly coercive states, the appreciation for the one note of reason injected into an otherwise emphatic ideology, and so on), you still can't wipe that grin off your face.

And then there's that final paragraph in which Black pulls it all together, the paragraph Pit Schultz cut and pasted and jettisoned out to the nettime mailing list, and which I have cut and pasted again to show you now, trimmed as much as I can stand it:

"Libertarians complain that the state is parasitic, an excrescence on society. They think it's like a tumor you could cut out, leaving the patient just as he was, only healthier. They've been mystified by their own metaphors. Like the market, the state is an activity, not an entity. The only way to abolish the state is to change the way of life it forms a part of. That way of life, if you call that living, revolves around work and takes in bureaucracy, moralism, schooling, money, and more. Libertarians are conservatives because they avowedly want to maintain most of this mess and so unwittingly perpetuate the rest of the racket. But they're bad conservatives because they've forgotten the reality of institutional and ideological interconnection which was the original insight of the historical conservatives... A glance at the world confirms that their utopian capitalism just can't compete with the state. With enemies like libertarians, the state doesn't need friends."

One of the nettimers unveiled this gem in the rough to a friend who replied, "Even if every single good thing in my life, including my own genetic makeup, was a direct result of government action, I would still be a libertarian." Now that's commitment. It is the sort of commitment that didn't pose much of a threat when Black wrote his essay back in 1984 when libertarians were still fringe. But the times, they have a-changed, and so have the libertarians.

Liberals (in the American sense of the word, not George Will's) are going to have to deal. The libertarians are here. They write some of our favorite software, oversee the production of some of our favorite machines, publish our favorite magazines, and direct the money we have given them to some of their favorite causes. It's time to talk.

Sticking by our own principles as ever, of course, but lo, we share many of these with the libertarians. Glenn Raphael, a libertarian of liberal heritage, has outlined ten on a web page he calls, "Top Ten Political Issues Liberals and Libertarians Can (Sometimes) Agree On." Numbers ten and nine, predictably enough, have to do with freedom—press and religion. No problem there on all sides. Eight, cut military spending, cheers all around. Seven, drug laws, just don't do 'em.

Six, "Stop trying to be the world's policeman... Liberals either expect foreign policy goals to 'serve corporate interests' to the detriment of doing the right thing or they expect the government to ignore the interest of local populations in order to further goals like 'stability.' And you know something? They're right!" See? Isn't that nice? Some of these people are ready and willing to talk.

Five, immigration; in sum, Pat Buchanan, you're full of it. Four, people enjoy all sorts of sex; let them. Three, voluntary military service; okay, kind of a done deal, but should the issue arise again, we can link up on that one, too. Two, abortion, or as Rafael says, "I like to call myself 'pro-choice on everything'." Fine. Over to you, Glenn: "And the number one political issue Liberals and Libertarians can often agree on is... One, That Newt Gingrich sure can make an ass out of himself."

It's a start.

In "Rage Against the Machine," that article for *Fast Company* by Ronald Brownstein mentioned in the *Rewired* interview with Paulina Borsook, the "other side" is represented by the "Techno-Communitarians," an unwieldy label referring to a group of high-tech Midwesterners who may well be on to a strategy that will work as whatever changes online technology has in store begin to take effect.

"Rather than elevate the heroic individual," Brownstein writes, "Techno-Communitarians celebrate the team." And although, like Bill Clinton, they'll profess that the era of big government is over, they'll never relinquish the essential role government has to play in conjunction with the forces of business and the needs of society as a whole. Communitarianism existed long before the Net did, and even Greg Smith, who wrote a book on it, *Community and Communitarianism*, admits that the concept is still rather vague.

Perhaps that can be taken as a sign of bafflement in the face of a new age, or perhaps as a sign of a new sort of politics on the verge of taking form—a sort that will be more able to absorb and address an age-old set of issues currently being radically redefined by the leaps into a new millennium prodded by technology.

"Sometime over the last two years, someone somewhere must have decreed that the intellectual buzzword of the 90s was to be 'communitarianism,'" Fareed Zakaria wrote in *Slate*. "Communitarianism was supposed to be a third way, neither liberal nor conservative, that charted a new course for philosophy and politics." Sound familiar? "But...it has become a collection of meaningless terms, used as new bottles into which the old wine of liberalism and conservatism is poured."

Still, something is going on. Serious thinkers put off by libertarianism nonetheless see a need for a new approach. In "Brand New Politics," *HotWired* columnist John Heilemann tells an interesting story about Stewart Brand, the co-founder of "The Well" who was an invited guest to the Progress and Freedom Foundation's annual speech-fest in 1995, but not in 1996. Most probably because last time around, Brand had patiently waited out countless denigrations of government, relentless rhetorical slander until at last he broke out with, "What about the GI Bill, which paid its way in four years and has been pure profit ever since? ARPA and computers, ARPA and the Internet, ARPA and God knows what else? ARPA and the Santa Fe Institute! Two million bucks, far beyond any other source for SFI. NASA and all manner of things. The Naval Research Lab and etc."

These comments came to mind when I came across a report in *The Economist* on what ARPA was up to during the summer the magazine that would ignore it was floundering. Quantum computing. Nevermind binaries, some scientists are beginning to suggest, the truly radical innovation may lie in some sort of organic, sub-particle structure we are not even sure about yet, but the potential looks interesting.

Now what private company, embroiled in a battle over this week's plug-in feature enhancement of its web browser is going to spend either the time or the money to bother with something as abstract or non-profitable as what might or might not turn out to be in the twenty-first century as profoundly revolutionary as the Internet has been at the tail end of the twentieth?

Of course, by that time, if the technolibertarians have their way, only the "successful" will even be aware of the next revolution, much less be in a position to take part in it. Already, as the Techno-Communitarian and an executive vice president of Sybase Inc., Mitchell Kertzman puts it, we are headed that way, and the libertarians would only speed up the process. "I believe the extrapolation of where we're going is Mexico, some Caribbean island, or Brazil, where the very wealthy live behind

guarded walls to protect themselves from the people who work for them...
I think it is terribly dangerous."

Contrast that with Rossetto's hunky-dory snapshot of the present in
which people are living longer and better, cities are on the up and up,
and a "New Economy" is being born. And those who don't see things his
way need to "pull their heads out of the 19th century." Maybe it is time
technolibertarians pulled their heads out of the twenty-first, out of their
computer screens and dreamy models of functioning anarchies and took
a walk through some of the dicier neighborhoods of the late twentieth.

Anyone selling you a vision of the present so out of whack has,
intentionally or not, got an even more botched vision of the future to sell
you at a slightly higher price. Louis Rossetto is heading that sales force.
If you are buying, check out who gets short-changed.

"What seems to be evolving is a global consciousness formed out of the discussions and negotiations and feelings being shared by individuals connected to networks through brain appliances like computers. The more minds that connect, the more powerful this consciousness will be. For me, this is the real digital revolution—not computers, not networks, but brains connecting to brains."

Louis Rossetto

Chapter Thirty

What "Kind" of Libertarian— An Interview with Louis Rossetto

By the time I approached Louis Rossetto for comments on a story I was writing about the collapse of Paulina Borsook's book contract with HardWired immediately following her interview with Rewired, he had already read an early draft of that story. That in itself is a long story; suffice it to say, e-mail spreads very quickly.

A few sharp messages were exchanged, but things cooled off after this one from Rossetto, which serves as good an introduction as any to the interview:

"I'd be willing to talk about Borsook, David, but only if the discussion includes the charges and allegations about *Wired* she's been making for the past year—and has been given a free pass on by the people, like you, who would like to believe them. In other words, I want to get into 'And you know, I've heard horror stories....' And she goes through a few, the scene after the Jon Katz review was killed by Kevin Kelly, the ones she touches on in "wired_women." So there is this thing about how they have their "worldview, or actually religion." 'Don't contradict with facts, please.'

"Yeah, I want to get into the 'horror stories.' I get the feeling that the people who empathize with Paulina's 'worldview, or actually religion,' don't want to get 'contradicted' with the facts when it comes to *Wired*. I think maybe it's time to inject a little reality here."

Piecing together an interview conducted via e-mail, or regular mail for that matter, is something akin to trying to make a coherent narrative out of a three-ring circus. Discussions of various points split and branch off, but are all carried on "simultaneously." I've tried to capture the flow without letting it get too choppy or losing any of the content or context.

David Hudson: When people talk about *Wired*, its politics, its ideas, how the business is run, it very rapidly gets personal. Never ceases to amaze me.

Louis Rossetto: From my side, it gets personal because no matter how far it's come, in many ways *Wired* is still the same company it was when twelve people invested their passion and suffered a whole bunch of pain to bring out the first issue almost literally four years ago. There's no cover of bureaucracy here. You make a charge against *Wired*, it's not rhetoric, it's an accusation against a real person.

DH: How do you respond to the accusation that there's "too much Louis in it?" One often hears, especially now that *Wired* has so many projects going on, expanding into other media, etc., Look, the guy can't have a hand in everything, and yet he tries to.

LR: I have two major responsibilities. I'm the editor-in-chief of *Wired* magazine, where I've been very hands-on since I co-founded it. And I'm the chief editorial officer of Wired Ventures. In effect, all creatives ultimately report to me, and I'm ultimately responsible for all content.

That doesn't mean, however, that I'm hands-on in all projects. That would be as counter-productive as it would be physically impossible. What I do is manage a creative process through an organization run by senior creatives.

Sometimes in that process I am very present—especially when we are creating new brands and products. Even there, however, there's no fast rule; a major new "HotWired" initiative was recently presented to me after it was already pretty fully baked. Often I'm completely absent; I'm pretty much hands-off on a large majority of the content that we create here.

Which, in point of fact, was the case with Paulina's book at HardWired. I didn't even know it was happening until Peter told me it was one of the books for next year, and then I only found out after the fact that it wasn't. Which is similar to my relationship to "HotWired," where I read the content on the site for the first time on the morning it's posted, like most of our members do.

Which is entirely normal for an enterprise with three companies, dozens of different projects and products in production, and 335 employees spread across four offices.

DH: [Quoting from a portion of the early draft] "*Wired* is robbed of 'any credibility as anything other than a glossy stooge for out-of-whack libertarians'." And for color, [let's] set it next to Mark Dery's assessment of *Wired* as "a bully pulpit for corporate futurists, laissez-faire evangelists, and prophets of privatization."

I think what gets a lot of people so riled up about *Wired* is that it's been enormously successful, has literally become a cultural icon doing just that—not simply giving voice to the Gilders, Tofflers, and so on, but actually serving as a mouthpiece for them.

And I think these same people sense the Net slipping out of their hands. They sense a very rapid evolution over which they have little or no control from the realization of the Net's many-to-many potential to the old "top down" media models.

LR: Perhaps the most telling sentence here is that "what gets a lot of people so riled up about *Wired* is that it's been enormously successful."

I call this the MelodyMaker syndrome. In the UK, MM used to be the arbiter of what was cool in music. They discovered new bands. Then they hyped them until they started to get a modicum of commercial success. Then they turned on them and denounced them for any number of sins. Mostly that they had became popular. Success envy. Why don't people like success? The question is more about the people who don't like success than the people who are successful.

DH: People love success. Around the world, they pay Hollywood hundreds of millions of dollars a year to have success stories told to them. Especially those "come from behind" and "up from nothing" stories. That's why *Wired*, at first glance, usually the only glance mainstream media bothers with, is such an exhilarating story on the one hand.

LR: People love it, and hate it. There's a reason why envy is in the top seven sins.

DH: A small group of people squeezed into an office in San Francisco building an empire; it's the stuff of legend, the American Dream come true, and I certainly don't have to tell you people admire you tremendously for that accomplishment.

On the other hand, what people can't stand is having the hero turn on them, being told to either hop aboard the steamroller or get flattened into the road. Because there are a couple of different kinds of successful people, right?

LR: *Wired* never set out to be anyone's hero. All we wanted—and still want—to do is report accurately on the future that's arriving. The *Wired* editorial line today is exactly the same today as it was when it launched. We believe as strongly in Mitch Kapor's vision of a Jeffersonian Democracy in cyberspace today as when we published it in our first year. We have fought very hard for freedom in cyberspace. *IDG* and *Ziff* haven't, the *New York Times* hasn't, *Mother Jones* hasn't. We have turned on no one.

Wired reports on the world that's really out there, not the world that the PC left or the Christian right would like to believe is out there, nor the one that the cynical/mindless media distortion machine would have us believe is out there, but the one that's really emerging today.

That world is in the midst of a profound revolution driven not by disgusting political ideologies, but by the people creating and using convergence technologies to solve problems and create opportunities in their business and private lives. That is the overwhelming fact of our time. To deny it is to live in a fantasy world shaped by 19th century or older social nostrums that border on religions. I don't believe in religions.

This new world is characterized by a new global economy which is inherently anti-hierarchical and decentralist, and disrespects national boundaries or the control of politicians and bureaucrats or power mongerers of any; and by a global, networked consciousness that is creating a new kind of democracy for achieving social consensus that is turning the bankrupt electoral politics we are witnessing this year into a dead end. These two factors are not about top down control to accomplish either selfish or noble ends, but about a global hive mind that is arriving at a new, spontaneous order.

There are a lot of people who are upset about this emerging world. Especially the right and left of the traditional political spectrum, who have invested centuries in attempting to achieve political power in order to control the state to accomplish their particular agenda. Pat Buchanan/Mark Dery, they are the opposite sides of the same coin —people stuck with 19th century social thinking who are unhappy with the emerging new world.

Each attacks us with their worst epithets: "godless pornographers" from the right, "prophets of privatization" from the left. Both are most upset that the world is moving out of even the possibility of their control, indeed, out of control period.

"Stooge," "bully pulpit," "mouthpiece." The rhetoric attacking *Wired* is laughably hyperbolic, from the idiotic piece that the *Baffler* ran to the most current criticism. What ignorance. *Wired* has been an incredibly independent voice since our founding. We have sucked up to no one, have bowed to no one.

If we have attracted readership and advertising, it's because we resonate with our times, not because we are kissing ass. *Wired* is not about regurgitating 19th century social thinking. If people want that, they are free to look at the *Nations* and *National Reviews* of the world, there are plenty enough of them; indeed, I would probably say that all of the rest of media is stuck in that place. *Wired* is about talking about this erupting future. Economists, philosophers, artists, scientists, technologists, and business people—and yes, Gilder and Toffler—are talking about this future, and we report on them.

If there was anyone on the left that had any original thoughts about the future, we would report on them too, as we have on the Krokers. But the sad fact is there aren't many at all, and I mean the word "sad" precisely.

DH: Really? The mailing lists I subscribe to seem full of them. To be fair, a lot of my fellow subscribers work at *Wired* or "HotWired." Probably a dumb question, but I have to ask: Do you pursue new ideas on this side of the fence as actively as those on the other?

LR: Story ideas at *Wired* come from two sources: internal and external. The majority of ideas that get turned into stories come from the outside. They are brought in by editors, and anyone else at *Wired* with an idea. If you have an idea, send it in.

As Paulina herself admits in the interview with her you published, the left is, let's be as charitable as Paulina, "exhausted." It has no new ideas. Instead of embracing the erupting future, it flirts with neo-Luddites—in other words, the most reactionary tendencies in our society. Again, as Paulina herself admits, to the "lefty" groups she feels affinity for, the fact that she is even conversant with this domain makes even her a perceived threat.

This lack of new ideas is perhaps mirrored in Borsook herself, who instead of wanting to write a book about a positive, "lefty" view of the future, chooses instead to make a career out of attacking "cyberlibertarians."

DH: Isn't this a tad presumptive? Doesn't Paulina in fact spend most of part 2 of the interview explaining why she's drawn to them, why she feels that the "cyberlibertarians" have plenty to say worth listening to, that they matter?

LR: And I was actually surprised that she admitted that. But the reason you wanted to talk to her had nothing to do with her grudging appreciation of "cyberlibertarians," it was her opposition. The point anyway is the inability or unwillingness to forward a positive agenda for change.

Again, the fact that anyone thinks the Net was ever in "their hands" in the first place is itself an indication of a certain twisted addiction to control. The Net was never in anyone's control, and it still isn't. It is, as the Federal appellate court put it when holding the CDA unconstitutional, the most democratic medium ever invented.

This medium is evolving, as it has from the day the first byte moved across it. If you think the corporate world has a clue about what's going on, that it can "control" it, go ask Microsoft how they let Netscape become the fastest growing software company in history.

DH: And then once they felt it breathing down their neck, are even now swatting it dead like some pesky fly.

LR: It's totally unclear how this Microsoft/Netscape thing is going to turn out. If you know, you can become one hell of a rich guy. Netscape is not going away. And Microsoft may have bitten off more than it can chew. Microsoft is still less than 20 K people, with under $7 billion in sales. That's a fraction of one of the large media companies, much less the other forces that could be said to be arrayed against them, from the million of users at the bottom who are skeptical, to say the least, about the desirability of their running everything, to the commercial interests like the telcos and banks who have absolutely no interest in letting Microsoft have a monopoly.

In addition, the battle for the desktop is a lot more complicated than the battle of the browser. The fact the browser battle got to the cover of Time indicates perhaps that the story is over. The new battle is in push media and the active desktop. And there again, it's not clear who's going to be the major player.

The Net is, and will remain, many-to-many. Top-down media models do not work, and are not present on the Net today. There aren't three networks. There are 500,000 web sites. You do not need to talk to the programming director of NBC to put *Rewired* out on the Net. All you have to do is get a computer, and buy access, at a derisory cost compared to what it used to take to get a press, develop the distribution channels, etc. People who talk about the arrival of top-down control don't know what they are talking about.

DH: The sad irony they're picking up on is that the voice of what was supposed to be our "revolution" is telling us to let the top run wild and do its thing.

LR: The sad irony is that the group which used to shout "Power to the People" don't really trust the people, and continue to insist that "controlling" this revolution is necessary, much less possible.

Because the reality is, this revolution really is "out of control." And the more out of control it is, the better. The top isn't "running wild," as anyone who has spent any time talking to so-called media leaders, it's running scared. No one knows what the Net is going to look like six months from now, much less five years. And the larger the company, the more "top" they are, the more clueless they are.

No, this obsession with the "top running wild" is a characteristic kneejerk reaction of the left when confronted with the idea of freedom, the same way "child pornography" is the kneejerk reaction of the right when they think about freedom. Each obsession is a product of the dark corners of their respective psyches. On the one hand, that the successful might continue to be successful, on the other that somewhere, someone might actually be enjoying themselves.

And sorry, both are wrong—and neither is going to get space in *Wired*.

DH: That's why the mishap over Paulina's book reverberates the way it does. *Wired* (Hot, Hard, and so on), with all its tremendous influence, comes off looking as if its stifling an important perspective on probably the most decisive factor determining how this revolution's going to turn out.

LR: Look, the question is no longer what sort of statists we should be supporting—republicans or democrats, communists or fascists. The question really is what sort of libertarians we should be supporting. There is no alternative to a world that's out of control. Central power not only doesn't work, it's not even possible anymore.

The financial markets are entirely out of control of any one or combination of states. And as Dylan put it, money doesn't talk, it screams. And it's screaming at states that they better not do anything stupid, or it's going to trash their economies. (It's saying the same to companies too, for that matter.)

DH: Oh, Louis, Ouch! "While money doesn't talk, it swears..." ! (Rhymes with, "Obscenity, who really cares...")

LR: Ouch is right. I've been quoting that for years. Short term memory loss has apparently turned into long term memory mismanagement. State power today is impotent, and will get even more so, until, as Barlow has put it, the Congress will be as relevant as the House of Lords.

What "kind" of libertarian? At the moment, a lot of the new ideas are coming from market-oriented libertarians. Of course, that is only one strain of the libertarian tradition. The older strain is actually left-libertarianism, which predates Marxism. The Haymarket Martyrs, for instance, whose death is celebrated on 1 May as the International Day of

Labor around the world, were left-libertarians, and anti-Marxists, for that matter. Indeed, the Marxists systematically destroyed the left-libertarians, culminating in actually exterminating them in Spain during the Spanish Revolution. Read George Orwell about his experiences in Spain.

If "lefties," as Paulina puts it, really want to have an impact on how the revolution is going to turn out, they should stop fighting the inevitable, recognize that like the earth is not the center of the universe, the state is not the engine of social change, forget about trashing the cyberlibertarians who are probably their allies in fighting the existing social order, rediscover their roots, and begin developing a truly progressive vision for the future.

DH: With a few minor changes, that's kind of a paraphrase of the entirety of part 2 of the interview, isn't it?

LR: Maybe. I would perhaps insert after "social order:" start fighting the real enemies. To me, those are enemies of freedom, whether that's media companies, telcos, and cableco's seeking to maintain monopoly privilege, the Christian right seeking to censor free speech in cyberspace, or the PC left which is still pretty much addicted to the idea that intentions are more important than results and that state power is actually a good thing, rather than a major problem.

You can ask any of the people I discuss politics with at *Wired*, and they will tell you that I have despaired at not being able to publish modern, progressive, "lefty" social analysis. Because, as even Paulina admits, there frankly isn't any. Blaming *Wired* for that is like blaming the weatherperson for the weather.

DH: People who recognize and relate very deeply to Paulina's point of view can't help but ask again: Are you trying to "cover" the revolution or be the driving force behind one particular element of it?

LR: Covering the revolution is itself being an agent of change. But let's not let this get out of perspective. I may think deregulation of telecommunications is good because it will result in competition and more supply, but, hey, *Wired* had very little impact on what happened in Washington last year. If we had, the law wouldn't have turned out the way it did (like, with CDA?). Some kind of larger forces are at work here, forces with incomes counted in 10+ digits. *Wired* is still a small magazine, with limited influence in the current centers of power, not least because the currently powerful are techno-illiterates.

Again, however, I return to: what is the alternative to the ideas that *Wired* covers? What is the other "particular element" we are not covering? If not deregulation, what? If not free speech, what? What is the cogent alternative? The right regulation? Just the correct speech?

We don't cover the fossilized left any more than we cover the fossilized right, for precisely the same reason, they have nothing to say about today, much less tomorrow. They are the status quo, or worse, and that is not what *Wired* is about. Again, you want to read that, you got all the rest of the media to consume.

Wired is about critical optimism. It is about saying that the universe is out of control, and that's okay. It's about embracing the erupting future. It's about rebuilding civil society in the 21st century. It's about transcending political practices and labels, and encouraging a new kind of democracy that grows out of discussion of genuinely new ideas.

DH: "Out of control." Kevin Kelly has indeed put forward a set of fascinating ideas—how do you respond to the charges of social Darwinism many interpret in them?

LR: I would respond by saying, like, pull your head out of the 19th century and take a look around. Kevin is describing how the world is working today, not the way social or religious creationists would like to believe the world works. He is saying that technology is becoming biological, and biology is becoming technological. Which is absolutely true. Again, blaming the weatherperson for the weather is just plain stupid.

DH: Would you go as far as the "techno-transcendentalists" (Rushkoff, Barlow)? Will the two realms actually merge into a single global mind?

LR: Fifty years ago, Teilhard de Chardin spoke of electric technology as being part of evolution, of the earth clothing itself with a brain. I think the metaphor is pretty accurate. A single global mind? Probably not any more than there's a single human brain inside our skulls. We actually have a bunch of different "minds," which negotiate with each other. What seems to be evolving is a global consciousness formed out of the discussions and negotiations and feelings being shared by individuals connected to networks through brain appliances like computers. The more minds that connect, the more powerful this consciousness will be. For me, this is the real digital revolution—not computers, not networks, but brains connecting to brains.

DH: Can the Net evolve away from the democratic model?

LR: Anything can happen. But right now, there are no signs that it is becoming any less democratic. What is happening is that commerce is arriving on the Net, as it arrives anywhere humans congregate. I don't think that's a bad thing. People who do think it's a bad idea need to explain why, not fall back on kneejerk (and ultimately hypocritical) reactions to anything commercial.

DH: Hypocritical? I honestly don't understand. In what way?

LR: Because commerce is inherent in human life. Everybody engages in it. And everyone needs to be part of it to survive. Even the Unabomber needed to go to the store. Treating it like it's heresy, like there's some pure world out there that it violates, while at the same time living off it, one way or the other, is hypocritical.

DH: Here's my main question, then. You're saying *Wired* is neither right nor left, but represents something new, a third alternative. This is very exciting and appealing obviously as the electorate, in its "throw the bums out" mood, swings every two years between its seemingly very limited choices.

But how does "out of control" translate in real, what-to-do-about-it terms? Isn't it, so far at least, just the New Right's wide open market approach dressed up in cyber-cool?

LR: There are really only two alternatives: trust the universe, or trust the politicians and bureaucrats. Right now, most people who have been educated believe that governments are necessary, and that electoral politics is the highest form of democracy. Indeed, they equate electoral politics with democracy. And that may have been true when these ideas of representative governments were formulated in opposition to the high-handed rule of monarchs in the 18th century. That equation of democracy with electoral politics is entirely inappropriate now.

People believe electoral politics is democracy because they have been brainwashed, period. Children are collected in public schools, they are taught history, which means basically they are taught the history of the state, or rather the history of a particular way of looking at their state, and that idea is continually reinforced by mass media and the structure of the game. Democracy in America? It's quadrennial kabuki paid for with tax dollars administered by politicians and bureaucrats ultimately for their benefit, and for the benefit of the economic interests who influence them. As Jerry Brown said, there's only one party in Washington, the Ruling Party.

The fundamental question: Is what we got now really democracy? Indeed, what is democracy? Democracy to me is not an electoral process, it's a social process. The social process is about creating and discussing ideas, and arriving at a consensus about how we'll behave with each other. Discussion is the essence of democracy. Electoral politics used to be part of that process. It no longer is, and no amount of so-called reform is going to change that. In a world kept ignorant by mass media, presided over by politicians who have no interest in discussing ideas, there is no serious discussion of real issues in the traditional public spaces, as Jon

Katz has pointed out in *Wired* and "HotWired." Because the system is inherently decadent and corrupt.

Now an alternative has emerged. It is networked communications. A higher proportion of the populace is engaged in discussion of fundamental, crucial issues, on a higher level, than at any other period since the Committee of Correspondence during the American Revolution. This is real democracy. Democracy is what occurs in the Net, in our homes, offices, factories—it is not politics. Politics has always been the tail on the dog. In 1996, this election is proving that it's now the tail that's wagging the dog.

I believe the current political situation is inherently unstable, and that we are on the cusp of a massive change. And that change will entail the continuing decline of state power, and the gradual emergence of a new democracy founded on an ongoing, high level discussion in the nets of the world. That democracy is then an evolving social consensus, which may or may not find its way into law. But that democracy will be a lot more powerful than the combined collection of 70 K pages of the Federal Register.

DH: A quote from Richard Sclove [author of *Democracy and Technology*]:

"Karl Polanyi, in *The Great Transformation*, explained 50 years ago that truly unfettered competitive markets are unfailingly a human and social disaster. They trammel people, communities, and natural environments in devastating ways, and have always resulted eventually in compensatory regulation to try to clean up the mess, ameliorate some of the suffering."

Would such lessons, drenched in history, have any bearing in the 21st century?

LR: On the most primitive level, thousands of people carry on a plebiscite about the market every day. They decide to leave the countryside and move to the city. Despite the horrors of the favelas, despite the grimness of being at the bottom of the social order, they continue to stream into cities—to the market. They do it because they perform the calculus and decide that the benefits outweigh the costs, they're better off. If Polanyi was right, the mass migration would be going in the other direction.

Change has costs, no question. Massive change has massive costs. The world as we know it is being overturned. There's lots of dislocation. People are hurt. But on the whole, society is benefited. There's a reason there are five billion people alive on the planet today, and it's not because a politician or bureaucrat planned the whole thing out.

DH: This sort of opens a Pandora's box of case-by-case quibbling— we could, theoretically, get into ticking off specific countries in the first through fourth worlds and citing different reasons for different migrations. For weeks.

But instead, let me just say, as someone who appreciates the role of free markets in society, in conjunction with other factors, that I find this paragraph pretty scary. You're not only saying that it's okay that entire populations are uprooted and forced to abandon the land (where the real resources are still, even in the digital age) and try to make do in already congested, depleted cities, but that it's the market that's left them no choice.

Okay, I'm tweaking your words, but my real question is, doesn't your example actually only prove Polanyi was right?

LR: I'm saying that people always have choices. I've traveled extensively through the Third World. A lot of it is outside the money economy, as it's been for millennia. They live, in that pre-money economy, as well (or as miserably) as they ever have. Meanwhile, there's a money economy which exists in the cities. Relatives come back and tell them about it. They decide to leave for the city. The city is hard, horrible maybe— but not so horrible that they turn around and return to the pre-money economy they came out of—because that, relatively to them, is even more horrible.

This is not about force. Force is what Jackson did to the Seminoles. Force is Stalin deciding that the Volga Germans should be "uprooted" and driven to the middle of Russia. Force is what the Serbs did to the Bosnians. The migration to the city in most of the Third World is about people deciding on the micro level what is best for them.

And let's get over the mythology of the land. As the grandson of generations of small peasant farmers, I don't think there's anything romantic about living under the same roof as the cows and pigs, or eeking out a living by scratching in the dirt. I repeat, very few people, once they are exposed to the money economy, voluntarily return to ancient ways of surviving. And certainly no one who has grown up in the money economy voluntarily returns to subsistence agriculture.

DH: As one of those "lefties," I'm with you all the way on free speech, of course. Isn't there more to the left than regulation (which, yes, I would argue has its place—admittedly, it's a tricky formula)?

LR: The sad fact of regulation is that it's never a ceiling, it's a floor— on which the regulated stand. There has never been a regulatory board that hasn't become a tool of the supposedly "regulated." Wishing it were otherwise, hoping that someday, somehow we can find the right "tricky" formulation of words and people who could accomplish "good" regulation, doesn't make it so.

And yes, the left is more than regulation. It's worse. Much of the left is stuck with a belief in the inherent superiority of central planning to accomplish social ends. Regulation is only one part of that planning. But central planning—the belief that a technocratic elite can run society like a machine—just doesn't work. Not only doesn't it work, it's been shown in many situations to be an abomination. And in a networked world, it is now a virtual impossibility.

DH: You realize, of course, you're going to ruffle some feathers placing the "technocratic elite" on the other side of your argument, though I'm sure that doesn't disturb you. No question here, just an observation.

LR: Technocrats, of course, don't have to know anything about technology, and often don't.

DH: Minimum wage...a floor worth preserving?

LR: Minimum wage, a religious artifact worth fighting over? If you could make people wealthy by passing a law, why doesn't Congress just raise the minimum wage to $20 dollars an hour, a $100? Because, surprise, the laws of economics have yet to be repealed. You raise the cost of something, you diminish its consumption, it's that simple. You raise the minimum wage, and those people who still have a job are better off, and those whose job has suddenly become redundant because the business cannot absorb the cost, those people are unemployed.

If the real purpose of a minimum wage was to ensure a decent living for the lowest paid—instead of a public relations wank by a bunch of well-paid politicians and their political co-religionists—then the solution would be to pass an income subsidy law, instead of trying to mandate that the cost of that subsidy be borne disproportionately by certain businesses, and ultimately individuals, who will pay with their jobs when those jobs are extinguished because those businesses can't afford the increase.

The minimum wage is kabuki, pure and simple, the theater of politics. Ask yourself why it was brought up in this, an election year, when the Democrats don't control Congress, instead of the first year of Clinton's term, when they did.

DH: What about positive activism toward goals such as universal access...?

LR: Universal access is only an issue in an environment of a certain kind of scarcity. Do we ensure universal access to air, water, food, clothing, television sets? No, we only do it to regulated, monopoly communication services. That monopoly is going away with deregulation. The increased supply of telecommunications services (wireless, cellular, satellite) is driving the cost of access to affordability for the entire population.

Access is a non-problem. I keep comparing it to television. Should we have had government mandates to ensure universal access to television? Cars? No, because even though at the beginning they were restricted to elites, it was the elites who helped amortize the development costs and pave the way for the mass market. A good example of how bad mandates in telecommunications can be is the example of Minitel in France, which put a 1200 baud computer in everyone's home, and retarded the development of a truly useful Net in France by 10 years.

DH: "Do we ensure universal access to air, water, food, clothing, television sets?" You know, actually, we do. In a variety of ways. Excepting the obvious exception of TVs, most of us view the first four you mention as inalienable rights. The UN has even tried to cast these rights into some sort of global Bill of Rights, without a whole lot of success, of course, but the symbolism of the attempt means something to a lot of people.

LR: Universal access is the mandated provision of service. Far as I can tell, not even the government has figured out how, or had the audacity, to mandate the provision of air, water, food, or clothing—as in forcing some company or individuals to provide them to the population at large at artificially low prices.

On the other hand, the government has surely tried to subsidize the provision of some of those goods, which is another story.

DH: If information technologies actually do become the economic lifeblood of the 21st century, is it morally right to deny access to anyone?

LR: Look, it really comes down to how compelling this technology really is. Is it compelling like a newspaper, a television, or a car is part of the economic lifeblood of the 20th century? Why don't we have provision for universal access of newspapers, televisions, and cars? Mandates from the government to force corporations to supply newspapers, televisions, and cars at below market rates to those people who demonstrate that they can't afford them?

The idea is ludicrous, because the supply of those products is unconstrained, because they have become mass market, because they can be obtained at all sorts of price levels, because people want and need them, and manage their own personal finances in order to get them. And if there is a very small minority that can't actually afford them, we directly subsidize their purchase through welfare.

What makes the Net any different? Either it is so compelling, like a car or television, that everyone needs it, and hence everyone manages their finances to get it, or it isn't, in which case, why should we want to mandate the delivery of a service that isn't essential?

You keep talking about telecommunications services like this was the 1930s, and the wires haven't reached the farms in Oklahoma yet. This is 1996, and AT&T is offering free Internet service, you can make a telephone call anywhere in America for a dime, and you can find a perfectly competent used computer to connect to the Net in the classifieds in newspapers for about the cost of a television. And there isn't just one wire coming into your house anymore; indeed, telecommunications services are not even being delivered only by wires. They are coming by cellular, PCS, satellite. More supply means even lower prices.

Universal access is a non-issue, more kabuki.

DH: Getting schools and public spaces wired...?

LR: An equivalent at the turn of the century would be automating blacksmith shops. Schools are obsolete. We should be doing all we can to liberate children from the slavery of the classroom, not wiring their jail cells.

DH: Okay, I'll bite. How does education work in the future?

LR: Like the saying goes, "If schools had the responsibility to teach people to talk, we'd be a nation of mutes."

Most of what we learn, we learn because we're curious, not because we are in a classroom. The vast majority of what we learn, we learn outside the classroom. What we mostly learn inside a classroom is how to fit into a hierarchy, and how to sit in one place for eight hours—in other words, how to be good industrial workers.

The whole system, from top to bottom is obsolete. You don't need education factories. You don't need to enslave children to "make" them learn.

The school system is the last vestige of 19th century notions of social planning, central planning at that. I envision a lot richer education environment when families can purchase education services like they purchase everything else in their lives. I can't fully imagine what that environment would be like, since its development has been so seriously retarded by the monopolization of education money by the current education establishment. But I could certainly envision one that relied heavily on networked learning, education companies, and new socializing institutions.

The fact is, the era of mass production is over, except in the schools. They're like the Soviet Union, an impossible idea whose sell-by date is way past.

DH: Putting the Net to use as a tool for empowerment?

LR: What can I say? Just because you have good intentions, doesn't mean you are going to achieve good results. And just because I don't wear my good intentions on my sleeve, doesn't mean I don't have intentions as pure as yours. Helping to spread the digital revolution seems to me to be the best way to create the most social good, the most wealth, a better civil society.

The way to help the spread of the digital revolution is to prepare people for the erupting future, and to help the spread of the Net. The Net spreads by more supply being available, with prices being reduced. More supply is available when companies compete to create new technologies and deliver more bandwidth. That's why I think de-regulation is good. Also because regulation just plain doesn't work, and increasingly just plain can't work in a networked world where the Net, to paraphrase Gilmore, recognizes attempts at control as damage and routes around them.

That's what *Wired* is about. Throwing up restraints to that spread seems to me what the PC left and the Christian right are about. The left would like to control it to make sure no one is successful, and the poor are protected. The right would like to control it to make sure no one is sinful, and the children are protected. Both are wrong.

DH: Is there a role for government when monopolies do arise? It happens. And aren't consumers, and as a matter of fact, the telecommunications industry as a whole, better off for the break-up of AT&T?

LR: The role of governments in breaking up monopolies is way overrated. The largest Justice Department antitrust case ever was against IBM. Cost both parties tens of millions, and burned up thousands if not tens of thousands of human-years. At the time the case was started, IBM was a colossus, with 400,000 employees in most of the countries around the world, with a majority share of the global computer market. It was the best run, the most efficient, the richest company on the planet. Lots of people argued it was a monopoly. The government took it to court.

We know the ending of the story, of course. The government lost the IBM case, yet the company is no longer the dominant player it was. In fact, its competitive position deteriorated so seriously in the past ten years that it shed the majority of its employees, and lost $75 billion in shareholder value—that's the GNP of Sweden. Why? Clearly not because this monopolistic company was broken up by the Justice Department. But because it was unable to maintain its monopoly in the face of rapid technological change, and insurgent, smarter companies.

And yes, we are better off for AT&T having been broken up. What's forgotten in that story, of course, is that AT&T was a creature of the government in the first place. At the turn of the century, AT&T was gobbling up local phone companies. The government started thinking about an antitrust suit.

Instead of fighting it, AT&T invented the notion of a regulated monopoly. It said to the government, don't break us up, regulate us. And that's exactly what happened, until MCI, which wanted to get into the long distance market, prodded the Justice Department into filing suit.

In other words, the monopoly broken up by the government was the one it sanctioned in the first place. In the intervening years, AT&T lived fat. Regulation for them was cost-plus. The entire deal was anti-supply-side, and the only thing that kept the United States from having the worst phone system in the world was the fact that the rest of the world went the United States one better (or worse), namely, they had nationalized monopoly phone systems. The beginning of this digital revolution can probably be marked by the foundation of MCI.

I can say categorically that we should not tolerate monopolies. But I find the examples of monopolies that grow out of markets few and far between, and then temporary at best. On the other hand, monopolies are products of governments, and they endure for decades. Just look at Europe, where there are still government phone companies with national monopolies charging extortionate rates and delivering substandard service.

Meanwhile, there's a whole line of economic thinking today which is arguing that temporary monopolies can actually be good. Think VHS. The fact that a standard gets set can offer downstream benefits that far outweigh the temporary costs.

DH: [Some of the] more technical matters do bring up some questions closely related to some of the things you've talked about regarding the Net and what it means for a new kind of democracy. To some, for example, the very term "push media" signifies a decrease in interactivity. Sounds a bit "top down." On the one hand, Java, ActiveX, and so on are very exciting. They ought to make the web a lot more entertaining. But at the same time, they will most likely encourage "viewers" to kick back and take in the show—not participate.

LR: If the only thing push media was about was re-creating television, I'd agree it's not very exciting. On the other hand, it would be no worse than television, and it wouldn't keep people from just passing through that layer and returning to the web world, or the news groups, etc.

But my feeling is that push media is about adding moving pixels to the interactive mix. Right now, interactivity via the web is about serving and consuming documents. Life is not about documents. It's fluid, moving, emotional, and reactive in real time. Push media starts to approximate the mental image we've always had about what could be good about television, and what could be good about interactivity—something visually stimulating, and something you could easily and creatively interact with.

DH: The browser and the desktop, one in the same? Sounds convenient. But the convergence gives some people pause. On the one hand, they worry about a single company, whichever it'll be, monopolizing their means of access to and experience of this global conversation (or show, whichever way it goes). On the other, it makes a PC less personal— what I'm getting at is, how can we come to terms with being "out of control," surrender to the universe, and yet maintain individual freedom and personal choice?

LR: I think they're getting media forms mixed up. Access to the larger Net will be essential to being able to sell any interface, as AOL has discovered. It's not like television, where there are only a limited number of frequencies being doled out by the government to corporations who are guaranteed to get large because of that scarcity (monopoly grants, again).

The Net is more like a newsstand, or lots of newsstands. Stocking only two magazines is not going to draw a lot of business.

But then let's get a little more precise here. I would like to make a distinction between media and democracy. Media is information and entertainment. It's rarely been discussion. Media is professional and propaganda, and has cloaked itself in free speech, but it's primarily a business. A business that a lot of people support by spending their money and attention on, but mostly a business none the less. And business, by its very nature, ends up concentrating into larger and smaller players.

Beyond business, however, is the discussion space of the Net. That discussion has not diminished since the arrival of professional media on the Net. On the contrary, there's more of it than ever. Probably because the medium is still really mostly about brains connecting to brains. I don't see that discussion diminishing just because professional media now starts to make the Net entertaining as well. In fact, I suppose you could make the argument that by making the Net even more attractive, it will draw the rest of the population into this huge discussion.

Finally, to loop back to the question of technology, I think in five years we are going to look at this discussion about browsers and desktops as being distinct entities and think it was pretty quaint. Connectivity is unstoppable. A computing device that's not connected to a network is like a bee separated from its hive, to use Kevin's analogy. Computing devices would be better thought of as connectivity devices, and of course the desktop is going to vanish into whatever software device—browser or Marimba tuner or Pointcast—that is that year's hot flavor.

DH: If networked communications are to be an alternative to electoral politics, I guess the most obvious question is the most pertinent. How? Do you see a consensus building out there on any single issue other than the CDA (which you've got to admit is a special case in that, one, it was so blatantly absurd, and two, we all had a shared interest in its defeat)?

Otherwise, it's endless, circular argumentation that almost inevitably degenerates into personal attacks, flame wars, and so forth. Maybe I'm looking in all the wrong places. Do you see tribes laying down their weapons anywhere out there?

What I hear here are magnificent, beautiful ideas. But I don't see them being put into practice. Do you?

LR: Hey when you're at a keyboard, you can't hold a weapon. All you can hurl are ideas. And in the end, I'm a believer that the best ideas will win out, because the universe does not reward an inaccurate assessment of reality.

I don't think the CDA is a special case. It was an assault on what the arrogant political establishment thought was a small, hapless minority. And this minority, namely us, if we had reacted like every other minority by holding protest marches, lobbying politicians, infiltrating local party organizations, etcetera, etcetera ad nauseum, would still be bound by this disgusting law as we spent years trying to change the minds of a political generation that is terminally out to lunch.

Instead we used the Net. And we turned the entire thing around.

This is not an exception, nor a trivial example. Keeping the government out of cyberspace is crucial to the Net's development, and the development of the New Economy and global consciousness. To me, that one single battle, in what is still a very large war, was an incredibly important turning point.

More broadly, I think we just have to get away from this idea that passing a law is somehow the end goal of democracy. It's just not. It's increasingly the booby prize, the indication that a solution has been locked in for a problem that may no longer exist, with the new law itself now a problem.

I also disagree that discussion on the Net is all circular argumentation. It's discussion. It's struggle. It's ideas brewing. Some of these are very big ideas. It takes time to diffuse them, work them all out, for people to get their minds around them, to contest them, reject them, or accept them.

The very fact that this discussion is beginning is a triumph. That you cannot point to any one "law" that was passed because of it to me means that you are looking at the wrong measure of its success.

In fact, this explicitly "political" discussion being conducted on the Net today is only part of the evolution of non-electoral decision-making and new consensus building. Let me put it another way, the way Walter Wriston puts it in the current issue of *Wired*. Networks have created a daily plebiscite on government policy, held by money managers and currency traders sitting in front of over 300,000 terminals around the world. There's no little screen that pops up when Clinton commits to a balanced budget in his first term and asks: thumbs up or thumbs down. No, the plebiscite is whether those managers buy or sell U.S. government securities or currency. If they do, the dollar is supported and Clinton is, in effect, backed. If they don't like what he's doing, they sell dollars, the dollar starts to move in the wrong direction, and Clinton has to change course.

This financial hive mind is not restricted to thinking about governments. The same thinking is applied to companies, who also have to behave responsibly to retain the support of this community.

And the same sort of hive mind is evolving in other disciplines as well, whether that's legal, educational, medical, or probably even religious. To me, it is the evolution of this hive mind that is more important than any one particular law you can point to and say today, "The Net made that happen."

DH: "Helping to spread the digital revolution seems to me to be the best way to create the most social good, the most wealth, a better civil society." On the one hand, this strikes a chord and I couldn't agree with you more wholeheartedly. On the other, I hear the word "revolution" being coopted to serve the "same as it ever was," only more so.

LR: We disagree. The world is changing radically, on every level. The Cold War is over. IBM is no longer the king of the hill. Microsoft is worth more than General Motors. Large power blocs are breaking up. 40 million people are connected to the Net. New business creation is accelerating. Netizens have actually rolled back a government assault on our rights. Telecommuting is a reality. People are living longer and better. Cities in advanced economies are becoming less polluted. Power is diffusing out of centralized institutions. We are emerging into a much less rigid, much more fluid world. Global consciousness is arriving. A New Economy is being born. This is most assuredly not more of the "same."

DH: The brilliance that went into *Wired*'s conception and packaging immediately made it the most widely recognized voice of that revolution, an incredible position of power, and as some would see it, responsibility. If it were on *Wired*'s agenda, how would you go about communicating that the coming transition, be it an evolution or a revolution, is inclusive rather than exclusive to those who fear being left out?

LR: I suppose I haven't felt it necessary to explicitly spell this out because I find the possibility of everyone not being included to be literally incredible.

Kevin talks about the fax effect. A single fax is worthless. Two faxes, you start to get some value, you can actually send something to someone else.

Indeed, you start to realize: Hey, the more people who have faxes, the more valuable this thing is, the better my life is. I'm motivated to encourage other people to buy faxes because the value of fax machines increases with their diffusion, and not just linearly, but geometrically. At that point not only is the fax company a promoter of faxes, the users become evangelists as well, and hence hasten the spread, the creation of mass market, the plummeting price of fax machines.

This imperative to include people, to make sure they are connected, is a part of a new kind of economics. It's one that's based not on scarcity, but on ubiquity. Simply, more people who possess certain goods and services means more wealth for all, as opposed to the old economics that said value came from the scarcity of an object, whether that was information, expertise, or money. All the incentives, then, are for the companies and participants in this revolution to be trying to pull people in, make them part of the New Economy.

The idea that we need to worry about anyone being "left out" is entirely atavistic to me, a product of that old economics of scarcity, and the 19th century social thinking that grew out of it. Mass communication, mass production, mass poverty, mass markets, mass society, mass media, mass democracy—that's history. Ford and Marx are well and truly dead. We are living in the 21st century.

A more appropriate concern looking to the future is the obverse of the worry for people being left out—namely, the consequences of everyone being connected. An entirely appropriate line of criticism of this Revolution might explore what it really means if five billion brains are connected together. Is this the ultimate, horrible, dystopian nightmare? (Or perhaps just less horrible than the world we are leaving behind?)

DH: Your example of the hive mind self-regulating the world of finance certainly describes one aspect of the way things get run, but there are checks and balances. As a matter of fact, the Crash of '87 could be described as something of a mini-prelude to the "dystopian nightmare" you speculate on should five billion brains get connected. Put speed and panic together and disaster is likely to escalate geometrically.

LR: Perhaps. But then again, the Crash of '87 hasn't repeated itself. On the contrary, the market has never been higher. Perhaps because the lessons were integrated back into the process. In other words, we learn.

But you're right, of course. Who knows where all this is going in the long run? I just think at this stage it's best to approach it with a certain critical optimism, because the possible negative outcomes that've been forwarded are mostly about fears or ideological biases, rather than rational examination of the issues.

DH: Would you do away with the Federal Reserve as well?

LR: At the moment, the Fed is one bank in a multi-bank global monetary system. My guess is that its influence on the domestic and world scene is going to diminish with the arrival of e-cash. It already has with the arrival of network money trading. It's not a matter whether I think that's good or bad, it's just happening. Better that we should understand what's going on and think about how we can preserve our financial security in a more complex world.

DH: And then the law. I'm tempted to ask about so many sets of laws, it's hard to select a reasonable number that'd be fair to ask you to respond to. Just these, then: labor laws, consumer protection, and the most basic criminal laws. How does the hive mind deal with murder, for example?

LR: Laws don't control 95 percent of your and my behavior, the uncodified norms of how we live together in civil society do. Laws are what happens when society reaches consensus. Laws don't create consensus. Italy is full of tax laws. No one follows them. Highways have speed limits. If they're too low, no one follows them.

The law is neither the only nor necessarily the best method for ensuring justice in society. Laws are only as effective as the faith people place in them to actually control behavior. Clearly, the justice system in this country is in crisis. With the war on some drugs, we have a criminal system which literally creates criminals. And the civil courts have become a huge welfare system for trial lawyers.

And specifically, how does the hive mind deal with murder? I don't really know, but you might ask OJ.

DH: Finally, services. What would be the bare bone set of government services you'd retain, if any?

LR: David, I don't have a thousand point program for how we get from here to the future. I just want to help start the discussion. Government is not going away. Governments perform all sorts of services—like the provision of legal and protective services, and others that you have pointed out—which are and will remain essential to human society. I'm just saying that in revolutionary times like these, we need to question everything, including that most sacred of sacred cows, the state. What is obsolete, what is really necessary? That questioning is going on in the business realm, and even in our personal lives—it should also be part of a discussion on the political as well. Ideas which we take for granted should be challenged. When Galileo said the earth wasn't the center of the universe, but revolved around the sun, he was considered a monster. Now it's conventional wisdom. Everything, as Barlow says, is in the process of becoming its opposite.

DH: Okay. The "horror stories." It would be foolish and highly unethical of me to bring up the names of anyone whose story hasn't already "gone public." I didn't in the published version of the interview with Paulina (the Katz/Kelly run-in seemed common knowledge enough), and won't now. But there do seem to be certain categories complaints fall into: paychecks have been cut with a curt "take it or leave it," writers' work has either been severely edited or killed altogether because it is not "politically correct"....

LR: I guess I take offense at anonymous charges being surfaced somewhere, then repeated somewhere else, then quoted in a third story as though they were fact, when they were never sourced in the first instance, and we never had a chance to rebut them.

Take Katz/Kelly. As I recall it, Kevin had a problem with a story Jon was working on. He felt it did not move beyond the arguments Jon had made in his last piece. He tried working with Jon on it, others tried working with Jon on it, in the end, it didn't work. That doesn't mean we don't respect Jon, that Kevin doesn't respect Jon, it only means that that particular story didn't work for us.

Was this the most elegant way of dealing with this particular situation? In retrospect, probably not. But Kevin meant no disrespect, and Jon continues to work with us—on *Netizen*, on stories for the magazine (the July cover was his), and with "HardWired." We would all like every interaction we have with everyone to be perfect. Sometimes they're not.

Writers write, editors edit. That's the way the world works. However, no story that I am familiar with "was severely edited or killed altogether because it is not politically correct." The only political story I intervened in was David Kline's piece on government. When I first saw it, I thought it was basically your standard Kennedy-liberal justification for government meddling.

We have a question around here: what's the revolution of the month? Kline's was no Kroker/Dery analysis. It reminded me of what I used to read in *New Republic* when I was in college. In other words, conventional wisdom. I have no problem with people who believe in conventional wisdom. There are plenty of venues where it gets exposure all the time. In fact, just about all the rest of media. What I wanted was more meat, more bite. I marked it up, Kevin talked some more with David, David did another cut, which added another layer on top of the liberal arguments he had already made. I was still unsatisfied with it. I was overruled. It ran. I still think it's not a very compelling reason for believing we need government. But the fact is it ran.

In all cases, "politically correct" is not the standard here. Being smart and new is. Back to my original editor's statement in our first issue. "Our first instruction to our writers: Amaze us." That still stands, even about politics.

And finally, one of *Wired*'s 10 heuristics is: "Legendary customer and contributor service." We are still a long way from achieving it. But we really try. Every issue, we have probably 150 to 200 contributors. They are handled by the 40 people who work in edit and art, and then another 10 in accounting. That's a lot of personal and commercial transactions. Multiply that by the 48 months we've been in business, and we're talking about a large number of people we've worked with, a lot of interactions. I wish every one was perfect. In this life, unfortunately, that's pretty much not possible. But my guess is that if you took a survey of *Wired* contributors, you would find that the overwhelming majority feel very good about the relationship they have with *Wired*, and want to continue to work with us.

DH: ...there's a cultish inside/outside thing going on, wherein anyone who speaks of the inside on the outside gets it.

LR: This is plain wrong. Who "gets it?" Gets what? What is there to tell about the inside on the outside? This just sounds paranoid.

DH: And then, the personal thing. We've brought it up before, but really only as it pertains to people identifying *Wired* with you. It works the other way around, too.

Here's a very public example. Jon Katz has his reasons for not wanting to get involved with Wired TV (*The Netizen*, or whatever it'll eventually be called). When interviewed, he states them. At the same time, his genuine admiration for you personally is unmistakable.

Yet there you go, into a very public forum and attack him on such a brutal and personal level. His physical appearance? Why?

LR: This is one of those "When did you stop beating your wife?" questions. I did not attack Jon on "a brutal and personal level." <http://www.netizen.com/cgi-bin/interact/view_ stitch?msg.25901>

Even lovers can have quarrels, and even in public. It's a funny kind of persecution where we love the guy and publish him continuously.

In that particular instance, I repeated a comment he made to me about why he didn't want to be in the *Netizen* TV show. Among the reasons he gave was his personal appearance, as though that disqualified him from appearing. I was trying to say that his personal appearance was irrelevant, that old television aesthetics were irrelevant, they were not part of *Wired*'s television effort, and that we wanted him because of the force of his ideas. Which we are trying as hard as we can to spread in as many venues as we have access to. In essence, I could barely take the appearance issue seriously, and had no idea I had stepped over any line with him until he e-mailed me the next morning. At which point I apologized to him, telling him what I'm telling you, namely that I had no intention to insult or embarrass.

DH: Let's tie this into the article I'm working on now. Never mind the ethics involved, no matter how "tired," does this make good business sense? If, now that the market's looking a bit healthier, you're getting ready to start the IPO process again, no matter which way you slice it, this doesn't look good or bode well for *Wired* as a long-term investment.

Because when employees are tossed out on their ear or generally abused, in public or private, especially the eloquent writer ones, they tend to get vocal and publish *Wired* rants left and right. Some rants are good for *Wired*. They make it look like that spunky publication that gets people all riled up. But a lot of rants, a steadily increasing number of rants, is going to give investors pause, right?

LR: What's wrong with this rant is that it's long on allegations and short on facts. It's utterly unsurprising that after our four years in business, some people don't like us. Nor that they would vent their dislike in public forums. Just because it appears in type, however, doesn't make it true.

What I object to is repeating Paulina's allegations about "horror stories" without documenting the stories. Paulina saying there are "horror stories" isn't good enough, she may not be an unbiased observer here (an understatement, to say the least). You need to dig out the "horror stories" themselves. Otherwise, all you're doing is repeating unfounded allegations, spreading bad memes.

At which point, I get frustrated. Because you're not talking about "vague stories by disgruntled contributors about alleged slights to people who work with *Wired*." You're stating as fact that there are "horror stories" at *Wired*, without a shred of proof. Forget about naming names, you can't even describe what constitutes "horror" here, much less quantify it. Instead, you give credence to a harsh accusation, and pass the bad meme along, forcing us to either have to live with an egregious misperception about *Wired*, or try to chase it down and combat it in every venue where it is casually quoted and passed along.

DH: There's a linkage between what many perceive to be the cold politics of libertarianism and the cold shoulder shown to "defectors." That linkage is central to the article. Is it a fair judgment?

LR: This whole discussion began with a story you were writing about Paulina Borsook and *Wired*, the "defector" you are apparently referring to (how she can be a defector and contributor at the same time is, of course, a leap of logic itself). From her assertions as to what transpired with Peter and "HardWired," you are trying to prove a general thesis about *Wired*. If I were you, I would question the assertions in the first place, and then the conclusions you draw from them.

I have no interest in talking about Paulina. I do challenge, however, her comments about selfishness. According to Paulina's argument, the very fact that people don't believe in using the government to correct social ills is QED a manifestation of their selfishness. It's like she read her Rand too closely.

Just because you believe state action is often immoral, and even more often ineffectual if not actually dangerous, doesn't mean you are "cold," or wish ill of your fellow human. On the contrary, you may actually believe that voluntary interaction is a more moral, and ultimately more efficacious way of ensuring justice and a better life for more people. And just because you don't rush out and become a social worker, doesn't mean you aren't contributing in a major way to improving the world around you.

As to "defectors" and "cold shoulders"—I repeat, after four years, we have worked with thousands of people. We believe we have treated and will continue to treat all of them fairly. Beyond fairly, well. They don't all agree with us; indeed, they often disagree with us (*we* even disagree with us); the vast majority still work with us.

DH: Also central to the article is a certain vicious circle; the worse *Wired*'s image becomes, the more irrational and cold the treatment of people who are seen as in the way; which in turn, worsens *Wired*'s image, and so on. Bad business, bad PR and bad blood. Fair or totally out to lunch?

LR: Totally out to lunch. Maybe the formulation is: The more *Wired* succeeds, the more frustrated its detractors become, the more vicious their allegations, the more they try to tarnish *Wired*'s image, and so on— all the while *Wired* participates in a virtuous circle, producing great content from a great work environment, which attracts satisfied users, retains employee loyalty, and establishes deep ties with an ever-widening group of valued contributors, and so on.

DH: Louis, many of the things you've said in the last couple of messages have made me stop dead in my tracks and think. Hard. This is why I value *Wired*. A friend was telling me the other day that he disagrees with just about everything *Wired* stands for but hopes to God it never goes away. I'm with him.

LR: I appreciate your comments, David, thank you. Clearly, I've enjoyed our exchange as well. And I'm ready to discuss any other issues, and any other "horror stories" with you in the future. Indeed, I would appreciate the opportunity to discuss them before you pass them on to your readers or friends, instead of having to chase after them. I know *Wired* isn't perfect. I also know we do a pretty good job on a whole lot of dimensions. The highest complement you can give us is not that you agree with us, but that we made you stop and think. What more can a magazine of ideas ask for?

References

Barbrook, Richard. "Hypermedia Freedom," *CTHEORY*, Vol. 19, No. 1–2, May 15, 1996.
http://www.ctheory.com/ga1.1-hyper_freedom.html

Barbrook, Richard and Andy Cameron. "The Californian Ideology."
http://www.wmin.ac.uk/media/HRC/ci/calif.html

Black, Bob. "The Libertarian as Conservative," originally published in *The Abolition of Work and Other Essays*, by Bob Black, with no copyright.
http://www.c2.org/~mark/lib/libertarian.html

Boardwatch.
http://www.boardwatch.com

Borsook, Paulina. "Cyberselfish," *Mother Jones*, July/August 1996.
http://www.motherjones.com/mother_jones/JA96/borsook.html

Borsook, Paulina. "How Anarchy Works," *Wired* 3.10, 1995.
http://www.hotwired.com/wired/3.10/departments/electrosphere/ietf.html

Borsook, Paulina. "Nite-Crawler," *Suck*, April 12, 1996.
http://www.suck.com/daily/dynalink/96/04/12

Borsook, Paulina. "Sex and the Single URL," *Suck*, June 26, 1996.
http://www.suck.com/daily/dynatables/96/06/26/

Borsook, Paulina. "Something about Art," *Leonardo*, 1995.
http://wwwmitpress.mit.edu/Leonardo/isast/spec.projects/borsook.html

Borsook, Paulina and Andy Reinhardt, "beverly_hills.com," *Wired* 3.02, 1994.
http://www.hotwired.com/wired/3.02/departments/electrosphere/beverly.hills.html

Brain Tennis (Borsook vs. More).
http://www.hotwired.com/braintennis/96/33/index3a.html

Brownstein, Ronald. "Rage Against the Machine," *Fast Company*, 1996.
http://www.fastcompany.com/fastco/issues/fourth/politics.html

Burstein, Daniel and David Kline. "Is Government Obsolete?" *Wired* 4.01.
http://www.hotwired.com/wired/4.01/departments/electrosphere/government.html

Byron, Christopher. "Hype and inconsistencies? Potential investors beware: Mired in red ink, Wired giving it a go with an IPO," MSNBC.
http://www.msnbc.com/news/32779.asp

"Chez Justine" (An unofficial Paulina Borsook web site).
http://www.transaction.net/people/paulina.html

c|net's Rumor Mill, September 30, 1996.
http://www.news.com/Rumors/Entry/0,26,,00.html

Dery, Mark. "Unplugged," *Educom Review*, Vol. 30, No. 3, May/June 1995.
http://www.educom.edu/educom.review/review.95/may.jun/dery.html

Gehl, John. "Editors Just Want To Have Fun," *Educom Review*, Vol. 30, No. 3, May/June 1995.
http://www.educom.edu/educom.review/review.95/may.jun/gehl.html

Gitlin, Todd. *The Sixties: Years of Hope Days of Rage*, Bantam Doubleday Dell, 1993.

Griffin, Bryan. "Comments from a Libertarian, Mistakes and Misleading Statements," *Mother Jones Live Wire*, August 3, 1996.
http://www.mojones.com/Agora_1.01/parse_post.pl?LIVE_WIRE/LW2266/lw12397.post

Groendahl, Boris. "Wired Goes Germany," *InSight*.
http://www.rommerskirchen.com/insight/ventures.html

Heilemann, John. "Brand New Politics," *Netizen*, August 8, 1996.
http://www.netizen.com/netizen/96/32/index3a.html

Heilemann, John. "Westerly Winds," *Impolitic*, *HotWired*, November 14, 1996.
http://www.netizen.com/netizen/96/46/index4a.html

Huben, Mike. "Critiques Of Libertarianism."
http://world.std.com/~mhuben/libindex.html

Hundt, Reed—Chairman Federal Communications Commision and Vice President Al Gore. Speech to the Interactive Services Association's 11th Annual Conference, San Diego, CA., July 23, 1996.
http://www.isa.net/newsroom/hundt-ISA.html

Keegan, Paul. "Reality Distortion Field," *Upside*, January 1997.

http://www.upside.com/companies/wired1.html

Kline, David. "A Tale of Two IPOs: Why Wired's Failed and Cybermedia's Succeeded," *Upside*, November, 1996.

http://www.upside.com/online/columns/netprofit/9611.html

Koch, Jorg. "Wired," *Netzeug*, Wildpark.

http://www.wildpark.de/netzzeug/2wired/2wired_nz.html

Kress Täglich (German news service).

http://www.kress.de/tgl/index.html

Mercury Mail, "Broad Support for U.S. Child Food Aid—Charity," October15, 1996.

http://www.merc.com/stories/cgi/story.cgi?id=312731-ab6

Mother Jones, MoJo Wire polls.

http://www.motherjones.com/news_wire/soapbox/

Mr. Media.

http://www.mrmedia.com/mrmedia/Mr. Media

nettime.

http://www.desk.nl/~nettime/

Perelman, Lew. "Weird, Feared, Revered?" *Educom Review*, Vol. 30, No. 3, May/June 1995.

http://www.educom.edu/educom.review/review.95/may.jun/perelman.html

Pitta, Julie. "Wired's Reach for Multimedia Ring Falls Short," *Los Angeles Times*, October 14, 1996.

Raphael, Glenn. "Top Ten Political Issues Liberals and Libertarians Can (Sometimes) Agree On."

http://www.batnet.com/liberty/liberal/topten.html

Red Herring.

http://www.herring.com/mag/home.html

Rewired's two-part interview with Paulina Borsook.

http://www.rewired.com/96/0819.html

http://www.rewired.com/96/0821.html

Rosenberg, Scott. "Wired Unbound," *Salon*, October 2, 1996.

http://www.salon1999.com

Rossetto, Louis. "Response to the Californian Ideology."

http://www.wmin.ac.uk/media/HRC/ci/calif2.html

Watson, Tom. @NY.

http://www.news-ny.com/viewpoin.htm

Weil, Debbie. "The Hill Is Wired These Days, But Do They 'Get It'?" *Editor and Publisher Interactive*, July 1996, No. 2.

http://www.mediainfo.com/ephome/news/newshtm/wordbiz/wordbiz702.htm

Winner, Langdon. "Peter Pan in Cyberspace: Wired Magazine's Political Vision," *Educom Review*, Vol. 30, No. 3, May/June 1995.

http://www.educom.edu/educom.review/review.95/may.jun/winner.html

Wired.

http://www.hotwired.com/wired

wired_women, Home Page.

http://www.cyberwerks.com/wired_women/index.html

Zakaria, Fareed. "A devil's dictionary," *Slate*, July 25, 1996.

http://www.slate.com

Part VI:

Communities Real and Imagined

"As a single entity, the Net will not forge a community any more than a house or a public square would. It is those inside that space and what they are doing with their time there."

David Hudson

Chapter Thirty-One
Socializing (on) the Web

Brian Eno: A lot of the questions people ask me have to do with new technologies and what effects they have. What I'm interested in is the way new technology keeps generating new metaphors for us. So for instance, the Internet, in terms of content, is not all that interesting in my opinion, with exceptions, but in general it's not a place I would go to do my best reading. In terms of content it isn't a huge step forward yet. Structurally, it is terribly revolutionary. Content always follows.

John Alderman: Do you have favorite places to go on the web?

Brian Eno: I speak to one or two friends. That's the most important thing. It puts me in a community that doesn't have a geographical center or boundaries.

A grand, expensive, and ambitious experiment, the culmination of years of imagining and pondering and months of serious tinkering, launched at 11:11 a.m. PST on the eleventh day of the eleventh month of 1996—Howard Rheingold's Electric Minds was off and running, one of the most promising solutions proposed to meet the challenges currently facing online communications a long, long while. Why?

First, we can pretty much take it as a given by now that the web has just about finished swallowing the Net. By the time Electric Minds opened, AOL had all but thrown in the towel, placing its content on the web and becoming essentially an ISP with a few extras—so that was about it for the commercial services. PC or NC, when you turn the thing on in the not-so-distant future, your desktop is most likely going to be not just a Net connection but a web browser.

Further, any new gadget, publication model, or software program being dreamed up right now has the web in either the fore or background of that dream. Yet despite its lock on the future, the web's got problems, not the least of which is that it is not turning on a whole lot of people as yet. Techno-logically, the problem is simple to pinpoint: It is too darn slow. People get stuck, they turn it off.

After all these years of everybody saying so, bandwidth is still the number one hurdle to be overcome before any of these new online media attain the significance of the old in most people's lives. Survey after survey has turned up trouble. Although the Net is still growing, that growth is slowing. More tellingly, those who are on are using it less. And the far and away number one complaint among these users is speed.

Worse, in one of his "Stop the Presses" columns, "A Contrary View: Infrastructure Will Slow Internet Speed Improvements," Steve Outing presents the views of Robert Crandall, a twenty-year veteran of the techie side of the telecom industry. Basically, Crandall believes the solution to the bandwidth problem is a lot further away than the new media moguls would have us believe. Without delving into the details, in which Crandall does indeed seem fairly fluent, the gist of his argument is that any chain is only as strong as its weakest link. Because wiring every household with fiber-optic cable is out of the question in the near future, that leaves most people depending on twisted copper wires, which are in a lot worse shape than most people realize, Crandall asserts. They can handle voice and they can handle data at low speeds, but crank up the juice and they are overwhelmed.

Crandall is just as critical of the prospects for cable modems and other proposed solutions. There may be a ray of hope in wireless technologies or in Intel chief Andy Grove's plans for multimedia whoopie running on existing bandwidth, but of course, we would all have to buy fresh chips. So, what's doing serious damage to the CD-ROM technically is that you can't update it (and they're too expensive). What threatens the web is that, although you can update it, it doesn't zap (and, for a lot of people, it is still too expensive).

Boring content plagues both. But in theory at least, the web's boring content can be "updated" with engaging content. And even now, you can create a modest bookmarks file that will serve (oh, once a week or so) as a decent batch of reading material. Problem is, of course, a customized magazine does not a digital revolution make. But that is about all the web has been able to offer most people for the first three years of its existence.

So one of the challenges facing anyone who wants to make the web work is to make do with its severe limitations. To put some of the magic that had everyone so excited about the Internet a few years ago back into its present lumbering form. As Scott Rosenberg wrote in "After the Gold Rush," a sharp and sober survey of the state of the web that appeared before Electric Minds debuted, "two very different groups are emerging with different ideas of how to drive the web forward: call them the information peddlers and the community builders."

So far, peddling information has meant publishing—text—because that is what the technology can handle. Turn on your computer and read. It is the worst of several worlds. Your computer is not really computing any more. You are staring at a screen much like a TV, but there's no action. And who is comfortable reading while sitting up straight at a desk? Still, there is a hardcore bunch of us who can't help ourselves. Not enough to launch a self-sustaining industry, but we're there. The main attraction is enticing, though: peddling has never been easier. It is still limited to those with the means, but those limitations are less strenuous than they are in old-fashioned paper-based publishing. So the web holds out the opportunity to talk back.

But wait a minute. It is a lot harder to talk back now on the web than it was on the Net when our aesthetic expectations weren't so demanding. Many-to-many communication, what the Net was supposed to have been about in the first place, is still tough and impersonal if you want to go the publishing, information-peddling route. No wonder, as Electric Minds' business guy, Randy Haykin, has put it, "surfing is lonely."

How to bring back the ease and flow of that communication, as it was (and, of course, still is) experienced in the days of UseNet, Telnet, and the BBS is the second challenge facing Rosenberg's second group, the community builders.

Now, no one has probably done more for the idea of the virtual community than Howard Rheingold, a feat for which he has been both praised and ridiculed. Interestingly, for the most part, both the praise and the ridicule has been based on approximately the same interpretation of what Rheingold has said and written in the past. Virtual communities not only exist, the argument has run, they can create a sense of belonging for the individual and even challenge the powers that be, constitute a force for social change.

Here are Richard Barbrook and Andy Cameron in "The Californian Ideology" again to represent the political criticism of the idea of virtual communities:

Rewired

"On the one hand, the anti-corporate purity of the New Left has been preserved by the advocates of the 'virtual community'. According to their guru, Howard Rheingold, the values of the counter-culture baby boomers are shaping the development of new information technologies. As a consequence, community activists will be able to use hypermedia to replace corporate capitalism and big government with a hi-tech 'gift economy'. Already bulletin board systems, Net real-time conferences and chat facilities rely on the voluntary exchange of information and knowledge between their participants. In Rheingold's view, the members of the 'virtual class' are still in the forefront of the struggle for social liberation. Despite the frenzied commercial and political involvement in building the 'information superhighway', the electronic agora will inevitably triumph over its corporate and bureaucratic enemies."

If you are wondering what is really all that bad about such a position, and there is certainly good reason to wonder, basically Barbrook, Cameron, and others claim that the goals are lofty enough, surely loftier than those of the other targets of "The Californian Ideology," but that these goals are unattainable. We will get to that in a moment, but first Rheingold's reply:

"Got some e-mail from Barbrook praising Electric Minds," Rheingold announced somewhat triumphantly a few days after the launch. Barbrook was quite vocal in his approval of the project. "He and I corresponded a bit when I tried to tell him that I did not actually get together with Louis [Rossetto], Kevin [Kelly], John Perry [Barlow], and Stewart [Brand] for our California-ideological cell meetings. He admitted that was true, but feels I am still an 'anti-Statist' because I have reservations about the CDA." That would indeed be a serious misreading of a position in favor of supporting the First Amendment. More to the point, are virtual communities possible? In *The Virtual Community*, Rheingold argues that online technology can feed "the hunger for community that grows in the breasts of people around the world as more and more informal public spaces disappear from our real lives." Richard Sclove disagrees and explains why in *Democracy and Technology*.

First, no technology, no matter how virtually real, will ever measure up to live, face-to-face communication. You just can't replace the actual presence of another human being. "Electronic media decompose holistic experience into analytically distinct sensory dimensions and then transmit the latter. At the receiving end, people can resynthesize the resulting parts into a coherent experience, but the new whole is invariably different and, in some fundamental sense less, than the original."

This a very well-taken point. In many ways, friends made online are still strangers. But that is true of friends "in real life" as well. More importantly, the same breakdown of the self into a limited sort of representation to be reconstructed on the receiving end takes place in any mode of communication, even one as romanticized as letter-writing.

Next, Sclove has a few nasty things to say about screen-based technologies. People grow lethargic and start to decompose in front of those squares. To me, this is the weakest of Sclove's arguments in that watching television and actively engaging in an online chat are very different activities indeed. Further, he might run into some resistance from more than one media critic to the idea that taking in a movie or a TV program is a solely passive experience. On top of that, sitting on a front porch with friends is certainly communing, but no more physically demanding that curling up on the sofa with your significant other, a good video playing on the set.

"Third, a strength—but also a drawback—to a virtual community is that any member can exit instantly. Indeed, an entire virtual community can atrophy or perish in the wink of an eye." The danger Sclove sees here is that an individual can become too dependent on what ultimately amounts to nothing but an illusion of community. His subsequent claims for the psychological damage such dependency can incur do seem to be a bit of a stretch, but it is an argument worthy of consideration. At the same time, we have to wonder, especially at the close of the millennium, whether the fragility of any online community is greater or less than any other in real life.

The community of a small rural town in an underdeveloped country may be very strong indeed, but in many urban centers, and for that matter, sleepy suburban towns of industrialized nations—where, in fact, we find most of the participants in online communities—real-life communities are few and far between. Is it somewhat sad that we have to rely on technology to fulfill a loss technology is mostly responsible for, or is this a development to be celebrated? Does the sort of community Brian Eno is talking about experiencing himself actually exist?

"The machine age in developing the Great Society has invaded and partially disintegrated the small communities of former times without generating a Great Community... No amount of aggregated collective action of itself constitutes community." That was John Dewey in the mid-20s, in the middle of a different and yet not so different sort of technological revolution.

The arguments in his book *The Public and its Problems* are aimed at many targets, and one of them is clearly the optimism with which the network of roads and rails was cheered on, the confident belief—not merely the hope— that society's new connectivity would give rise to a great big small town where everybody knows your name. The link between the optimistic confidence then and now does not take much of a mental click to make.

Now, here I am calming a friend who was brand new to one of my own favorite online hang outs, the "San Francisco Bay Guardian Online." As a side note, I should add that for over a year, I have been participating in that fluid community from Berlin. I met folks while living in San Francisco, but the physical move a continent and an ocean away didn't mean I would have to lose touch. My friend had been wondering why one of the conferences there that looked lively enough at first was suddenly deathly quiet: "As you hang around for a while, you'll see that these communities evolve very, very quickly. People come and go. Someone flames somebody else, and either both get over it, or both disappear, or an all out flame war flares up. At any rate, you can't get too attached to any one place... You'll see people herd from one conference to another and a constant rotation of new names appearing and disappearing... It's a fascinating ant farm. And as one of the ants, I'm having an absolute blast!"

Looking more objectively now at these words I rattled off in a personal note, typing before I thought, and then looking at the Dewey quote, I am overwhelmed by the echoing rings of micro and macrocosms. Somehow, it slipped out that a single conference, be it on a BBS, UseNet, the web, wherever, is a community within the framework of another. To zoom in even closer, as I teeter back and forth from the viewpoint of someone very much within one community ("one of the ants") and the outsider's, bird's eye view of the whole farm, I'm doing so in a private e-mail. Are two a community?

If not, consider another conversation: I'm in Berlin, she's in Arizona, and he's in San Francisco. Every message is CC'd, and so far, there must be a hundred of them. How tightly can we zoom in before the concept of community dissolves?

Notice the factors with which we are dealing here: virtual space, time, and population. If you think space is irrelevant, consider the system operator who once showed me the nifty feature allowing him to see "where" everybody logged on to his system was hanging at any given time.

And time is taken apart and put back together in utterly unrecognizable ways. This three-way conversation I'm engaged in—add it all up and it might be the equivalent of a chat over dinner that lingers a while after the dishes have been cleared. But in fact it has been going on for months. And the bonds that take root and hold, the ones that have nothing to do with the number of words exchanged, permit me to say to myself, that woman in Arizona, the one I've never seen, yes, I know her. She's a friend of mine. But for how long? After the words and threads are played out, will the other bonds still hold?

Zoom out. If the idea of two, three, or ten people constituting a community is too abstract to be useful, the same warped characteristics of space and time apply to groups of hundreds, thousands of people assembled online—systems teeming with alliances of varying interests. And over time, alliances dissolve and reform as new ones in other spaces. Always. For all the sweet things Howard Rheingold has to say about "The Well" in *The Virtual Community*, when the new managers decided to spruce the place up a bit, many stalwarts of the community hauled off and tried to reconstruct a memory on a different system.

Zoom out again. Can tens of millions of people be a single community? In the Net's infancy, you could talk about a "Net community." Those online shared among them a whole set of characteristics. Only certain slivers of society had the means and the desire to play with the Net. But at the moment, the single defining characteristic of the Net community is that it is online and everybody else isn't...yet. Still, some persist in their talk of a Digital Nation with a coherent agenda. The problem with static visions of a Great Community is that they don't take into account the nomad in human nature, the itch that propels us to leave the comforts or the boredom of one place to seek out stimulation in another. Look at that Dewey quote again: "No amount of aggregated collective action of itself constitutes community." As a single entity, the Net will not forge a community any more than a house or a public square would. It is those inside that space and what they are doing with their time there.

"I'm still open about whether this community stuff is for real—or a dangerous illusion," Rheingold says in the talk that follows. "I think that the truth is somewhat more complex than, 'This stuff is a community' on one end, and 'This is a complete illusion' on the other end." The approach is far more sober than the one he is usually associated with. Either he has been misinterpreted by his critics or he has tempered his views over the years. One of Rheingold's hopes for Electric Minds is that it will provide a place in which to discuss this question and perhaps even provide evidence of whatever answers come up. And indeed, those answers will probably not align themselves with either of the extreme ends, pro or con. So whether such a thing as a virtual community exists in the idyllic form its name would suggest, there can be little doubt that something is going on when people "get together" online.

"Since I am a member of an online community," a writer e-mailed to me after seeing a column on the *Rewired* site about Electric Minds, "it's a topic of some interest. But I've always believed the old 'it's a community/ no, it's not' debate was moot. For me, it's like Santa Claus (or God, I suppose). An online community exists for you if you believe in it and want it to exist, because, I believe, the act of wanting it to exist and believing in it is one of the most powerful things anybody can do in creating a true community. Conversely, an online community vanishes like a puff of smoke if you didn't believe in it. In my view, to deny the existence of online communities is to declare your opposition to them."

Powerful words. But anonymous ones. The writer, a journalist who covered a particular pop cultural phenomenon around which the community he belongs to evolved, worries, along with the other members of the community, about too many other people coming in and stirring things up. He saw, for example, the Virtual Community Center on Electric Minds where hypertext links to various communities are gathered, where communities are profiled and discussed. He thought about adding his to the list, but thought better of it.

"As more and more people pour on to the online world, what communities do exist are becoming hidden ones. We no longer put up sign posts. We no longer evangelize. We welcome newcomers if they find their way to us, despite the difficulty and the camouflage. It means they were motivated enough. But who needs half-interested types just wandering to see if they like the place—or perhaps just looking for a place to create havoc? We've been scorched too often by those who seek only to prevent others from enjoying themselves. So we hide, and pray the barbarians at the gate don't find us."

An especially interesting, but far from unique, component of his community is that the members have gathered several times IRL, or in real life. Some members, in fact, have flown great distances to be in on these gatherings. Also interesting, and again, a fairly common characteristic of other such communities, when they gather "virtually," they no longer spend a lot of time chatting about that shared interest, the pop culture thing, that brought them together in the first place.

"We just talk about our day, or things that interest us. We console each other when a tragedy strikes. We cheer when one of us has a victory. And the group has sparked any number of loving couples. We're a family, and like all families we fight sometimes. But the community stays strong. But we have also been assaulted many times by those who have become aware that we are quietly enjoying ourselves and seemingly cannot bear the thought of that happening. So mentioning the chat room or its name in public folders is now a taboo respected by all." And by me as well.

Electric Minds is a very different sort of "place" than other online gathering spots. Rheingold is consciously trying to make it a collective web publishing venture as well. "Information" and "community"—two seemingly opposing buzzwords from the dictionary of Net hype—are jammed together on one site. That is the experiment, and the key ingredient in the mix is context. No one is saying with absolute certainty that it will happen. But if it stands a chance anywhere, most likely, it is here. Articles go up and people talk about them, but the content and the talk share virtual space on the same web pages.

And the interface works. Of course, everyone is going to have his or her minor criticisms. As someone who usually despises frames, for example, this is one of the few sites in my opinion where it really makes sense to have a couple of different windows going on, tiny as they may be. The proportion of info to the size of the window is right on.

The genuine innovations show up on the front pages of each of the broad areas into which the site is divided: content on the left, conversation on the right. But as Rheingold points out, it is not as easy as it looks. My guess is that we are going to start seeing a lot of imitations of interface designer Abbe Don's work. Lots of time, money and effort went into it, but as they say in the movies, it's all up there on the screen. But Howard Rheingold's experiment will truly be a success if the special effects are too real to notice, throwing the spotlight on the cast.

As a showcase, storefront window sort of medium, the web has encouraged a return to top-down, one-to-many publishing and broadcasting models, much to the delight of many a large company already used to disseminating its product, information, with a shovel. This is antithetical to the Net's most vital characteristic, its many-to-many model of communication, or in a word, dialogue.

This is not to say that all sorts of other exciting things had not been going on on the web before Electric Minds came along, but the general trend was in the wrong direction. Rheingold is certainly not single-handedly bringing dialogue back to the Net. Clearly, it never went away in the first place, and there have been some very innovative stabs at web-based conferencing for years. But what is significant about Electric Minds is that it has been a very high-profile move in the right direction. Advertising dollars, the media spotlight, and online buzz have been drawn to a project whose primary feature is conversation. Not just "interactivity" or "click here to discuss this essay," or "click here to e-mail the author."

Further, the conversation is meant to be cultivated and eventually harvested. As Rheingold says, "Just because you don't call it a column or an article doesn't mean that it's not valuable." If you have interesting things to say and end up attracting an audience, some of the site's revenues might be funneled in your direction. That is putting an important observation often made about online communication to productive practice. Howard Rheingold is flattening the medium back out again, at least his corner of it.

But it is tricky. Who chooses what is valuable? An editorial staff? By what criteria, and would there ever be such a thing as conversation guidelines available for those shaping a persona as a sort of audition for publication? And what if you think you are saying some pretty neat things but are not getting picked out, either for the front page or the potential digests of conversations aimed at the reader on a tight schedule? Rheingold argues that at Electric Minds, the editorial selection will keep the place interesting enough to attract an audience.

Hopefully, the process will proceed with as little friction as possible and will not interfere or distract from the main attraction—the full-blown, freely flowing conversations. Already, some terrific ones have taken place. I recognized one conference immediately as a sure hang-out. Media Shock, co-moderated by Steve Rhodes and Rebecca Eisenberg, is the conference that, as the co-written description puts it, "tours the craters of media-technology convergence, and looks at what happens when the worlds of technology and media collide."

Because I was interested in how moderators had been chosen anyway, these two presented themselves as prime candidates for a few questions. When Steve Rhodes, a media reporter who can hear a pin drop on the Net, was contacted about doing a conference, he said he would be "interested doing something on media or television with someone else since I think the best conferences have co-hosts."

But because Electric Minds is all about technology, it was decided that "a conference on media and tech might work, but they probably wouldn't add it until January [two months after launch]. Jen [Bekman, Director of Community Development at Electric Minds] contacted me a few weeks ago saying they had a bit of extra money in their budget and wanted to start the conference at launch. That was great—it was an important topic to be there at the start—but I have a full-time job, so I definitely needed a co-host. I'd been reading Rebecca's Read Me! [at her web site] since March when Suck linked to her. I visit a lot of Web sites, but I return to very few." Indeed, no one reads Rebecca Eisenberg just one time.

"I thought she would be a good co-host since she writes about media, consumes about as much media and popular culture as I do, and knows more about technology than I do. We got together on a Friday and talked about what we wanted the focus of the conference to be and brainstormed about some names." The name was plucked, naturally, from the web. They fiddled with an online thesaurus for a while to come up with this. When I expressed reservations about the "Shock" half (echoes of Toffler), Rebecca replied, "The word 'shock' is DA BOMB," and accompanied this very Rebecca comment with the following definition from Webster's:

3. shock n [MF choc, fr. choquer to strike against, fr. OF choquier, pro]... 1: the impact or encounter of individuals or groups in combat 2a: a violent shake or jar : CONCUSSION ... 3a1: a disturbance in the equilibrium or permanence of something... 5: sudden stimulation of the nerves and convulsive contraction of the muscles caused by the discharge of electricity through the animal body ...

Okay, it fits. "It did click partly because it was a play on Toffler's *Future Shock*," Steve Rhodes adds, "but it also describes the way a lot of people both in and outside the media industry feel right now." Indeed. So, Rebecca, what is it like to co-host? "I love sharing moderatorship. Steve is so much nicer than I am. From my view out here, Steve gives a lot of fact—and tons of useful resources and links!—and I rally a lot of opinion. That is not a set rule, however."

"It is going well so far," Steve chimes in. "I was afraid there would be too much traffic to keep up with when we opened, but it isn't part of one of the content areas so it is probably a little harder to find. There also are a lot of people lurking and we're talking about ways to try and get more people to post. I hope there will continue to be friendly disagreement. I've seen too many forums disrupted by one person."

So has just about anyone who has been a part of an online community!

UseNet is a perfect example of all that can go wrong when no one is guiding the community. Again, although the anarchic technical infrastructure of the Net works, anarchic human infrastructures don't.

In real-life human communities, there is a system of checks and balances we have been tinkering with since we stumbled out of the caves. Sometimes it works, sometimes war breaks out. Mostly though, on the day-to-day level, it rocks along. But this system cannot be transplanted as a whole on to the online environment. Short example: Two guys get in a fight in real life, the bartender tells them to take it outside. Online, how do you do that? Because if you don't, their fight eats up a whole conference or wrecks a chat room. And if that happens too often, people get a bad feeling about the place, and that is hard to sell no matter what else you have to offer.

Rewired

Rheingold has sketched out Electric Minds' "Rules of the Road," a set of policies that aim to allow as much personal freedom to the system's users as possible while ensuring that everyone's rights are respected and not infringed on by other users. All in all, establishing Electric Minds has been a delicate balancing act teetering between freedom and discipline, editorial content and conversation, online and offline publication. Several eyes are on the experiment Rheingold calls "The Social Web," watching and hoping that it can bring some of the magic back to the Net that was lost when the web came along.

Chapter Thirty-Two
A Talk with Howard Rheingold

A lot about Howard Rheingold can initially put off anyone born too late to have had much to do with the 60s. For all his up-to-the-moment technological savvy, his way with words and all he has done to bring the Net into mainstream consciousness, he can appear at first glance to still be carrying around too much of the outrageous, some might say naive, enthusiasm of a generation that hoped to change the world.

The thing is, he evidently can be an outrageous character, as evidenced by his famous wardrobe, and no, he hasn't given up hope that technology can be put to positive use. But what I have seen during the months since Electric Minds debuted is a mind wide open to new ideas and new angles on his old ones. Famous for praising the virtues of virtual communities, he opened a topic at Minds wondering out loud whether the whole idea wasn't "dangerous hooey." As host, he scoots from forum to forum jazzing up the conversations, quelling brawls when they break out with a friendly yet firm hand, and over and again, asking questions, seemingly far more eager to learn than to drop his own unique science.

In short, Howard Rheingold is one of the few among what might be called "the first generation digerati" who is not only willing to evolve with the times and revise his notions according to the new demands of rapidly shifting realities—he actually does so.

On November 9, 1996, two days before Electric Minds opened its doors to the public, I called Howard Rheingold to talk about the site, what makes it different, how it works, where the money comes from, and possible directions for the future.

DH: Let's start out with this. What in your view is different about Electric Minds? We've got a lot of web conferences out there. What's going to be different?

HLR: Well, I think what differentiates Electric Minds really goes to what the original vision was, which was to use the medium of the web not just to push older kinds of publishing models a little further, but to create something new that is a real integration of editorial content and user-generated content.

Now, people are using community as a marketing term these days. As you know, I'm a real believer in the responsibility of the community. I don't think you create communities. I think you can create a context for people to get together. And in our case, the context is technology and what it means. You give them the enabling technologies to enable them to communicate with each other publicly, and you create the environment in which intelligent conversations can emerge.

Hopefully, those intelligent conversations will lead to ongoing relationships, and that's where community can emerge.

Editorial content is a context for conversation among our audience. And rather than having a button at the bottom of the page that sends you to some threaded discussion, we really are putting the window to our conversations literally right up there on the same page, right next to the content. There is a window on to the conversation that invites you to jump into it. When you're in the conversation, there is a window into the content.

So, I'd say that that's the main thing that differentiates it. We really believe that there are a lot of intelligent, articulate people out there who know what they're talking about who are going to contribute to content that is just as valuable as the stuff we go out and pay your professionals and your names to provide.

DH: Yes, I like that window, too.

HLR: It cost a lot of money, time, and effort, which we didn't understand at the beginning, to make this actually work. Because we've got this pretty fancy Oracle Java database that serves up the conversation material and into the HTML page. But from the very beginning, the mission was, how can we really marry the content to the community?

And although, now that you can see it, the solution looks easy—you really divide the page in half and serve up pieces of the conversation on one side—it was something that we struggled and struggled and struggled with. Abbe Don, who is our interface designer, really came up with one of those solutions that, after you see it, it looks very simple, but you know, if it was that simple, why hadn't anyone else done it yet?

You go to "HotWired" or to "Salon," and they have lively discussions, but in terms of user interface, they're appendages to the content.

DH: Yes. Something actually that my friend Andrew Sullivan and I were talking about trying to do with *Rewired*, but you're right, it's tough, and we didn't figure it out. So that was Abbe Don, then?

HLR: Yes, she really cracked that problem. Now, it is one thing to say, Well, we'll put our content up on the left side. And on the right side, we'll get an editor's selection and an automatically chosen most active topic put up. It's another thing to do it, we discovered.

It costs hundreds of thousands of dollars, in fact. So that's where this integration of the database, the conferencing system, and the web site came together. If we didn't have to put those three technologies together, we could have launched at the end of the summer.

DH: So, it's very, very expensive. How does the revenue come in? I've read that you've got some sponsorships, and there'll be a bit of advertising...

HLR: Well, we're trying to push the envelope on the advertising revenue model as well. The idea here being, there's traditionally the Chinese Wall between editorial and advertising, and there's all the advertorial stuff, there's click-through banners, and that's very much predicated on traffic and having a large number. We're not really aiming for large numbers. We're aiming for a particularly intelligent audience who are knowledgeable about technology.

The theory there has been that perhaps we should go the PBS route rather than the network route. Instead of delivering a thirty share, we deliver quality programming to people who are interested in and who care about technology and actually buy technology, make buying decisions for companies about technology. Wouldn't that be something that the technology companies would want to underwrite?

Underwriting means they believe in the product. They want to associate their brand name with it. They're not necessarily going for the millions of impressions that they get from buying at Netscape. So the sponsors that you would see up on the site are people who actually believe in what we're doing. We showed them the demo, and they said, this is great. We want to be a part of that.

It's very tough out there going for ad dollars via the normal route. And frankly, 75 percent of the ad dollars go to 20 or 30 different sites, and the rest of the thousands of us have to scramble for the rest. Sun Microsystems and US West Media Group, Netscape, Oracle are very enthusiastic about what we're doing. So at the beginning, without any numbers, some of them gave us money. Some of them gave us technology we would not otherwise have been able to afford. And some of them are giving us traffic.

They all understand that should we succeed, we're going to be looking for money to underwrite it. That's one of the legs of the revenue model.

But we do have investment money which we are spending rather frugally. We don't have too much of a fancy office. We're slightly understaffed. We actually came in under our original budget to launch this thing. But the idea here is not that we are going to get to be a profitable business with a high valuation quickly. We are trying to create a viable publishing medium that has revenue that looks like the business model works, but we're aware that it's going to take us a while to build to that.

And so are our investors. Our investors are looking for the next Netscape or Yahoo!. Or let me put it this way, after they talked to me, any investors who were looking for a quick, heavy turnaround on their money were not interested. Patient investors who wanted a stake in where the medium might go were interested.

DH: And then eventually, as I've read, you will want to branch out into other media. Television and books, publishing, and so on. How much further into the future do you see that happening, and in what ways? Have you already looked into it?

HLR: Here's the thinking. We really want to concentrate on the core of confidence which is great content about technology and what it means. Now, that content can come in the form of a number of different media.

The web site and the community are really the center of it. It is a place where we aggregate great minds. It's a think tank. It's a place where people can come in over the transom and turn into contributors. You can probably see that by their nature that some of the serialized material that we're presenting could end up being in a book.

Now, I wrote a book twelve years ago called *Tools for Thought* in which I interviewed Doug Engelbart, Bob Taylor, Alan Kaye, Ted Nelson, and a lot of people who built the technology but are not as celebrated as the people who built the industry. Well, I'm going back and interviewing them, because it's an interesting exercise in retrospective futurism, and talking to them about the twelve years since we first talked.

And now we're spending a little bit of money to have a professional video crew there when I do those interviews. So, A, a transcript is meant for the web site to enhance what we're doing with futurism there. B, we have high quality video that could be used for broadcast, could be used for a video series that we sell as a package, and when streaming video becomes a possibility in the medium, we have material there. So we're trying to think ahead about how we can gather material.

But I vividly remember my days at *Wired*. The strategy there was explicitly that we've established a beachhead, now let's land as many troops as possible, and we'll take the entire continent. We're really not trying to establish an empire. We're trying to grow a business that attracts the best minds out there. We're going for the PBS/NPR/*Scientific American/Harper's/Atlantic* niche.

We want to be able to not simply be a web site and a community. We want to be able to reach people who read books or watch television or maybe buy a video. Now in terms of television, we've been talking with The Site about doing a pilot. Going out to some real virtual communities and getting some video on the real people in them. The first one we've scheduled is "Cyborganic," the second one is "New York Online," two very different communities.

All this is really in line with my mission, which is to elevate the level of discourse about technology. And I would love to build a thriving community. I'm still open about whether this community stuff is for real—or a dangerous illusion. But I think we need to have a place where we can have intelligent conversation about that. We've had a lot of unintelligent conversation about it. I think that the truth is somewhat more complex than, "This stuff is a community" on one end, and "This is a complete illusion" on the other end.

So whatever media we can use to reach people is consonant with my vision, and in the words of the marketing side of the business, it also helps to build a brand. Those are all means of doing cross-promotions.

This is all fairly new to me. I had a vision. Now, a vision, it turns out is not enough. You need a revenue model, you need a business model. I'm being pushed constantly by the marketing necessities and the business necessities. "What can we do to make money on this?" And my touchstone is, "What can we do to make money off this that's not going to get off the central mission?"

If I get off the central mission, why did I ever go to the trouble of doing this is the first place? I could still be writing books, being in control of my life, and making good money. So, it's a very interesting experience for someone who has been an observer and an analyst, a writer and an editor my whole life to get into the entrepreneurial necessities here.

DH: It must be. Very strange territory for me as well.

HLR: You learn to understand capitalism a lot better. I mean, on the one hand, the American Dream really is true. It doesn't matter whether you have a penny in your pocket. It doesn't matter who your parents were. If you've got a great idea, someone out there will give you a million dollars. Now, the string that is attached to that is that they're going to want ten million dollars in value back. Eventually.

So capitalism forces you into growth. You can't say, "I'm going to have my little boutique web site and have a nice little community." You have to say, "How is this going to grow into a 10 million dollar business?" Or more.

So that's where the inverse publishing—which is to cultivate the think tank, aggregate these minds, and to publish material that we refine and create together with those people—came from. Some people get the mistaken impression that we're going to sell people's conversations.

First of all, that's not in line with what I would do ethically. Secondly, nobody would buy it.

DH: I guess it depends on who's talking!

[Laughter]

HLR: Now, interactivity is a great way, if you've got the thick skin, to develop material. I've done this on "The Well" for a few years with my column. Putting up a proposed column before I file it. And people whack at it, and sometimes, people know what they're talking about. If you can stay open to that, and not get beaten up by it, it is—essentially, that's why I say a "think tank"—it is a way you can invite people to help you think about things.

DH: The organization, the architecture—who was the team that came up with that? In other words, you've got "World Wide Jam," "Virtual Community," "Meeting of the Minds." How did you go about that?

HLR: Part of it grew out of my old web site, "Brainstorms." There is this fellow at Pathfinder who does this dead sites, "the Dead Page," and he has listed "Brainstorms" as one of the dead sites. You know, I used to post every day. It became obsessive, for over a year. Sort of the Justin Hall religion, you know, you gotta post every day.

I had something called Digital Zeitgeist, my friends around the world, who were contributing for free. You will see that some of those people are now paid correspondents. They're in Tokyo, Frankfurt, and London. That really grew into "World Wide Jam," and as Mark Petrakis became the producer there, and I let go of my little baby. Yes, I recruited those people, and yes, it was my idea to do something like that, but now it needs a producer who can take it in his own direction.

The "Virtual Community" center really came from going to AOL as a potential investor. Just a casual conversation with someone involved there, saying, "Oh, Howard Rheingold, 'Virtual Community.' You know, we really need to be doing something about community." I mean, they sell community. But if you were just to wander into a chat room on AOL looking for community, you would have some rude surprises.

There are communities there. You need to know where to find them. And so, on the airplane back, Randy, my partner, said, "You know, there's a business there." And the light bulb really went on. He came up with the idea, and I ran with it, which is, let's create a Virtual Community Center. Again, I looked for someone who was knowledgeable on that and who was enthusiastic. It was Jill Davidson, and she produced that.

So all of these areas essentially were ideas that I had, but Abbe Don, together with her design team, said, "Okay, you've got an idea. How does this become a content area?" That in fact took months and months and months of hard work.

The other part of it is that we hired producers to do this. One of the things that we've learned and our friends have learned from "HotWired" and "c|net" and "Cyborganic" is that you need to have a producer who is responsible somewhat in the way that a producer in television is responsible. Making sure everything is done on time, all the material comes in on time, that the editorial direction the editorial director wants to take is somehow translated into story ideas, that story ideas turn into assignments, that illustrations go with the assignments—I had no idea!

Justin had convinced me that this would be like us sitting in my backyard tweaking our web pages on our portables. Except that there would be more people doing it. But it turns out that there's a qualitative difference between trying to make an economically viable web site of this size from fun old user publishing.

And it requires producers, and it requires a lot of thought about design. Its information designers, its user interface designers, its graphic designers, all have to work together. I've learned a lot about what I didn't know when I started out on this.

DH: About the size, can you foresee possibly whole new, other branches developing? Suppose hundreds of thousands of people come pouring in.

HLR: If hundreds of thousands of people come pouring in, that's a catastrophe. The success part of it means that we've got revenue. The catastrophe part of it means that we're going to choke on our own success if we don't take measures.

The measures I would take, if I had the funding to pursue it, would be to hire a bunch of good editors who would go to our conversations and every week give people the five-minute version. The two-hour version is still there. If you're a fanatic, and you want to spend two hours a week going through the conversation, they're there. They're not hidden.

If you would rather go through an editorial filter and have someone pick out those responses in those conversations, characterize them, and give you a link that enables you to go in, I think that's the only solution to the UseNet kind of catastrophe.

DH: Yes. It's kind of a sticky area, though, too, isn't it? Online conversations have always been about freedom and anarchic growth and all that. I just wonder about a certain group within a certain conference feeling that they're a part of the group, and then their conversations aren't getting picked...?

HLR: Yep. Yes, okay, there's your fear. What if you aren't picked? Well, one would hope that anyone who has something valuable to say is going to end up being picked. Either pretty soon or eventually.

I mean, we just have to be upfront about it. The editorial function is precisely to cut two hours down to five minutes. That's why people read magazines. They subscribe to get an editor's cut of all the stuff that might be about that subject.

On the other hand, our source of material is people stepping up who we've never heard of before and making good conversation. Now, presumably what would make them succeed is that the conversation is stimulating and something people would want to participate in.

To know that you might be picked for a sort of editorial congratulation I would hope would be an incentive. And if we become successful enough, I would hope that we would begin hiring people. Those who make the best conversations ought to become contributors. Just because you don't call it a column or an article doesn't mean that it's not valuable.

If you end up writing a thousand words a week and people pay a lot of attention to it, and it's high quality, then we ought to figure out a way to send some of our revenues your way.

Now, that all depends on success. And that's me, as the editorial voice, finding the revenue guys saying, "Listen, don't spend so much money on editorial. We need to make a profit!" But that's why I started this. If you're an editor and you want to have editorial freedom, you've got to be a majority stockholder. It's really structural, it's not personality, although certain personalities become publishers and certain personalities become editors. But it's structural that the publishers will want to maximize their profit and that the editors will want to maximize the content that they are providing for their readers.

Chapter Thirty-Three
Pomo Threads

Selbstdarstellung. Like so many German words, this one is *zusammengebastelt* (put together), building block-like: *Selbst* = self; *dar* = there; *stellung* (from *stellen*) = to place. So it would seem to mean "placing oneself." And it does. But naturally, as words do, it has gathered steam over time and taken on a vast realm of connotations. An actor is a *Darsteller*, for example. But what *Selbstdarstellung* boils down to is the presentation of oneself.

We all make a habit of changing the way we present ourselves in different situations and to different people. It's only human. We show different sides of ourselves to the police, to our friends, to our boss, to our lovers, to our moms. The Net has not invented this ability in us. Nor does it necessarily exaggerate it. But it does provide ample opportunity for us to exercise it.

It's a hot topic, and Sherry Turkle in particular seems to have struck a chord with her book *Life on the Screen*, all about "identity in the age of the Internet." There's something exhilarating about one of the doors online technology opens. Behind it, a full-blown masquerade party is going on. Step in as someone else, and you're free to do what you yourself would never do.

That's the fun part. The not so fun part is that the deception, no matter how playful, is a two-way street. With many, many lanes, some of them faster than others. Just as you might give the impression via chat, e-mail, MUD, or MOO that you are single when you're not to some nubile sex goddess, she in turn might be just another dirty old man. It's happened, and it's no longer news.

Nor is it news that behind the user ID you are flirting, trading gibes, or arguing politics with there may not be a human at all. That bots have been released, often experimentally, to roam some systems like party hosts bearing trays of conversational hors d'oeuvres. "You're looking swell this evening, Bob. How the hell are you anyway?" Some of these bots are awfully winning creatures.

But the Internet itself? In an article distributed via the nettime mailing list, Ted Nelson (yes, he of the Xanadu vaporware brouhaha and the man credited with coining the term "hypertext") suggests that spoofoids, "...any entity that tries to fool you about its nature, including its physical existence as a human being," are already out and about chatting us up in unsolicited e-mail, UseNet posts and the like. Why? They, or rather the real humans behind them, would like to get to know us.

Spoofoids, according to Nelson, are out after not only our vital statistics but the subtle workings of our minds: our opinions. And these could be very valuable indeed, not only to advertisers but for governments, be they foreign or our own. Now, I have a hard time swallowing this whole idea as being exemplary of the current state of affairs. Maybe I'm just not interesting enough, but behind all my unsolicited e-mail, there do seem to be real people. I do not, however, have a hard time entertaining the idea as a possible scenario for the future state of affairs.

I have met people online that I have become very personal with. People about whom I know nothing other than what they themselves have presented as evidence of their true selves. One summer, as a friend of mine and I were about to leap into a joint endeavor with another guy, my friend sent an e-mail: "Before we do this...do you trust him?"

It shook me. I actually broke out in a cold sweat, which I didn't know I could do—I had only known the phenomenon previously as a literary cliché.

But I realized that I had never laid eyes on this third party before. This party had pushed all the right buttons with me. He was witty, intelligent, and yes, complimentary but not given to blatant flattery. My perfect foil.

Or...was he indeed exactly who he said he was? I suddenly realized I had no idea. "Okay. I have a potentially tricky topic that I'd like to discuss here."

That is how the moderator of a conference opened what was to become a lively thread (or discussion) in the "underground" of the "San Francisco Bay Guardian Online," a free service offered by the weekly alternative publication and run by eLine Productions. The "GOL," as its users call it, is a far more wide open sort of community than, say, the Bay Area's most famous conferencing service, "The Well." You have to do something pretty outrageous to get thrown off the system, such as chat-bombing (sending out hundreds of invitations to chat live within seconds) or anything that threatens the technical functioning of the service.

It is an aesthetically pleasing place to enter. After you log on, you are greeted with a stylized street scene of San Francisco and the sound of a fog horn that segues into a car horn (at least that's what I hear, though I wouldn't bet on it). There is a typically San Franciscan Victorian right up front, and each of its windows sports an icon with names such as "Arts and Culture," "Politics," or "Styles." You can head off to conferences devoted to each of the city's individual neighborhoods or read the paper's articles at the kiosk on the corner.

Either because it is free or because the *Bay Guardian* is famously liberal, even for a town like San Francisco, the "GOL" attracts not only several thousand interesting, engaging, and thoughtful users, but a rotating yet persistent handful of troublemakers as well. Who knows what inspires these clowns to choose an alias, go in, and start making racist, sexist, or otherwise inflammatory remarks, but they do, and they are tolerated. Online editor Jon Maples insists on a no censorship policy, and interestingly, in the place of editorial weeding, the community often forges its own method of handling these pariahs. It will be collectively decided to ignore them. Their messages won't be read or responded to, and sure enough, more often than not, they get bored and go away.

When Andrew Sullivan was originally designing the system in 1995 in the basement of the Guardian building, he was very conscious of re-creating the feel of the physical city. He was also aware that most of the people who would be attracted to an online service hosted by the *Guardian* would not be the type to want to hang around all the conventional areas usually featured on your average BBS (such as "Arts and Culture," "Politics," or "Styles!"). So off to the left of that front and center Victorian, there is a manhole cover; it is lifted slightly, and from the darkness peers a set of cartoonish eyes. This is the porthole to the underground.

Click on it and your screen goes dark. Now umpteen pairs of little cartoonish eyes are staring out at you, each of them icons with translucent to opaque titles such as "flirt zone" or "Cosmo-shed." It doesn't take long to figure out that this is where the action is. This isn't to say that nothing goes on above ground.

On the contrary, my own favorite conference is up there, "film." For over a year, a steady band of regulars has been trading tips on movies they have seen, often before the official release date (more than a few of the participants write movie reviews for various publications around town) or gabs about the trends, politics, and personalities of the business. If I had to choose between reading reviews in the traditional media or checking in about one time each day to this conference, "film" would win hands down. They are that sharp in there.

But it is underground where most of what we are calling "community" goes on. Sure, there is quite a bit of flirting among users of all ages, though the twenty-somethings and under especially seem to have taken to the "GOL" as a sort of virtual dating service. But that is hardly all. The "GOL" has another pretty brilliant policy: If a particular personality posts regularly and seems to be gathering something of a following, give him or her a conference.

These personal conferences, shaped, run, and moderated by individual users take on a life of their own. "So-n-so's Hang Out" attracts those who have become friends or admirers of So-n-so, so the personality of So-n-so is the mood of that particular place. So it was in the conference of the moderator who brought up the "potentially tricky topic."

Now, I approached each of the participants of the thread and acquired not only permission to quote from his or her remarks, but also permission to use names. There was a bit of discussion about this, and more than one of us commented on the self-reflexive irony of the discussion considering the thread I wanted to pluck from the underground and slap on paper, but in the end, I have decided not to name names—or in the case of a few, aliases. It is just cleaner this way.

Funny, when "Electric Minds" opened, I was posting along, treating it sort of like the "GOL"—and it hit me several days later, Hey, this is on the web.

Anybody can come in, poke around, and read this stuff. Immediately, I thought of a few things I either wish I hadn't said or had at least said differently. The strange thing is, the "GOL" is public, too. Anybody can get an account, come in, and read about my Björk thing, for example, in the "Crushes on Greatness" conference—certainly mild and no big deal, but it made me stop and wonder, what's the difference, really? There is a difference, though. The community of the "GOL" is a shade more private than the web; the underground a step further; and this moderator's conference, a step further again. Technologically, there is no difference, but somehow, virtually, there is.

But on to the moderator's questions and the responses. The moderator is female, so she gets an (F) behind her moniker. The male respondents get, that's right, an (M).

Moderator (F): I am curious if and how being a part of such a public community/play-space has changed the way people express themselves and/or interact.

I'm wondering if anyone who is (or has been) engaged in any kind of online/offline romance or online/offline sexual relationship has found that they end up modifying the nature of their posts and public interactions.

Do you censor yourself because you are concerned about what your (online or offline) lover might read?

Do you feel a need to protect (or expose) online personalities if you have had a particularly good or bad offline connection with them?

Do you find yourself channeling certain parts of your personality in order to have an effect on past or future lovers?

Do you find yourself channeling certain parts of your personality online, regardless of the effect it might have on how others perceive you?

I'm curious.

[Well, immediately, one user, an (M), replied, "I think that all of your questions are wonderful, but, uh, if anyone should feel so restrained how will they feel comfortable posting about it in this conference, knowwhutImean?" To which she wrote...]

Moderator (F): Well, yeah. I know exactly what you mean...which is why I referred to it as a potentially tricky topic. I had initially thought that it might be silly to pose such a question in this space, but decided that I would go for it anyway since the possibilities seemed exciting and worthwhile.

I did hope that those who were moved to post on this, might either choose to answer some questions over others, or to post about those things they could share comfortably within a group without violating their own limits.

I also hoped that if some people were excited about this topic, but didn't want to participate under recognizable screen names, that they might make aliases with which to participate.

In any case, I was aware that it would be a tricky subject to confront, let alone to do so in the very forum about which I was inquiring. I'm still hoping that some brave souls will end up sorting through their thoughts and sharing them with us.

Thanks for pointing out the inherent contradictions in the question— although I was aware of them when I posted them.

[So already, the discourse was taking on a sort of pomo twist....]

User 1 (F): I have met one person offline so far, and that hasn't changed the way I present myself online.

This is the first time I've posted under this name. I have an alter-ego who appears under my real name who does post now and then. As "Hope," I spend most of my time exchanging e-mail. Hope is sexier and maybe more playful than my alter-ego; my alter-ego is much more cautious and concerned about her public image.

Now that I've been online for a while, I find myself wishing sometimes that I could consolidate personas so that people would know more about me. But I think it's too late to do that, because the personas have gone in different directions. Besides, as Hope, I have more freedom than I do under my alter-ego. I also find myself wishing that I had never signed on with my real name in the first place, but again it's too late, as my real-named alter-ego has already established a presence in her own right.

The only person who knows of both identities is the person I've met offline. We met here in e-mail under our aliases, and then gave each other clues as to our real identities. Soon after we mutually uncovered each other's identities, we got together in the real world.

I was wondering if anyone else had similar experiences with dual identities, and how it feels to them to maintain these different personalities.

User 2 (F): When I first started using "GOL," I used aliases as well as my real name. I didn't exactly post stuff that I wouldn't have posted under my real name, but there was an element of safety to it. And I did engage in some chats that I might not have if they had been under my real name. The anonymity definitely was important to me.

But the problem with doing this was that I had to keep a constant eye on which alias had posted what, and on not giving away information under an alias that might connect it to my real name. And even though I thought I was being careful, I slipped; more than one person figured out who I was, including someone I had chatted with that I had definitely wanted to stay anonymous with. There are a number of people on this BBS who are very good at figuring out aliases and who spend a lot of time and energy doing so. So I pretty much hung up the aliases, and now just use my real name. (The other option would have been to give up the real name and keep the aliases...but I didn't want to do that.)

User 3 (?): As for adopting a persona online, I don't think that it is being false. I think it merely gives an extra sense of freedom to pursue/ explore facets of yourself in a context of safety. Facets, not only sexual but intellectual as well, which might not otherwise be given free reign. (damn those horse tail posts). It is relatively easy to figure out the person behind the alias, if they have any sort of style, it comes through regardless of the name. I have used many aliases and my real name, and they are all the "real" me. It is no more false than the ways we all behave differently in different social situations, (i.e., work, home, etc.).

[But back to the original set of questions....]

User 2 (F): Yes.

A little while ago, I was playing with someone I met here on "GOL." I found that I was less likely to engage in outrageous flirting or public sexual admiration of other people on the BBS. It's not that we were monogamous or anything; it just felt rude and callous. I wouldn't talk at great length to a lover or fuckbuddy about how hot someone else was, and so I didn't post to conferences about how hot I thought other people were. (We never discussed this, btw, although if we'd continued playing we probably would have. My fuckbuddy never asked me not to do this, it was my own ethical decision.)

Mostly I was fine with this, but if we had continued playing it might have become a problem. It did interfere with the degree to which I could pursue other people on the BBS.

Fortunately, although we are no longer playing, we are still friends. But I can see how it would be very uncomfortable to stay on the BBS if you'd had a nasty break-up with someone you'd met here. I know that when couples break up, it often happens that one of them winds up with a sort of unofficial "custody" of their mutual friendships and social circles. I wonder if that happens with BBSs, too.

User 4 (F): I've been involved with two people that I met online, but because I generally don't post anything exceptionally personal, I haven't modified my public posting at all. The only thing I might have modified here was my answer when you dared me to break up with my girlfriend. She probably wouldn't have been amused, although we did break up. Last week though, not a couple of months ago.

I've only felt the need to protect people from others if they're dangerous or creepy, just as I would offline.

"Do you find yourself channeling certain parts of your personality in order to have an effect on past or future lovers?"

Nope.

"Do you find yourself channeling certain parts of your personality online, regardless of the effect it might have on how others perceive you?"

Nope. What you read is what you get.

User 5 (M): Well, Christina is not online. I probably relate more online about us in honest response to queries such as this than I might in ordinary conversation. Because I don't know any of my online acquaintances in the fleshly world, I take advantage of the anonymity to express occasional thoughts or feelings I could not easily discuss in a face-to-face. I think about this a great deal—I am sometimes tempted to unsend a post that I think might be too revealing (not that I'm exposing all manner of dark secrets); so far, I have always refrained. I think that there is a certain honesty in leaving it all out there for anyone to see. The feeling of exposedness is, for me, a major part of my reasons for posting anything of a personal nature. There is a confessional feel to it—I come to you, my online pals, for something like absolution.

Despite the fact that I spend a great deal of time prowling the singles conferences, I am not in the market for a partner. I may drop the occasional salacious comment, but I could never portray myself as an aggressive flirt online. There is too much of that sort of interaction that is lost in the primarily text-based exchange. I know how far I can go in real life; I do flirt, and think it is healthy to do so. But you all don't know me, and I am bound by my own moral code not to depict myself falsely. Obviously, others are in this online thing for other reasons, and have adopted online personas that allow them a certain latitude in their behavior.

I guess the point here is that while I appreciate the usefulness of anonymity, for my own reasons I find it more satisfying to give you my real name and tell you true stories about myself.

There; I came up with some ruminations that don't exactly answer the question. In school, I would have received an "F" for this assignment. However, I am interested in what others think about the anonymity/ secret identity issues that an online service gives rise to. Sorry to hog the floor.

Moderator (F): Well, here's my own response to my query:

I have had a number of relationships that developed out of first meeting people in cyberspace. I have noticed that the most important thing I have to be careful about is that I don't use public forums to communicate things to the individual in question. I have found that I need to make sure that if I want to send some sort of "message" to the person I am (or have been) seeing, that I need to do it in private e-mail and not use the public forums to express things that need to be expressed privately.

I have also learned that if and when I am posting things that regard our relationship, it is best to talk to the individual in question first (even if I am ensuring that no one else will know who I'm referring to). It's become important to me to get permission from any lover of mine before I talk about issues we are dealing with (or have dealt with) in a public way. That's one of the things I have been learning to negotiate in this new world of online relationships.

Interestingly enough, since I first got online 1993, I haven't dated anyone who isn't part of one of my online environments. So I can't say I've dealt with having an offline lover who might be concerned about what I post online. Then again, it poses another issue, since the people I have dated have shared my online communities with me. But I tend to be a fairly private person when it comes to those kinds of intimate details of my life anyway—sort of a juxtaposition, since I flirt and play publicly, but usually tend to avoid specifics about my relationships. So, in general, most of the censoring I do happens on a more internal level and has to do with my own sets of limits, rather than those developed because of a relationship.

Still, when I'm in a relationship, I tend to be a bit less flirtatious online in certain ways. I think my desire for public attention drops quite a bit when I'm getting regular attention from someone who's important to me. I consider most of my public flirting to be "throwaway" type of stuff...things that I consider meaningless. I avoid "real" flirting in the public forums—stuff that is based upon real feelings or real events I might have shared with someone. The kind of flirting that I do in public posts is more linked to my online persona than it is to who I really am or what I might really want.

Because I'm mostly protective of my private life, that usually extends to the people I know offline. I have had two or three bad connections with people in my past three years online. I usually think that bad-mouthing someone reflects more on me than the person I might be referring to. Where I have had some difficulty in the past is if I think the person is actually potentially dangerous. If someone is simply a jerk, I figure that people will find out soon enough. If they are actually a bad person and do irrefutably bad things to people, (things that may not be easy to detect at first), then I think that they lose their right to be protected by me and I have a much harder time with this issue. Still, I have yet to outright "warn other women" or go on a rampage about someone... although I have at times, been tempted to do so.

I do think that I tend to focus a much more playful and flirtatious part of my personality online. This medium lends itself nicely to the one-liner and to the innuendoes I like to toss out now and then. But I don't think it's really a conscious attempt to have an effect on others. I know that I enjoy the attention that my flirtatiousness inspires. I like being flirty and can enjoy that behavior in others online. But the thing that I usually like about it is that it's temporary and limited to online, and then I can bounce off into the real world and interact with people in a more solid and complete way. I view my little flirty public interactions here as little perks, and nothing more.

As I said in the first part of this post, I try to be careful to communicate private information directly to the person I might have a private relationship with, rather than using a public forum to do that kind of communicating. So I don't think the flirtatiousness that gets channeled online is for anyone else's benefit other than my own.

User 6 (F): Having been sort of almost stalked by someone online at one point and also having experience with being with someone in a relationship who is also online, I'd have to say in either case it didn't really change what I posted. I was aware they would read it, and that may have even made it a little more interesting, but I certainly don't think I have selectively deleted anything because a significant other would read it. I have found it a valuable way to find things out about a person in subjects we haven't come across in our own discussions. I can see individuals talking about things they enjoy with others with the same interests, perhaps not interests I have, and therefore can see them discuss it with others who are in the know of such things.

These days we enjoy the e-mail banter back and forth, and perhaps are able to say things hard to say in person; I know this is true for me. Communication is the key, and as long as we communicate about what is being said publicly online, there seems to be no problem. But then, my online persona is not so different than it really is, with this primary name. Others are used for other things, and reasons have been explained or are understood. If anything, the online community has made for a better relationship, more ways to play.

But, nothing beats real life interaction. Having the Internet as the only way to talk, or that and the phone, is a lot harder, and was the status of things with my little stalker until I finally met him, which made things more difficult.

[User 6 told me later that she was still in a relationship with another "GOL" user, that they had been together eight months and were still "...very happy. Would have not met without the "GOL," and I do sometimes write what I write online with him in mind. The Internet has been incorporated into our relationship on several levels." As of this writing, they are still happy, and hopefully will be ever after....]

Chapter Thirty-Four
The First and Last Miles

Remember that IBM commercial with the laptop-toting Amazon explorers? "Omigosh, we're lost," says one (or something to that effect), right there in the thick of exotica. No problem, the naturally sharpest and sexiest looking of the bunch announces. She whips that trusty top off her lap, and zap, within literally seconds, the screen has zoomed from an asteroid's-eye view of Brazil into a patch of jungle with a tiny blinking you-are-here button.

I don't know that URL. Nor have I ever seen a laptop of any brand with such Trinitron-like resolution. Or graphics that load like an MTV video.

Doesn't matter. If the old dramatic law establishing the suspension of disbelief applies anywhere, it is advertising. What makes the IBM ad curious as a cultural artifact is the use of another old dramatic trick: Deus ex machina, with an accent on the machina.

Technology, specifically a broadband wireless hook-up to one heck of a server, throws a lifeline to the civilized awash in uncivilization, reeling them back into the global fold. Whew. Not to be too picky, of course, but there is something amiss in this picture. The web's reach may be wide, but it isn't yet as wide as the world. Just which Amazon jungle-based ISP did this woman access?

Sure, it was probably a long-distance call, but it tickles the imagination to contemplate her dialing up a local BBS for maps of the immediate area, and maybe even a live human on the other end of the line who could talk the group back to the hotel.

The idea's not as farfetched as it might at first appear to the average Net cruiser as depicted in current demographic studies. Just outside the beam of the media spotlight, there is an active group of Net pros whose focus is not on Wall Street, but rather, worlds away. Not necessarily geographically, but at the very least, economically.

Their focus is on helping those for whom online technology represents a daunting other world, on helping them make this technology serve them, not the other way around—on community networking. And among them is Steve Cisler.

Steve Cisler's efforts, which began when he was instrumental in starting the Apple Library of Tomorrow grant program way back in 1988, are not about getting the Internet Shopping Network to the Australian Outback. They're about the use of online tech to help communities get a sense of themselves, online and off, "and that knowledge can be valuable politically and culturally."

Tossing e-mail back and forth with Steve Cisler can send you on your own private guilt trip, though he would surely never see it that way. But you've got to ask yourself, Am I taking time away from work on a program that will preserve communication in a dying language? From establishing local networks or at the very least awareness of their potential from Barnesville, Ohio, to Cuba, from Turkey to Chile, Venezuela to San Jose?

Still, the devil's advocate in me just had to ask, and it wouldn't be for the last time, "What's the point?" With winning frankness and patience, he replied he isn't 100 percent sure, though he has seen mighty convincing results of hands-on engagement. "For example, if Indians on a reservation are involved in the planning and assembly of the network and don't just leave it to outside consultants or a private firm (pretty common) then it won't seem so remote and uncontrollable to them. That happened with the Oneida of New York, and a librarian happened to be at the center."

Steve Cisler is big on librarians. And public libraries. That's where his own hands-on engagement with local information infrastructures began, and when he got involved with Apple, "I felt that any community network without library involvement was going to make a lot of mistakes with regards to information archiving and dissemination," but at the same time, he wasn't interested in seeing any particular library shifted as-is to the online environment. He wanted them to work with other groups in the community—that is, he wanted to see the whole of the community using online technology to communicate in ways they may not have been communicating before. That, after all, is what the technology is supposed to be all about.

"I consider the building and control of the First Mile to be a chance for local citizens to feel some sort of ownership as the Net explodes in industrialized and developing countries." First Mile? By that he means, "the most important connections: the ones from homes, schools, local businesses, libraries, and non-profits to the larger network and to each other."

As he pointed out in a post to the nettime list, these are usually, perversely considered "Last Mile," whereas the HotNamed sites he lists "get more attention, but are actually less important."

Kind of sends the devil's advocate packing, doesn't it?

Having devoted so much effort to getting disparate communities wired, rural and urban, Steve Cisler's now focusing on what wireless connectivity might do for those even farther out of reach. He's working on a proposal to the FCC that would designate 300 MHz for public, no-license use.

Even so, another e-mail message makes you wonder how wireless you can go. "The most important applications in community building are not technological. I've come to that conclusion, so I'm learning more about human network organizing and dynamics. The web, BBS, library automation systems are in support of that and should not dominate even though they are getting more attention than the face-to-face people part."

Reviewing *The Wired Neighborhood*, a book on communities and online technology by Stephen Doheny-Farina, Cisler juxtaposes virtual communities and community networks. Note the difference. Virtual communities are about groups of people who meet, often for the first time, online. An intangible bond grows. Significantly, the bond already has a fairly bankable foundation in that more than likely the people were drawn to each other in the first place by some shared interest.

The bond uniting those served by community networks is geography, period. There can be, but doesn't necessarily have to be, any sort of gushy aspect layered on top. People are intrigued by the high concept of virtual communities, but comparatively, the practical work of wiring existing communities isn't as easy a sale.

Although he finds *The Wired Neighborhood* a good read, and "while I may believe this topic is of paramount importance, I don't think the book will have the influence of Howard Rheingold's *The Virtual Community* mainly because the publishing world is more interested in the electronic trends and how society is being changed by them, than in community revitalization and development. Reporting on the new phenomenon of virtual communities is easier than describing the challenge of practitioners using new tools and technology to improve physical communities."

We'll look at both in this chapter. The issue of whether virtual communities are real or imagined may seem like mere philosophical quibbling to those whose lives have been affected by them. The reality of community networks is, fortunately, undeniable.

In May 1991, Dr. Thomas Grundner wrote his first newsletter to the National Public Telecomputing Network (NPTN), calling it his first "Letter to the Fourth World." At first glance, Grundner's definition of the "fourth world" bears an eerie resemblance to John Perry Barlow's elitist definition of cyberspace as some otherworldly nation state over which all laws, natural or otherwise, hold no sway.

A second glance reveals Grundner's "fourth world" to be an early and enthusiastic casting of community networkers as a community unto themselves, socially engaged on two fronts, plugged into the real world as well as to each other. Grundner had been something of an inspiration for the community network movement since late 1984, when he set up what was jokingly referred to as "St. Silicon's Hospital and Information Dispensary" in Cleveland, Ohio.

Essentially, it was a single computer hooked up to a single phone line. People would drop off a medical question and get it answered within twenty-four hours. This humble seed blossomed more or less into the first FreeNet in July 1986, and by 1989, the Cleveland Free-Net was a full-blown Unix-based network with tens of thousands of users. Grundner decided this success was reason enough to go national, hence the NPTN.

Almost exactly five years after the first "Letter," Grundner was tired, all but out of the picture, having resigned as head of the floundering NPTN (which, abandoned by most of its financial backers, eventually did file for a Chapter Seven bankruptcy in September 1996), but his enthusiasm hadn't waned one bit.

Anne McFarland, a mover and a shaker behind the Akron Regional Free-Net and then the Akron Community Online Resource Network, asked Grundner in May 1996 for one "Final Letter to the Fourth World." In it, Grundner totals up the score of hundreds of community networks and around half a million users, and seems pleased.

Although he is still as gung-ho about the reasoning behind community networks, he warns, "Make no mistake, the 'community networking revolution' has not been won—far from it. If anything, we are probably in a more perilous position now than we were over a dozen years ago when I first began my work." What's the problem?

The way he sees it, the problem is that many building these networks have lost focus, lost track of why they're going to the trouble and who they're going to the trouble for. Many have become distracted by the

Internet itself. If that seems ironic, he reminds his fellow networkers that their job is not to build "just a slick bus station to elsewhere. Yes, you should be connected to the Internet. Yes, it is fine to have links to wonderful and exotic sites all over the Web... All of this is terrific, but not if it undercuts the development of similar online resources in your own town."

The concept Grundner insists on over and again is "the radius," the idea that within ten miles of wherever you are, there is a real live human with an answer to just about any question you can come up with. It does seem awfully romantic and perhaps the radius model isn't meant to be taken concretely but instead is put forward to drive home a point. Grundner despises the idea of online communications as "a giant electronic brochure dispenser." Instead, he encourages networkers to realize the goal of getting "people in your community answering real questions posed by real people. That is the true power of this medium—don't cripple that power!"

In his first "Letter," Grundner ticked off seven beliefs commonly held by the "fourth world," but all of them are essentially derivatives of the first: "We believe that access to information is a fundamental right of every person in a democracy." A lofty but legitimate goal to strive for.

If the "information" of the first "Letter" seems a colder, more abstract issue than connecting people to people, clearly his primary concern in his "Final Letter," it may very well be that five years in the trenches have brought the true value of raw data into greater relief for Grundner. The point he stresses toward the end of his farewell is inclusiveness. "Every person" means everybody, rich, poor, and interestingly, maybe even especially the middle class.

What a healthy slap in the face it is to be reminded that "your ultimate target audience, in most cases, right now does not even know what a modem is."

About a third of the way into his essay "Community Networks at the Crossroads," Wally Bowen, still very active in community networking as executive director of the Mountain Area Information Network, utters this provocative statement: "Despite the media hype, the Internet will not change the dominant, commercial media order of the United States."

Bowen isn't the first to make such an assertion, and although you may not be hearing it the first time from him, it is nevertheless a sobering jolt to anyone intoxicated by the general assumption that the Net will shake up not only mass media but the masses themselves. But a distinction has to be made between what Bowen is talking about and what he isn't talking about.

He's not talking about the mechanics of distribution. That will change. E-mail by cellular phone, faxes on the beach, *Seinfeld* on a PC, sure, that will happen. What won't change, he's saying, and he points to the history of "public media" to prove it, is the power structure—that is, who's doing the distributing. "Although some technophiles argue that the Internet is inherently democratic and will subvert any attempts at commercialization and privatization," Bowen maintains, "this belief is based more on faith than on any historical or empirical evidence."

A large media company swooping in on the Net comes as no surprise. Many of us have been happy to be there to greet them. Let them all come and plop big fat web sites down on any domain they choose, we whoop, our arms open wide. Maybe some of their respectability will wear off on us, and besides, the electronic frontier is infinite. There is room for all of us, publishers, broadcasters, great and small. Precisely because the Net is not a finite bundle of channels like a cable service, Ted Turner cannot shut out an irksome geek like he can a Rupert Murdoch.

Right?

Well, not all of us are so certain any more. It isn't just that the technical wizardry—and the budget to back it up—required to attain and maintain a site compelling enough to escape extinction (or worse, that cry-in-the-wilderness status) are being yanked out of the reach of the run-of-the-mill start-up. The far more effective shut out comes when those providing the big content become the ones providing the big access.

In one of his weekly "Stating the Obvious" columns on the web, Michael Sippey has expressed his worries about major access providers such as @Home selecting content to stream to its customers and demonstrated how they would do it. Because @Home is about speed, the company will cache and update what it sees fit. The selection probably isn't consciously malicious; actually, it is only natural.

And Bowen follows this media evolution to its only natural next step. He points to a Wall Street analyst who predicts that, "The Internet will evolve along a similar path as broadcasting. By the end of the decade, four private data broadcasters will emerge that will bundle and package branded content on a global basis to a broad array of personal computers."

If this seems a bit dark, consider media mergers such as Disney and ABC/Capitol Cities or Time Warner and Turner Broadcasting as Exhibit A in his case. Now that hardly anyone looks at the Net as some organic beauty grown outside the concerns of commerce any more, all but everyone is trying to strike on the best way to squeeze a buck out of it. There are basically two ways, Bowen reminds us: sell audiences to advertisers or sell products to consumers.

Whichever web model one of these two methods is plugged into, some derivative of advertising, subscription, or sponsorship, none of them are proving particularly successful, to put it mildly. But, we all keep our eyes on the future. By this point, it should be clear that the only survivors will be the ones with the deepest, most durable pockets.

And yet, and yet... Bowen is a community networker, and he is aiming this reality check directly at his fellow community networkers. Chin up, folks. Not only is there a way to survive the coming old world order, community networks can even thrive alongside it. If the Net's mainstream evolves into some sort of "shopping mall/amusement park," with its all but free entry fee for the consumer ("subsidized by advertising and pay-per-view/pay-to-play revenue"), "community networks will live or die based on their relationship" to it.

One of the keys will be deciding at the outset to embody an alternative in terms of both content and access. Remember, the two are inseparable. Therefore, after you have laid out what a community network can do that the Net can't—and that's bunches—build it and they will come...to you, too. Bowen foresees most people in the future maintaining at least two accounts, one local, one global. Just as people subscribe to a national newsweekly and a local paper or watch CNN and the local evening news.

People will value an electronically reconstructed public space, the very space we've lost as the twentieth century has worn on. Pointing to Juergen Habermas's analysis of this loss, Bowen essentially portrays what I'd call "massification" as the culprit. There's a limit to how many people can constitute a community. At some point, the individual gets lost in the crowd.

But to regain this lost public arena, a community network will have to do more than slap on the name of its hometown. It will have to be easily and conveniently accessible. Bowen's example: If the public market is harder to get to than the mall, if "you've got to change buses several times, take a few back roads and go farther out of your way," the townspeople will naturally flock to the mall.

Bowen's second criteria for successful community networking is public ownership. Only when the public has a vested interest in their own network's success will it actually evolve into a viable alternative. He points to the hopes cable television raised, the many failures and one success as an example of how to make it work.

"Morganton, N.C., discovered that the coaxial 'load-control' cable used by their municipally-owned water or electric systems could also carry a video signal. These communities now offer a full array of cable TV channels plus public, education and government (P-E-G) access channels. The citizens pay their monthly bills to the community-owned and operated cable system. The revenue stays in the community to support and maintain the operation."

What you are up against as a community networker is the well-financed wow-power the media conglomerates will be jamming on to the mainstream Net. Anyone tuning into the dazzle and then the local will be tempted to stick to the dazzle—unless the local offers the very community most people got wired for in the first place.

Still, there may be a way for communities to grab the dazzle and maintain control over their own networks as well. Bored, dissatisfied, or just plain baffled by the magazine model of web publishing, new media companies, many of them forged out of companies that used to be about something else altogether, all stumbled over precisely the same alternative model at about the same time. Microsoft, AT&T, AOL, from the distant mountaintops they came, descending on local communities to go after newfound gold rumored to be tucked into the foothills. Local communities, it was murmured, have real people in them, some of whom care more about how their kids' high school softball team scores against the next town's than they do about how Congress scores points against Clinton or how Clinton simply scores. Fortunately for the new media giants, there were already scattered little entities in this business, so weakened over time by rising costs and shrinking consumer bases that it would be a cinch snapping them up and having them churn content for them.

Newspapers. How sadly old-fashioned, worn, and torn they looked to the way new media machines roaring into town, smacking their chops. Piece of cake. Easy as pie.

Well, here's pie in your eye, fellas. In column after column, Steve Outing, who writes "Stop the Presses" for *Editor and Publisher Interactive*, has been chronicling what happens when the over-eager and over-confident chomp down on more than they can chew. AT&T's Home Town Network? Chopped. They're still in the game with CitySearch, not to be confused with Microsoft's CityScape.

According to Outing's fellow columnist at *Editor and Publisher Interactive*, Jodi B. Cohen, a lot of those old media editors took a look at what Microsoft has to offer in return for autonomy and balked. Microsoft came at them in a variety of ways, too, and it got embarrassing after a while. If the content is not for sale, how about the editors? How about a nice spot on MSNBC?

Maybe newspapers are beginning to realize they are in a far better position than it may have at first seemed. Not just a better bargaining position. They are starting to ask themselves, Do we need to bargain at all? Maybe this whole new media thing is a lot of smoke and mirrors, not all that tough to handle alone.

Recently, Outing reported on the "KOZ Community Publishing Solution" (CPS), a DIY web presence for communities. Basically, you plug it in and the town's groups (clubs, teams, cliques, official organizations, and so forth) and individuals come in and report "event listings, little league scores, homework assignments, dates for soccer practices, etc.," in other words, information people actually care about.

Cox Interactive Media (CIM), the arm of media conglomerate Cox Enterprises that extends into online matters, was the first to buy. Cox owns the *Atlanta Journal-Constitution*, so that's where they started, and a dozen other cities were to follow in quick succession.

This is the webbed community that doesn't come prepackaged. One that allows for bottom up content with its forms for the customizable database, that doesn't need a particularly large staff to oversee operations, that also lets folks exchange personal messages, and finally, that's got the name of a homegrown business on it, all of it paid for with local advertising, which, according to David Bennahum, amounts to $66 billion in the U.S. alone. This is the community people are already a part of, and Cox is banking on its members preferring to keep it that way.

As if that weren't enough good news, consider this angle. The community maintains control over just how much of itself—its real self, not the restaurant ratings and movie show times—that it will allow to open up to the rest of the world. That, too, may be more advantageous than it seems at first glance.

There could even be a nice bit of money in a community's decision to make the move to the web, according to one member of the San Francisco Bay Guardian Online. Goes by the name of nessie. Interestingly, right at the top of the game plan of all these big-time national local services is San Francisco. nessie thinks the GOL could wipe the floor with them. Why? Because the community's already there. The others are going to have to start from scratch.

"There's thirty million virtual tourists out there just waiting to get in and spend money. Tourism, you may recall, is the main local industry." Further, the GOL already features San Francisco's main attraction, its people. "We are tourist attractions. Us, not the Bridge, not Coit Tower. Us." Maybe it's a stretch. But it is an interesting one. If the Net really is about people, a radical idea the big companies are beginning to perceive, and step by step, come up with new ways to capitalize on, and that is where the money is going to come from, nessie thinks the GOL is sitting on a gold mine.

"All those folks with the cameras and check books didn't come here for the skyline; they come here for us. We're the attraction. It's the people of San Francisco who bring in the tourist money. The view is just window dressing. If they came for the view they wouldn't come here; they'd go to the Berkeley Hills. Now there's some fine views. The view in this town ain't shit to anybody who's ever been riding on Grizzly Peak Road and Skyline Blvd." Now, how else is some out-of-towner going to pick up on that tidbit?

"Nah, it ain't the view; it's the colorful natives in our colorful native costumes, selling our colorful native talents, our colorful native bodies and our colorful native drugs. That's what fills the hotels and the coffers. With GOL Web access that's what will fill the pockets of anyone smart enough to post ads here. But they won't come for the ads; they'll come to watch us and our colorful native antics."

What is someone on the other side of the world looking for when they check into one of half a dozen guides to San Francisco? Sure, maybe hotel reservations, theater and concert tickets. But what is he or she really after? "If all you want is a convention, go to Salt Lake," says nessie. "Wanna get loaded and laid? Come to SF. Wanna have 'friends' when you get here? Meet us online first."

You've got to admit, it is a fresh angle. No guide book online or off features the addresses of your friends.

Chapter Thirty-Five

What's the Point?
An Interview with Eight
Community Networkers and
a Mayor

Well over two decades ago, a small group of volunteers led by Lee Felsenstein and Efrem Lipkin set up a couple of computer terminals in a store run by the publishers of the *Whole Earth Catalogue*, a record store, and a public library in the Bay Area. After they were wired, Berkeley's Community Memory Project, one of the first community networks (if not the first), was born.

In part, Felsenstein and Lipkin were motivated by the desire to prove that technology could be put to positive use. Remember, these were the days of Vietnam, Mutually Assured Destruction, and a lot more rhetoric about the military-industrial complex than we hear today. Not only is technology no longer a dirty word, it has grown kind of sexy over the decades.

A lot of *Whole Earth* went into "The Well;" black vinyl has given way to silvery digits; and the new San Francisco Public Library features snazzier terminals, access to the world, and its own web site. Are community networks as retro as the wah-wah pedal?

What's the Point? An Interview with Eight Community Networkers and a Mayor

Rewired

Slipping on my best devil's advocate attire again, I put several questions along this line to community networkers via the Communet mailing list. Probably asking for trouble, but that's not what I got. Instead, I found the answers to be representative of the spirit and hands-on hard work that has gotten well over half a million people dialing into their local community network.

Participants:

- **Carole Klopp**, President, DANEnet Board of Directors http://danenet.wicip.org/about.htm
- **John Johnston**, Executive Director, FairNet, Fairbanks Alaska Community Network
  http://www.fairnet.org
- **Craig Silva**, Electronic Outreach Program Officer, Victorian Health Promotion Foundation, Melbourne, Australia
  http://www.vichealth.vic.gov.au/
- **Brenda C. Henderson**, Coordinator, Work Force Development Projects, Tennessee Tomorrow, Inc.
- **Dick Dowell**, Software Valley Information System
  http://svis.org
- **Dave Farley**, Grants and Development Officer, Office of the Mayor, Pittsburgh, Pennsylvania
- **Steve Snow**, Project Director, Charlotte's Web
  http://avery.charweb.org/home.html
- **Brian E. McLaughlin**, Volunteer, Central New York Community Network
  http://www.cnynet.org
- **Dan Speer**, Mayor, Pulaski, Tennessee
  http://www.usit.net/hp/giles/GCEF.html

DH: What's the point? With so many commercial ISPs, large and small, fighting for new customers, surely everybody's going to get online before too long. Why approach a government or a business and ask for money to set up a system that is already on its way? Is community networking a well-intentioned reaction to a scarcity that no longer exists?

Carole Klopp: However, a scarcity does exist. Most rural areas are having an extremely tough time getting access to the Internet alone, forget any networking. Perhaps where you are, access is great. It is here in Madison, but I know we are definitely the minority. Look at the figures nationally. I believe it runs about 25–30 percent [with] access. I would propose that a lot of people are currently disenfranchised because the Internet was contrived for reasons other than communities networking. Additionally, because of the current setup, communities are also being held hostage by our friendly telcos—who have the wires and will or will not wire you. I'm not sure the "too long" you use in your question is just around the corner for some—it may be down the road about two miles.

John Johnston: Commercial ISPs are not available to everyone in today's society. Although their services may be more reasonable, cost-wise, than in the past, not everyone can afford the cost of a computer and related software. You ask, "What's the point?" Simple, everyone in today's world deserves the ability to have access to knowledge and resources not available to them in any other form. Why? Considering the fast growth of the electronic world, every individual will need to learn the basic use and handling of a computer.

Nonsense you say. Well, next time you go to McDonald's, ask how the cashier rings your amount owed or how a warehouse worker calculates his inventory. These are jobs which have been traditionally "low paid, manual labor" categories. This is no longer the case. The general public is entitled to the knowledge and training only available from community networks in the same manner as public libraries and schools.

Craig Silva: Ownership of the hardware confers certain rights and responsibilities. Primary amongst them is control of content. To some extent it's similar to newspapers such that in the end the owner gets to say what is published. This is different from a community network democratically deciding what it will publish. However, to return to the main point, I believe that unless community networks provide the same level of service as the commercial ISPs they will be marginalised. It is clear that the provision of telecom services will eventually be monopolized by the big companies. This of course will have the desired effect of diminishing the control of the telecom service provider over content and refocus discussion on community networking on content.

Brenda Henderson: In the past community networks have been designed to deal with three issues (local access to the Internet, local content, and free access for those who cannot afford access to technology) with one solution, the community FreeNet model. With the rapid growth of commercial Internet Service Providers, the issues need to be dealt with separately. The Association of Community Partnerships, a Tennessee-based association, takes the position that gaining local call access to the Internet *is* a basic issue that can best be addressed through a partnership with a commercial ISP. Building local content for and about the community can only be done effectively by collaborative efforts within the local community. Free access for those unable to afford technology is best done by local funding for public access points (the library, the housing project, the local bank lobby, and so on). Individually addressing the

What's the Point? An Interview with Eight Community Networkers and a Mayor

Rewired

issues prevents fostering a "well-intentioned reaction to a scarcity that no longer exists" in this fast paced world of information technology.

Dick Dowell: Many, many around our country will not have such access for a long time. We in West Virginia are entirely rural (the only 100 percent rural state in the U.S.). We will have to force access to the furthest reaches. And, many, many cannot afford access at current ISP rates—so there has to be some way of leveling the field.

Communities will not go down the path of community/civic networks unless someone facilitates it. At the local level, getting started without help is a Herculean task. We need to have catalysts (facilitators) to start these networks so that folks can begin to sample what they can achieve through them. There are a vast many out there that have no idea what can be accomplished with the aid of such capabilities.

Communities need a push/assist to go in the proper direction.

Dave Farley: Scarcity is not the problem here. It is the ability to ensure that everyone can have access to information through the use of computers and Internet technology. Governments, for example, have the advantage of being able to ensure such things, in fact, do occur, whether they do that by themselves or with private sector partners.

Steve Snow: If you ask this, you misperceive the role of community networks—at least as some people describe it. In Charlotte, NC, we are distinctly different from ISPs:

1. Text-only dialup (no personal PPP)

2. Free e-mail

3. No personal web space (currently)

4. Focus on under-served communities for

    a. Training

    b. Access

    c. Support

5. Focus on institutional development, especially nonprofits and small governments that are unable to support their own MIS/Internet staff

6. Public access—more than 150 PCs throughout the community and in the region—to our system

Everyone will not be online before long. The truth is that people who lack the means also are less likely to see the value of being online for their children. Educate, educate, educate.

There are deep and long-winded answers to the question of involving government at all. I favor government seed-corn and then modest support, but not major government or business support. The real issue is this: Who should control the sharing of information resources in your community: the telcos, the cablecos, government, or the people?

DH: Okay, a big one. How does "getting wired" actually help a community? Other than keeping up with the Joneses, what's tangibly gained?

Craig Silva: Effectively it is like providing a new playground for the community. The new space creates room for new relationships to develop. Community networks are a necessity to stake a claim for community in cyberspace.

Carole Klopp: Information is power for those who have it, and sought by those who don't have it. How many times have you said, "if only I had known, I would have done it differently." I have on many occasions. So, although some will talk about encouraging and developing communities, I would add the power of information. Communities that are wired have gained the edge over those not wired. As a matter of fact, we have a community in our county who saw a business locate their main office there based in part on their web page. If that isn't power, what is?

John Johnston: Do you consider the knowledge gained from reading a book at the library or by exchanging ideas with pen pals on the other side of the world "keeping up with the Joneses?" I live in Alaska and my involvement with our community network brings me in contact with a variety of folks from every walk of life. I have received letters from elementary school classes wanting to know what Alaska is really like and can they come and see a real bear, moose, or caribou. This kind of contact would not be possible without the assistance of the electronic world and community networks. This international exchange of information and knowledge also enhances a sense of world unity which is the only way our current world can prosper and grow.

Dick Dowell: Electronic commerce, ready access to information, wider access to education (Internet in the classroom), better communication (asynchronous communications advantages), self documentation, better use of time, cheaper, and so forth, for starters. The biggest benefit is that it directly supports the growth of existing and new businesses, thereby creating/sustaining jobs and thereby creating real wealth in the community. The new technologies afford an opportunity for a community to take stock and reinvent itself.

Dave Farley: Citizens get to communicate among themselves and with other groups and institutions in many different ways that in principle

What's the Point? An Interview with Eight Community Networkers and a Mayor

Rewired

cannot be controlled by either government or by private interests. These types of communication are really at the heart of democracy, and we should support them. The face of the communication that occurs will depend on what people want to talk about. Although we may all believe there are some important things that we wish people would talk about, it is really none of our business what topics they eventually select.

Brian McLaughlin: I'm one of a group of volunteers working to develop a community network for Syracuse, NY, and the surrounding six-county area. We are working to "uncover the hidden wealth" that lives in this area—the specialized, non-profit, small-budget groups that give both a sense of "belonging" to the people involved, and reflect the range of "possibilities" to the larger community. There are groups to help battered women, groups to help people start businesses, groups to offer after school activities for children, fraternal organizations, professional organizations... What many of these entities have in common is, one, a desire to be "more visible" to the community, and two, no (or very little) money.

Most of these organizations disseminate information by word of mouth, person-to-person, and the Central New York Community Network is attempting to "extend the grapevine." We frequently will find related sites for these organizations, which offer them the prospect of networking within their own interest group. At the same time, they improve the capacity of local people with shared interests to find them.

Ultimately, we hope the range of organizations we have accessible will reflect the community we live in, from agriculture to microelectronics, with a focus on local-to-local (regional-to-regional) connections.

This is one of those "soft" quality-of-life issues, like infrastructure. It may not be too sexy by itself, but everyone certainly appreciates it when it's there!

Dan Speer: Pulaski has been "wired" for about eighteen months, not to keep up with the Joneses but to give our community the opportunities that most rural communities just don't have. We felt, and still do, that the technology can be used to improve the quality of life for our citizens and will improve our education system, improve communications between citizens and government, improve health care, and offer new economic opportunities. We also felt that we could offer the technology and build a model that would be economically sustainable. Also, we have built a Community Information Service (CIS) that addresses local issues and reflects our community heritage and pride.

Steve Snow: This is digital cotton in the South. Economic development. It will become a major educational tool for distance learning and also a major civic action tool for civic engagement and democratic participation. It is not there yet. People who look at what is being done today and wonder about whether it is worth it need to step back about six feet and look at the larger picture; this is the bleeding edge of a new medium, no less; it will have all the functional potential of any current medium and some additional components as well (especially interactivity). It is not the Holy Grail. It has big limitations, and currently these systems are more limited than they are functional.

Brenda Henderson: We believe that proficient use of information technology is a basic skill requirement of the twenty-first century work force. The extent to which community life can teach this skill will produce workers that require less training on the job and will lower training costs for industries locating in the community.

Rural communities can be target locations for "down-sized employees" providing niche market services deliverable primarily over the network. The quality of life and cost of living is attractive to many. These jobs don't pollute or require additional capital investments in infrastructure with the exception of information technology infrastructure. The average salary per job created is much higher than a typical manufacturing job, plowing more money into the local economy. In a sales tax economy such as Tennessee's, local businesses are vulnerable to worldwide market competition. The extent to which they can meet local needs with a new marketing approach and extend their market beyond the local area via Internet marketing will increase survivability. Gaining confidence and learning about opportunities before a crisis is an easier way to go.

DH: Everyone seems pretty convinced the web is the future of all networking. Doesn't any community network have to be web-based, too?

Craig Silva: If the Community Networks don't provide the accepted level of service, they will be marginalised.

Carole Klopp: Although I'm not a techie, my techies tell me that the web has exploded and to do otherwise would be like using a beta VCR. It apparently is as simple as that for our group.

Brenda Henderson: The reason many community networks are not web-based is based on the fact that many are competing with commercial ISPs who are paying taxes to local and state governments. To provide subsidized web-based services where the local or state government is a party to the subsidization is not the politically correct action to take. The compromise has been to provide only text-based access to serve those who can't afford access to technology. The Association of Community Partnerships believes these populations are best served by providing Public Access Points with web-based access. Otherwise, over time, your

What's the Point? An Interview with Eight Community Networkers and a Mayor

Rewired

user base will erode and the network cannot be sustained without additional revenue streams from the community.

John Johnston: Community networking is a system to exchange ideas, knowledge, and information. Sure, it would be nice to provide everyone with a free graphical browser, WWW-based. However, if we can just provide them with the means to gain the knowledge they desire and deserve we have accomplished our goals.

Dick Dowell: Right now we have a web page and a BBS-based Internet service. Most of our users don't have Internet access, nor do their computers support present GUIs. Moreover, most of the traffic is text, so why pay the very high penalty for graphics? Plus, the file transfer capabilities of the BBS technology is much superior. We are moving to the latest technology in this field in which the web page is directly linked to our BBS (try us at telnet svis.org, 198.77.8.11), which will be the best of both worlds. Final thought: Most of our folks cannot afford to be online very long. If we build a service that severely limits online activity, the costs of the service are dramatically reduced. When one needs to be online, go to the library, to Kinko's, or to some other compatible facility (we are pushing high-end technology community centers) and do your high-end processing.

Dave Farley: We are a pictorial society, and that's how we communicate, convince others of things (viz., advertise), inform, and so forth. The need for words is not going to evaporate any time soon, in my view, but pictures and interactivity are key improvements that should be part of any community network.

Steve Snow: I think so. But it depends on what you mean by web-based. If you mean only graphical, then I think you are wrong, in the near term, at least. Ultimately, the old machines will melt away and all will be pictures (analogous to black-and-white versus color TV; or color snapshots versus black-and-white snapshots—it's more expensive to get black-and-white today).

But part of the value of the web is that HTML supports both text and graphics. So a thoughtful system operator won't cut out citizens by being so focused on the cute and clever tools that non-graphics users can't find utility in the system and its information.

PPP to the world is not, in my opinion, the current answer to the world's problems (see my answer to the first question). Aside from graphics versus text, there is a great role for BBSs that can act as locally rich systems at very low cost and provide gateways to the Internet for e-mail and other things, including web-based information (you might not know, David, that you can do just about everything you need to do—including getting web pages—simply by using electronic mail).

DH: Who should fund community networks? A government (any or all levels?), a business, a dedicated community fund, a combination, all or none of the above...?

Craig Silva: It should be the community itself, but that of course includes government, state and local and even perhaps federal. This issue is about sustainability. Where a community network is established wholly by external funding, the likelihood is that the funding will eventually be cut and the network will die. Where a community is not willing to sustain a community network, the question must be asked as to whether there is a real need in comparison to issues of housing, health, and poverty, and also whether the community network is doing its job.

Carole Klopp: I believe a community network should be funded by all levels of government and businesses—depending on your site and focus. As you may have guessed, every community is not exactly the same. Some of us are the ISP for our communities, while some of us (such as DANEnet) are the community network, leaving the ISP business to the ISPs. We are currently looking for funding from the state, the county, local governments, schools, non-profits, and businesses. We think that providing free universal access to free public information is our responsibility and we are assisting government in their job. We can't and shouldn't expect government to do everything—and we don't.

John Johnston: Funding of a community network is everyone's responsibility. Do we question who should fund schools, libraries, our highways?

Brenda Henderson: We believe that equitable partnerships can be developed to encourage ISPs to offer local call access to the Internet. We believe that building local content can also be a local partnership between businesses such as local newspapers, radio, TV stations, local libraries, and the entire community. And although most information is free to the subscriber, there may be enhanced information services that may emerge. We believe that public sector entities should fund Public Access Points, but that does not preclude businesses from providing access for employees at the work site for use after work hours.

Dick Dowell: There are many different models. In Iowa, the state invested heavily in the state network. Problem: state-run. In Kentucky, the RBOC and the state got together. Problem: some laws prevented private use. PBS is pushing their view, AT&T, MCI, AOL, and so on. We think that the non-profit approach is the best and that the enterprise must be funded from the business community—through demonstrated value adding services provided—and that is the approach we are taking.

What's the Point? An Interview with Eight Community Networkers and a Mayor

Rewired

Here is the approach. Our focus is on creating jobs through technology—in the business of creating and growing business. We are the contracting agency for a new national program which will be putting shared used information technology centers in all the U.S.' fifty states and four territories. Each of these centers must have a business plan to be self-sufficient from user fees within a three-year period of time. Each federal/other funded site will be the hub of activity for other sites, the plan for which, including interoperability with other existing and planned systems (that is, schools, medical nets, and so forth), must target giving affordable access and training to all the citizens of the state (and adjacent economic areas).

Each of the sites will be a business incubator without walls—including a community support infrastructure. We will be in the business of supporting business in traditional ways (business consultants): cost saving, business planning, financing access, you name it. We'll work on a contingency basis with the understanding that our "profits" will be directed to the business incubator and related functions, including the expansion of the community networks to reach the goal that all citizens will have the access we have outlined.

Who pays? Business pays through the profits generated through growth. Government can support from the new revenues, and so forth. However, you must start with "there is no free lunch."

Steve Snow: I see a self-sustaining mix of support that includes some grant money—especially local and state money— for ongoing project development. I think the best networks with the best ideas that actually work will always be able to get some grant support for new and/or well-defined applications of the medium. Government plays a role because of the access to government information and civic enablement that takes place; in other words, all of the above...and more. Community networks should look to their communities to generate revenue for services they provide.

Dave Farley: All of the above. That's what we've been doing, and it's paying off.

Regarding Steve Snow's comments, we agree with the approach that's being described here. In fact, Steve may remember from a few years ago that I spent some time talking with him and other Charlotte's Web folks at a street art fair at which my wife was an exhibitor in Charlotte. The Charlotte's Web approach and basic philosophy has inspired us in Pittsburgh, and we hope we're continuing to do complementary things as a result. With respect to the role of government, however, I'd like to add that sometimes government must prod communities to do things such as computer networking. And not merely as extensions of existing institutions, either. That's a particularly evident challenge in places such as Pittsburgh, which is just breaking out of historical sets of relatively static institutional relationships for every civic effort. When I was outside the government back in the 1970s (and largely ignorant of how to make it work for the citizens, besides to stay outside and criticize it), I tended to share some of the same skepticism about motives and control as I often see expressed on [the] Communet [mailing list]. Some of that is deserved, but some of it is clearly not deserved. We believe that government can, indeed, lead the development of community networks, and that, in fact, it has the mandate to ensure that access is available to all the citizens as part of its overall, public responsibility to promote the welfare of the polity. That's why we're taking a prominent role in this stuff.

DH: What are the ultimate goals of your network? Competing with larger content providers? Linking people, building, or reinforcing a community? A sense of place? Or linking the community to the whole— that is, making sure your community is not left behind as the rest of the world goes online?

Craig Silva: Linking people, building, and reinforcing a geographical community.

Carole Klopp: Gosh, we are just discussing this now at our board meetings. We are not interested in competition—but collaboration. We feel that the provision of free public information is essential to the entire community and, yes, we don't want our communities left behind. I believe most "nets" are grappling with this as we speak and none have a simple answer.

John Johnston: The ultimate goal is to develop a system in which ideas and knowledge can be exchanged by all persons. Not just those with the money to afford it.

Dave Farley: All of those things except, perhaps, competing with larger content providers. We're really not interested in having the largest collection of information, because that's something the local libraries do well. Libraries are partners with us in the community.

Steve Snow: All the above except competing with larger networks. We see ourselves as conveners of our region around information and communication resources. We don't consider ourselves competitors but rather civic builders, enablers, and sharers of information and communication. We try to create opportunities for people to make connections and the means for those who lack it so they are not left out.

DH: Where are your access points? Surely you can't give everybody a computer...?

What's the Point? An Interview with Eight Community Networkers and a Mayor

Rewired

Carole Klopp: Why not? We take old computers, fix 'em, and give them away to the have-nots. Granted, we haven't done a lot, but our goal is to provide local access. We are located in community centers, libraries, schools, and local government. If we have to give a computer to a local city clerk to get her online, so be it, we will. Access is key. Information is essential. The two go hand in hand.

Craig Silva: Libraries, schools, and malls.

Brenda Henderson: The primary goals promoted by the Association of Community Partnerships are linking people, building or reinforcing the local community, and linking the community to the whole—that is, making sure the community is not left behind as the rest of the world goes online.

John Johnston: We don't need to provide everyone with a computer. Sure, it would be nice but not cost-effective. We have addressed this question by establishing Public Access Sites. These sites are similar to libraries or schools. Anyone can enter a Public Access Site and "surf the net" for education or pleasure. We are enhancing this by providing free Basic Computer and Internet training to residents of our community.

Our site locations are chosen by group needs. We have established one at our Borough library for the general public, at our local Seniors Center for the elderly, and at our local service center for people with disabilities.

Dick Dowell: Why not every household? We are a state of 1.8 million. We are targeting nine to eleven walk-in shared use community information technology centers. Each one can support about 2,500 folks using the center twenty hours per week. We plan dialup access (lower end) to the sites. We'll have a mini walk-in station in each of our 55 counties. Each of the main sites is the locus of an incubator and a community/civic net. These are expanded through the 55 county seat sub stations.

The national backbone is ATM to the desktop, completely open systems, fully interoperable with existing and planned systems.

The short straw in all of this is the human. The technology is all there today.

You may wish to review our 10th Anniversary Newsletter on our home page (for more background on what we have been doing and who our supporters are).

By the way, we have some international members (and would welcome others), and are in the process of planning (with others) satellite systems to support international distance learning initiatives.

Dave Farley: Libraries and schools, of course. But more than that. We're using community learning centers, settlement houses, YMCAs, public housing facilities, recreation centers, church buildings, social agencies, community-oriented police stations, civic clubs, banks, drugstores, and so on.

How many total sites and terminals?

Fifteen sites online now, and ten more coming on line by the end of 1996. In 1997 we will add many more. Based on the model that we've been pioneering here, we plan to have about ten neighborhood networks (each one of which might have ten or twenty other, smaller sites linked to them) all across the city.

All sites have at least two PCs, laser printer, scanner, high-speed modem, and an array of software. Four sites are LANs with between ten and twenty PCs each, lots of different kinds of printers and scanners, ISDN, and some fancy video conferencing stuff in one of those sites. All the LANs are hooked up through a neighborhood hub on a T1 to the Pittsburgh Supercomputer Center now. Eventually the city government will become its own ISP, and will take on the traffic from those neighborhood networks.

Parallel development of municipal or municipally administered sites (community learning centers, recreation centers, public housing, and police stations, for example) is occurring through the use of dedicated capital funding, and we link those sites into the neighborhoods as neighborhood networks are being built. We pretty much create the family of sites in a given neighborhood from receptive places, so the networks don't look exactly alike, and we don't expect them to. We also have put some technical time into linking up existing and new equipment, so that we are able to validate the financial investment of others that may have predated our involvement. That makes it easier for people to participate, and it enhances our constituency broadly speaking for these kinds of collective technology forays and for proliferating them all over town.

Steve Snow: Well, I actually see some value in making sure everyone has a computer, but I am in the minority on that. We refurbish older computers here and place them with community leaders in fragile communities. We train, train, train, and then support what we deliver. There are literally millions upon millions of computers in this country that could be living useful lives and doing useful work, but they aren't being used in part because people are too tied to the "picture" image of computing. I say get people connected when it makes sense for them; help people understand and find value in using this medium, regardless of the level of the tools; help people discover their personal value—the value they have to share with the community via this medium—and give them the means to share it. Then you will begin to see the transformative power of the medium.

What's the Point? An Interview with Eight Community Networkers and a Mayor

Rewired

This is a medium of hope, not of technology; the technology is merely a vehicle for people's meaning and value.

Brenda Henderson: We encourage the local community to discover the best places to locate Public Access Points. The natural place is the local public library, the local school lab, a community center, and public housing. But businesses are encouraged to provide service in the employee break room or training room based on corporate objectives.

Dick Dowell: Let's make sure that everyone has access. And, I see no reason we cannot have one—or the equivalent thereof— in every home.

References

Alderman, John. An Interview with Brian Eno, Pop, June 5, 1996.
http://www.hotwired.com/popfeatures/96/24/eno.transcript.html

Apple Library of Tomorrow.
http://www2.apple.com/documents/alot/alotsites.html

Bennahum, David. MEME 2.10.
http://www.reach.com/matrix/meme2-10.html

Bowen, Wally. "Community Networks at the Crossroads," June 1996.
http://www.main.nc.us/about/cmtynet.html

Cisler, Steve. A review of *The Wired Neighborhood* by Stephan Doheny-Farina, Community Networking Currents, University of Michigan School of Information.
http://www.si.umich.edu/Community/currents/

Cohen, Jodi B. News Bytes, *Editor and Publisher Interactive.*
http://www.mediainfo.com/ephome/news/newshtm/bytes/bytes.htm

Dewey, John. The Public and Its Problems.
http://psych.colorado.edu/~bmarmie/dewey.html

Eisenberg, Rebecca. Read Me!
http://www.cyborganic.com/People/rebecca/readme/

Electric Minds.
http://www.minds.com

Figallo, Cliff. "A Report From the Hinterlands: Netizens Interviews Steve Cisler," October, 1995.
http://gnn-e2a.gnn.com/gnn/netizens/cisler.html

Grundner, Dr. Thomas M. "Letters to the Fourth World," Vol. 1, No. 1, May 1991.
gopher://acorn.net:70/00/FreeWorld/About_NPTN/initial.tmg

Grundner, Dr. Thomas M. "Final Letter to the Fourth World," May 1996.
gopher://acorn.net:70/00/FreeWorld/About_NPTN/final.tmg

Guy, Neil. "Community Networks: Building Real Communities in a Virtual Space?"
http://www.tela.bc.ca/tela/ma-thesis/contents.html

Guy, Neil. "History of Community Networks," Chapter Five, "Community Networks:
Building Real Communities in a Virtual Space?" 1996.
http://www.vcn.bc.ca/people/nkg/ma-thesis/

Mountain Area Information Network.
http://www.main.nc.us

Outing, Steve. "A Contrary View: Infrastructure Will Slow Internet Speed Improvements,"
Stop the Presses, *Editor and Publisher Interactive*, September 11, 1996.
http://www.mediainfo.com/ephome/news/newshtm/stop/stop911.htm

Outing, Steve. Stop the Presses, *Editor and Publisher Interactive*.
http://www.mediainfo.com/ephome/news/newshtm/stop/stop.htm

Rheingold, Howard. *The Virtual Community*, 1993, p. 6.
http://www.well.com/user/hlr/vcbook/vcbookintro.html

Rosenberg, Scott. "After the Gold Rush," *Salon*, November 4, 1996.
http://www.salon1999.com/oct96/web961104.html

San Franisco Bay Guardian Online.
http://www.sfbg.com/bbs/windex.html

San Francisco Public Library.
http://sfpl.lib.ca.us/

Sclove, Richard E. *Cybersobriety: An Excerpt from Democracy and Technology*, New
York: Guilford Press, 1995, pp. 79–81, 108.
http://www.amherst.edu/~loka/sclove/virtual.htm

Sippey, Michael. "The Problem with Private Internets," Stating the Obvious, September
30, 1996.
http://www.theobvious.com/archives/093096.html

Conclusion
People Are the Killer App

The observation comes, once again, from Andrew Sullivan. Andrew and I had been exchanging views on just about all the subjects that pop up throughout this book since we met in San Francisco in early 1995. We met online, on the free online service he was building from the ground up, the San Francisco Bay Guardian Online. I'd posted something about an exhibition I'd seen at the recently opened San Francisco Museum of Modern Art in one of the conferences during the beta phase.

Something I said must have caught his eye and he dropped a note in my mailbox. Turns out we had a lot in common (except our age; this overachiever is almost ten years younger than I am). Besides art and politics, we both thought a lot about the media and the nitty-gritty of publishing, and of course, we'd both been online junkies since the day each of us first sampled the world in the wires. So we met a few times, not nearly often enough (our ragged schedules never seemed to jibe), and far sooner than planned, I moved with my family back to Europe, to Berlin.

In another age, we might have written a few letters, and most probably, our relationship would have faded with the sleepy pace of the transatlantic postal service. But in this one, I was able to plug my modem into the wall and get in touch within days of arrival. And the messages flew back and forth and haven't stopped.

Not an unusual story these days. Maybe the bit about launching a zine on the web called *Rewired* and running it from opposite ends of the ocean is slightly unusual, but for the most part, similar stories abound. What is important is that we've been able to communicate instantly despite the half a globe or so that separates us geographically, and after the initial investment in the equipment, it hasn't cost all that much. Also important, neither of us considers this magical, though it often feels like it.

Will we look back 10 or 20 years from now and call what has happened in telecommunications over the last decade a revolution? Or will the lines of development between the Net and cable, telephone and wireless communications seem all the fuzzier in retrospect as they surely will be in the future? Impossible to say. Histories are perpetually argued over and revised anyway.

One thing we can say with certainty about the present is that things are happening mighty fast. Decisions are being made now that will have a tremendous impact on this priceless—in the truest sense of the word—means of getting together and talking to each other. It would be disastrous for any of us to throw up our arms and decide that we have no control over our own futures. Because if we don't take control, however much we're capable of (and let's not suffer any illusions in the opposite direction either), others will.

The effects of an "out of control" approach to any endeavor, whether it be in the field of technology or any other, would be nothing less than disastrous. Because even if a vast majority of a population were to be convinced to kick back and let matters run their course, someone somewhere would know very well that all of human history is a tale of struggle over the reins of power, which not only exist but must inevitably fall into the hands of those most able and willing to snatch them.

There have been times when kings or dictators made no bones about what they were after, and there have been times when churches and soothsayers have lulled a populace into submission with the "out of control" mantra, only to quietly slip into power after that submission had turned into sleep. The best of times have been had after the majority has been awakened, when more people than not realize that if they don't act, don't take control for the ultimate benefit of the many over the few, it won't happen. And the few will run off with the loot, most of it the product of the many.

Were the future according to those who would advise us to keep our hands off it to come about, we would most likely find ourselves in a period more resembling the darker ages of our past than in some of the better days the Net and its related technologies might have in store. Because these technologies open a door that maybe, just maybe, leads to a more democratic society of greater equality, we need to be wary of anyone telling us that it is no use getting up and walking through it—of anyone shutting it in our faces.

A wide range of issues is brought up in this book. It would be ridiculously wide if I had set out to explore each of them to the hilt, get to the bottom of each and every one of them, and come back up with the last word. Instead, I hope to have provided an overview of many of the debates currently going on regarding this set of technologies and its impact on our lives. The line of argument in each case is hardly ever the sexiest one to take. There aren't many zippy slogans in this book. Sobriety is not a particularly celebratory or deliciously nihilistic position to take, but nonetheless, I hope it's an attractive one. Its time has certainly come. In fact, it is a little late, though not too late.

If you view the commercialization of the Net as evil, for example, maybe you will consider the point of view that it is surely a necessary one if this medium is to survive. If you're a big fan of *Wired* magazine, I hope you picked up on my appreciation for what it has done in raising vital issues, despite my jabs at it. If you think the idea of community without direct personal interaction is bunk, perhaps you can appreciate some of the benefits a slightly lesser form of communication can bring. And so on.

Above all, what I hope you've come away with is the sense that it was people's interest in and attraction to one another that made the Internet take off like it did. People are still this technology's greatest asset, its "killer app," the term applied to a function or piece of software that makes it irresistible.

We need to keep an eye on this thing. There's no need to allow it to evolve into another one-to-many, top-down medium. We've got plenty of those. This one could be unique.